Dear Colleagues,

I am very pleased that we are providing all staff with a copy of the book Frontlines to mark our 150th anniversary.

The book, written by Reuters journalists, past and present, captures the spirit of the special company for which we work.

These days we are all familiar with the importance of Reuters in the financial markets; Frontlines reminds us that we have a major role to play in helping to liberate people as well as markets.

I hope you will enjoy reading these stories and viewing the photographs with your families as much as I do with mine.

Regards,

Tom

# FRONTLINES

snapshots of history

# FRONTLINES

snapshots of history

REUTERS

*Published by* **Pearson Education**
London • New York • San Francisco • Toronto • Sydney • Tokyo • Singapore
Hong Kong • Cape Town • Madrid • Amsterdam • Munich • Paris • Milan

PEARSON EDUCATION LIMITED

Head Office:
Edinburgh Gate
Harlow CM20 2JE
Tel: +44 (0)1279 623623
Fax: +44 (0)1279 431059

London Office: 128 Long Acre
London WC2E 9AN
Tel: +44 (0)20 7447 2000
Fax: +44 (0)20 7420 5771
Website: www.business-minds.com

First published in Great Britain in 2001

© Reuters 2001

Published in association with The Tagman Press

The right of Nicholas Moore and Sidney Weiland to be identified as Editors of this Work has been asserted by them in accordance with the Copyright, Designs and Patents Act 1988.

ISBN 1903 68401 3

*British Library Cataloguing in Publication Data*
A CIP catalogue record for this book can be obtained from the British Library

10 9 8 7 6 5 4 3 2 1

Designed and Typeset by George Hammond Design
Printed and bound in Great Britain by Rotolito, Italy

*The Publishers' policy is to use paper manufactured from sustainable forests.*

*To the late Sidney Weiland, who inspired this book,*
*and in memory of those who gave their lives for the Reuters report*

# CONTENTS

# ACKNOWLEDGEMENTS

THE INSPIRATION FOR this book belongs to the late Sidney Weiland in association with fellow former Reuters correspondents Anthony Grey, Aleco Joannides and Gerald Ratzin and it was in large measure shaped by Sidney, who drew particularly on the wisdom and experience as an editor at Reuters of Jack Hartzman. The project, as it went forward after Sidney died in 1999, owed a particular debt to his wife Rosemarie and son David, who gave it their blessing and who edited Sidney's own distinctive chapter; to Bridget Bagshaw, our copy editor, for her good humour as well as her diligence as she prepared our final text; then to Martin Drewe at Pearson for accepting the proposal, and for his guidance and inexhaustible patience as we put the book together. We also wish to thank Izabel Grindal and Elaine Herlihy at Reuters for their support for our proposal.

Perils necessarily attend any collective venture of this kind, not least in deciding which themes to follow and stories to cover. For each of the forty odd bylines, a dozen or so others – many just as strong – could have been included. Concerns of space, continuity and context also meant that, as individual pieces were welded into a whole, some intrusive editing could not be avoided. We have traded on the goodwill of our authors.

We have been most grateful to David Cutler and Mair Salts of the Reuters Editorial Reference Unit, to Amy Schofield for her work with Martin on the photographs, to our designer George Hammond and to Michelle Clark who read the proofs.

We would also like to thank the many other colleagues and friends who have given their help or advice, among them: Salim Amin of Camerapix, Youssef Azmeh, David Betts, Jack Clayworth, Monica Cook, Michael Cooling, George Jackson, John Entwistle, Jim Flannery, Alex Frere, Roger Green, Robert Hart, Ian Jones, Stephen Jakes, James Jukwey, Evelyn Leopold, Paul Majendie, Mark Meredith, Ingrid Montbazet, Michael Nelson, Martin Nesirky, Alan Paterson, Michael Reupke, Rudi Saks, Abigail Sekimitsu, Linda Sieg, Alexia Singh, Arthur Spiegelman, Keith Stafford, Alan Thomas, Gill Tudor, David Viggers, Andrew Waller, Samantha Wheeler, Geoffrey Womack and Mark Wood.

THE FURTHER AWAY the disaster – goes the old newsroom adage – the bigger it has to be. A more elegant expression of this idea comes from a style note that Reuters issued to its correspondents in 1883, when it described the news that it considered suitable to include in the service of those Victorian days:

'Fires, explosions, floods, inundations, railway accidents, destructive storms, shipwrecks attended with loss of life, accidents to British and American war vessels and to mail steamers, street riots of a grave character, disturbances arising from strikes, duels between, and suicides of, persons of note, social or political, and murders of a sensational character.'

News values may change but it will always be difficult to convey the reality of a country on one side of the world, without over-simplifying it, in a way that suits the taste of readers on the other. Foreign correspondents feel this keenly and they love to write in-depth pieces to put things in perspective. Indeed, they often write their best copy when they have leisure to study their subject properly, but by then the spotlight has often moved on. They may not be published.

Reuters journalists suffer the same frustrations, although their position is a little different. They are not writing for a single publication. There is always somebody who is interested.

Wherever the action is, Reuters is always there, lacking any particular prejudice as it follows events, and it is also true that such a consistent news agency presence can throw light on things that might otherwise escape the attention they deserve. It may indirectly assist freedom of expression where this is restricted.

While Vaclav Havel was in opposition in the former Czechoslovakia, news about him from organizations like Reuters established his existence in the mind of a world readership and may have protected him from arrest. We know of other politicians who have been in jail or even on death row who feel that regular reporting helped prevent them being forgotten, or obliterated.

In times of crisis we have a more direct impact because we report in real time, not to any particular deadline. We are among a few organizations that cause presidents to be woken up in the middle of the night.

We may do more than ring alarm bells; leaders under pressure and their antagonists may be influenced by a dispassionate view. For example, we believe that Nasser drew heavily on Reuters during the 1956 Suez crisis. A correspondent who covered that story, Aleco Joannides, describes in these pages how the chief news editor sent him a briefing letter that emphasised how the objectivity of his despatches should be beyond criticism.

A steady news source may also restrain hasty actions that might be taken in the heat of the moment.

Not that we get at the whole truth everywhere. In the half century after World War II, many important events went virtually unreported. Little contemporary journalism exists on the Pol Pot massacres. It was difficult for Reuters even to enter Indonesia in the early sixties, so that the killings which followed its abortive communist coup in 1965 were never properly reported.

The ability of governments to conceal the truth began to decay in the seventies. Organizations like Reuters were agents of this change but bigger forces were at work, such as the spread of literacy, prosperity and the increasing sophistication of global communications. At first, obsession with the Cold War had a blinding effect; Yuri Gagarin went on what was no doubt intended to be a spying mission. Only later did people begin to realize the wider ramifications of satellite technology.

At the same time, the isolationism that sustained new post-war nations – and the despotic regimes of eastern Europe – was gradually superseded by a more outward-looking stance in the quest for trade, wealth and innovation.

It is arguable that Reuters induced change by participating in the financial revolution of the seventies, when the Bretton Woods system of fixed currency values gave way to floating exchange rates. This all started with a screen service called the Reuter Monitor, which harnessed information with computer technology to give instant valuations to users across the world. The Internet is now carrying the revolution in financial information to the individual investor.

The information age has suddenly shrunk the world beneath our pens, our keyboards. As an organization we do not claim that we have a special moral mission to make human beings understand each other better. Nevertheless, that has often been the effect of what we do.

The contributions by a just a few of our correspondents to this book – an informal initiative of their own – show how they chronicled some of the events that we remember from the end of World War II until the dawn of a new millennium and how they felt when they were doing that.

In this, our 150th year, I hope you will enjoy reading these testimonies by men and women who have worked for one of the most exciting companies in the world.

PETER JOB, CHIEF EXECUTIVE, REUTERS

# INTRODUCTION

I WAS COVERING a summit meeting of the Warsaw Pact in Bucharest for Reuters in the hot Balkan summer of 1966 when I first began to realize that, through the nature of their work, experienced foreign correspondents inevitably become walking time-capsules of modern world history.

I was standing amongst a group of journalists from the world's major newspapers, news agencies and television networks inside the splendid air-conditioned throne room of ex-King Michael of Rumania in the former royal palace. Before the summit went into a closed session to debate some new political or military challenge to NATO – the final communiqué spoke darkly of possibly sending volunteers to fight American forces in Vietnam – we were given a rare opportunity in that sumptuous regal setting to photograph and scrutinise a drab assembly of the all-powerful, uncrowned heads of communist Eastern Europe.

Grim-faced and haughty in their dark lounge suits, the communist leaders were ranged around a crescent-shaped table on either side of the bulky florid figure of the Soviet Union's Leonid Brezhnev – among them old revolutionary war-horses such as Janos Kadar of Hungary and Walter Ulbricht of East Germany. Present too was a comparatively youthful newcomer, Nicolae Ceaucescu, the recently appointed Rumanian leader, who 23 years later would be ignominiously executed by close comrades in a building a few streets away as European Communism crumbled with breathtaking speed.

Aged 27 and just settling into my first Reuters assignment in East Berlin and Prague, I felt a sense of privilege at being present as a witness at this historic scene in which truculent working class revolutionary leaders – heroes or despots according to your point of view – were lording it smugly before the world's press in the throne chamber of a deposed Balkan monarch.

Then, and in the days that followed, as I worked and dined for the first time amongst senior members of a large international press corps, I understood fully that journalists who have covered significant international news stories carry within them unique and vivid first-hand impressions of history as it happens.

Through interviews they obtain intimate portraits of national leaders, they experience the atmosphere of capital cities and battlefields in moments of crisis, they become privy to the machinations of self-serving political or religious factions and encounter the suffering and heroism of ordinary men and women caught up in the dramas and tragedies which shape our world.

Such journalists compete fiercely until their dispatches are sent – or 'filed' as they are accustomed to say – and deadlines met. Afterwards they relax affably with one another as they swap anecdotes of their experiences, often ironic or farcical. This casual table talk made a lasting impression on me in Bucharest that summer – sitting, as we often were, beside the pool on the terrace of the faded Hotel Lido. I thought then what a pity it was that such conversations were not more often recorded and presented to a wider public.

That is why thirty years later I have counted it a privilege to contribute to this book, written by some forty foreign correspondents, all of whom at some time or other worked for Reuters. Their stories have a flavour of 'table talk' conveying a sense of what it was like being a witness to great events whilst also illuminating history for both general readers and specialists. Our basic brief was: tell the personal story behind the headlines.

Millions of people have become familiar with Frederick Forsyth's thrillers and must often wonder, as they read, where he draws the line between fact and fiction. Freddie and I were cub reporters at the same time in the early sixties on the *Eastern Daily Press* in Norfolk and he later reported for Reuters from East Berlin prior to my own assignment there. Here with his usual stylish aplomb he memorably describes the undoubtedly factual drama of his own arrest by Stasi secret police in communist East Germany – but not before he had outwitted them to get his story.

Sandy Gall, whose craggy face became familiar in millions of British households during a long spell co-presenting the News at Ten on Independent Television News (ITN), was a Reuters correspondent in the sixties. His fascination and regard for Afghanistan and its people, and his courageous solo trips into dangerous territory behind the fighting lines over the years became a distinguishing feature of a remarkable career that began at Reuters. Here he describes his horrific experiences in the Congo and in a death cell of Idi Amin, which have a particular resonance for me because of the two years of solitary confinement I spent in Peking as a prisoner of the Red Guards during Mao Tse Tung's Great Proletarian Cultural Revolution.

In sharp contrast is Derek Jameson's lively account of how he started a life in journalism as a Reuters copy boy, a tale which amply demonstrates the indefatigable Cockney brio that would take him to the editorial chairs of the *Daily Express* and the *News of the World* before he became a radio and television celebrity presenter. Award-winning television reporter John Suchet has a wry tale about his experiences as a Reuters trainee in Paris.

Other chapters tell the stories of men and women who reported headline news across half a century from the D-Day beaches of Normandy to the release from jail of Nelson Mandela. We learn what it was like to stand on Mao's toes; to report from the ringside at a Muhammad Ali fight; how it felt to grab a bicycle to communicate a news flash announcing a dramatic OPEC oil price rise; and what it took to stay cool as Wall Street crashed on Black Monday in 1987.

The late Sidney Weiland, who inspired this book, was a distinguished Reuters bureau chief – a cigar-chomping writer of impeccable style. From Moscow he became a master of interpreting the arcane secretive world of the communist bloc using tenuous scraps of information he gleaned from assiduously cultivated Cold War contacts. Sidney could turn out a clear interpretative story in next to no time where there were very few known facts – and perhaps for this and other outstanding qualities he was affectionately known among colleagues and competitors alike as 'Sizzling Sid.'

His most famous scoop was to reveal first to the world Nikita Khrushchev's historic secret denunciation of Stalin. This and other stories made him a legend on the Reuters wire.

Sidney famously detested the word 'hack' because he held that there was honour in good journalism. During his retirement and after a heart transplant, he travelled the world to teach his profession as he believed in it, at schools of journalism and other lecture venues. Sidney died in 1999 but his conviction of the importance of the foreign journalist's role became the mainspring for this book. It is both a tribute by his friends and colleagues to his lifelong dedication to his craft, and an illuminating kaleidoscope of historic moments.

ANTHONY GREY

# D-DAY: A BEACH IN NORMANDY

DOON CAMPBELL

FRONTLINES 1

## D-DAY: A BEACH IN NORMANDY | DOON CAMPBELL

# At 09.06 on the dull grey morning

of 6 June 1944, I landed in Hitler's Europe. It was a wet landing. The ramp of the invasion craft was steep and slippery, and I fell chest-deep in the sea. The commandos charged on. My pack, heavy and sodden, seemed made to drown me. Then a shove from a burly corporal gave me a toehold on Nazi-held France. We were ashore on Normandy. I was just 24, and I had been born with only one arm. Yet now here I was on D-day, among the 15 Reuters correspondents assigned to cover the biggest sea-borne invasion in history. The beach ahead was a sandy cemetery of mangled bodies. The big guns of the Allied fleet thundered behind me. This was war in its totality: theatrical and terrifying.

**D-Day: Royal Marine Commandos storm ashore at Aubin-sur-Mer, Normandy to open a second front and hasten the end of World War II**
06 June 1944

© Hulton Getty

PERHAPS VESUVIUS HELPED ME to get the D-Day assignment that I had dreamed of. In something of a lull, when I was covering the war in Italy, the volcano erupted. I remembered that General Mark Clark, the personable commander of the US Fifth Army, had told me never to hesitate to use one of his Piper Cub spotter planes, and so I flew over the spectacular show of Nature's anger, grander even than the fury of the mortal battlefield at Monte Cassino. The London editing desk loved the colour story and, in the quaint news agency 'cablese' of the day, it telegraphed: 'Vesuvius flight enterprisingest. Grand descriptive. You shortly homecoming for new assignment.'

Then came a private and personal letter from the headquarters of General Bernard Montgomery, who had just been made field commander of the Allied invasion force that was going to land on D-Day, telling me to be at a conference in London on 16 May 1944.

I'd last seen Monty in Italy when, after saying goodbye to the army of Desert Rats that he led there from his North African victory at Alamein, he squatted on his caravan steps to thank the war correspondents for their 'help, kindness and patience'.

Here he was again, the same confident cocky Monty, at the conference in London and giving a pep talk to British, Commonwealth and American journalists who would form the invasion press corps. He addressed us from a stage, carpeted with army blankets, where he had stood on the previous day to brief an audience that included King George VI, Winston Churchill and the Supreme Allied Commander, General Dwight D. Eisenhower of the United States.

'I think it will be a terrific party,' Monty told us. 'And I am absolutely confident we will win it.'

Monty would later end a rallying message to his 21st Army Group invasion force with this verse:

*He either fears his fate too much*
*Or his deserts are small*
*Who dare not put it to the touch*
*To win or lose it all.*

I often wondered where he got the much-quoted lines. Fifty years on, his son Viscount Montgomery would tell me they were by James Graham (1612–50), Marquis of Montrose, a Scottish soldier and royalist.

After the Monty pep talk, a top-secret directive put war correspondents on 36 hours' notice to slip quietly from family and friends to join the rest of an invasion force of almost 160 000 men, behind the barbed wire of isolated transit camps.

AN ELEGANT SILVER-HAIRED COLONEL, Philip Astley, first husband of Hollywood actress Madeleine Carroll, read out our assignments:

'Campbell, Reuters, Marine Commandos, D-Day.'

'Yippee,' I almost shouted aloud!

One reporter, aggrieved that he was not in the assault wave, protested, 'But this is the biggest story since the Crucifixion.'

'Yes,' snapped one of Monty's intelligence officers. 'And they managed that very well with just four correspondents.'

Next day I went to join some 2600 officers and men of the 1st Commando Brigade – the elite of British shock troops – reinforced with 200 Free French and led by Lord Lovat DSO MC. He was a tall slim stylish aristocrat, yet a humane and sensitive, as well as fearless, fighting soldier who led his men from the front.

The fellow Scot, who was head of the clan Fraser, smiled without conspicuous enthusiasm. Then he raised an eyebrow, not at my one arm, but at the three bags that an orderly had deposited with me. When I explained that I had brought 'a few civilizing comforts from the Cassino front in Italy', you could almost hear him thinking, 'Thank God he seems at least to have seen some live action.'

'You will get everything you need in a commando pack,' the brigadier said.

'Including a typewriter?'

'Yes. Including a typewriter.'

Lovat graciously invited me to wear the commandos' green beret, the proud symbol of the record of these battle-hardened men of every class and size – miners and managers, cooks and clerks – who had fought in the fjords of Norway, jungles of Madagascar and the desert sands of Africa. Trained to concert

'Campbell, Reuters, Marine Commandos, D-Day.'

pitch, they sprawled or squatted on grass banks or in shallow trenches under a canopy of trees. The scene to a 'son of the Manse' like myself had Galilean touches. At a church parade they sang a favourite hymn:

> *Eternal Father strong to save*
> *Whose arm hath bound the restless wave*
> *O hear us when we cry to Thee*
> *For those in peril on the sea.*

We were set to go. No more football in gym shoes or stump cricket, or games swinging like Tarzan in the treetops. Dinghies were inflated and tested, bayonets sharpened, magazines oiled, first-aid kits handed out. Lovat promised his men the cutting edge of the battle – 'Who dares, wins' – then ended his address with an aside to the Free French, whose Gallic panache lent colour to the ranks, *'A chacun son Boche. Vous allez nous montrer ce que vous savez faire. Demain matin on les aura.'*

Buses took us to the tiny vulnerable landing-craft and what has been described as the 'grotesque gala ... more like a regatta' of the embarkation. We got a sense of the scale of the invasion. By August, two million Allied troops would be in France. As our armada sailed into the darkness, Monty's old desert adversary, Rommel, the German field commander, was at home in Bavaria on his way to see Hitler.

I WAS HYPED UP. What mattered was the story. A ghastly thought kept recurring. Suppose a mine or rocket or shell sank the boat and killed any chance of getting a dispatch back to Reuters. The news – how to convey even a tiny detail of this mighty mosaic – transcended everything. What to do if I found myself in the drink? Should I take off my artificial arm? I could hardly float and much less swim with George, as I called it. Too late now. My pack was so full it could not have taken an extra toothbrush.

Between 03.00 and 05.00, maybe a thousand Allied aircraft were overhead. Spitfires and Mustangs strafed the beaches, as the bombers – Flying Fortresses, Liberators and Lancasters – cascaded bombs on the defences. Then at 05.30, Admiral Ramsey's battleships began to hurl their one-ton shells at batteries around Le Havre, each salvo screaming over us like an express train coming out of a tunnel. A smudge of smoke marked our landing place. Some commandos tried the breakfast of hot cocoa and oily sardines. Others were too seasick.

AT 09.06 OUR RAMPS WENT DOWN and we struggled through the water to that charnel-house of a beach, where the blood clotted the sand and shells had scattered the mangled limbs of the dead, and we followed Lord Lovat, who had gone ashore with his Scottish bagpiper some 25 minutes earlier.

I trod warily, to avoid mines, in the footsteps of those men who had already surged forward to the brooding German-held woods. The brigade objective was to smash an exit through Hitler's 'West Wall', destroy a battery and garrison at Ouistreham and then link up with airborne units, who had dropped by night on vital bridges over the River Orne and the Caen Canal to secure the Allied left flank. The commandos had to fight all the way and the corps commander said no troops had a more momentous task.

We'd heard that 140 German guns could hit Sword Beach. 'Get off it and keep moving,' was the order. I edged along the illusory shelter of a shattered garden wall to a ditch where medics were treating the wounded. We dodged death in that shallow furrow. I wrestled to get out of my crippling Bergen pack harness and almost furtively undid the straps. No. The salt water hadn't wrecked the typewriter, but every time I tried to use it, an 88-mm shell or a mortar exploded and clods of earth clogged the keys. So I tore a page from an exercise book and scribbled my dispatch in pencil under the dateline, 'A ditch 200 yards inside Normandy':

**We dodged death in that shallow furrow.**

Every minute more men and guns, tanks, vehicles and supplies are landing ... First prisoners have been taken – I counted 60 lined up in front of me: young men who looked staggered at the weight of Allied shipping. Our planes dominate the sky – not one *Luftwaffe* sighted. For the moment, with the wounded, I'm staying behind in a ditch where we claw at the soft earth for more cover from German shells and mortars. Moaning Minnies sometimes fall too close for comfort.

Then I crawled back to the beach – dropping flat on my face every few yards and moving forward again as the German gunners reloaded – where I gave a naval officer £5 to take that grimy scrap of paper back to England and post or telephone it to Reuters at 85 Fleet Street. It never got there. Did he survive?

Sometimes now I marvel at my parsimony. A fiver was what a Boer War correspondent paid an engine driver to circumvent Boer censorship and win the classic Reuters scoop of 1900, by hiding his story on the relief of the siege of Mafeking in a sandwich he was carrying for his lunch. Allow for inflation and £50 might have been about right for that naval officer on Sword Beach in 1944.

The Germans hosed us with fire. Medical orderlies and stretcher-bearers did heroic work. The noise deafened. The pace as the landing went on was frenetic. Only the dead knew peace.

My conducting officer, Captain Hamar Bagnall, who belonged to a very *pukka* regiment, thumbed us a ride inland on an armoured car and I was soon scrambling with a borrowed entrenching tool to try to dig a foxhole in an orchard as German bullets whined by. The ground was rock hard and we decided to beat it out of there, which we did just in time to escape some of the 50 tanks that the German 21st Panzer Division threw in on that sector as they began their counter attack to try to re-enact Dunkirk and hurl the British back into the sea.

Nearer the beach again, where it would be easier to send further despatches, I found a deep dugout in a garden in Ouistreham. It was damp and smelly and could have had rats, but it was a place to flop after being shot at for 12 hours, so I shivered and sneezed there through an agonizing night as the German riposte faltered. By one of those flukes that sometimes help to decide battles, the panzer crews had been flabbergasted at a crucial moment by the sight of 250 British gliders landing a final wave of airborne troops.

When it got really dark, the *Luftwaffe* appeared. I saw one plane shot to bits in the beam of a searchlight. Another fell in a flaming ball.

At dawn I found a villa where an old lady with silvery grey hair and a Red Cross badge motioned me to a chair where a German officer had sat a few hours earlier – a piece of hard black bread lay on the table – as soldiers with tommy-guns flushed out a sniper on a nearby roof. Snipers were everywhere, up trees, in hedgerows, attics and steeples. They were becoming a nuisance.

Then I heard a banging at the door. It was Leonard Mosley of the *Daily Sketch* in the maroon beret of the airborne troops – with whom he had dropped behind German lines at 01.00 on D-Day. We acquired a Jeep and rode up to find the commandos again on a dusty road across a kind of Walt Disney fantasy of a landscape, scattered with dozens of pancaked gliders.

Lovat was there – with the Germans 100 yards away – a rifle slung across his shoulder, strolling about a farm that was now his headquarters as nonchalantly as if he had been on the moors of his Highland estate. He was proud of his men. He had swung up the road at the head of them, to achieve their '100-per-cent-successful' link with the airborne troops, with a piper on either side of him. What style. What qualities of leadership. This was the stuff that fires men's spirit in battle.

> … a kind of Walt Disney fantasy of a landscape, scattered with dozens of pancaked gliders.

MONTY DID THAT TOO. Six days on, he briefed the war correspondents to tell us, 'We have won the battle of the beaches.'

Holly and fir trees and sweet-scented white blossom surrounded the caravans of his tactical HQ, where he went on to confirm something that many had suspected: that the Germans were using female snipers.

'There are some very stout-hearted German women,' he said, 'and women snipers have been killed while doing their stuff.'

Every fresh village or mile of an Allied advance that often met with fanatical resistance was a new cameo of war. Beef instead of horseflesh, where Navy shells had killed 400 head of cattle. One night we made a billet in a château where a *vicomtesse* made a noble meal of German salted meat, Danish butter and black bread, artichokes and cider, coffee and cream. Then there was Bayeux – a town that battle passed by, where Chanel No. 5 and silk stockings could be found at bargain prices – and, before long, a liberated Brussels with its cabarets and champagne.

Always somewhere was the savage obscenity of war. We saw the slaughter of von Kluge's forces in the Falaise Gap, which Eisenhower would later call a scene from Dante, where you could walk hundreds of yards and step on nothing but decayed flesh.

The advance drove on until, in March 1945, it was time for the Allies to drop airborne forces across the Rhine and enter the heart of Hitler's Germany. Besides D-Day, that was the only assignment I solicited as a war correspondent and it would bring me eyeball to eyeball with a very sudden kind of death.

IT ALL BEGAN AFTER A NIGHT in a Brussels night spot, where the bubbly was as flat as the hostess, when an army dispatch rider with a homing instinct for the place brought a cable for Charles Lynch, a distinguished Canadian journalist and then, like me, a Reuters man. His face registered his reaction as he read the London cable.

'Let's see,' I said.

'Are you prepared to undertake important but hazardous assignment which may involve parachute drop?' it said.

I was by now Reuters chief correspondent, 21st Army Group, and I had pulled Charlie back from the Canadian front for a few hours' rest and relaxation in the fleshpots of the liberated Belgian capital.

'Look Charlie,' I said, 'the war's nearly over. You've got a wife and family back in Canada. You owe it to them to get back in one piece. Let me handle this with London.' Charlie reluctantly consented and I drafted a cable that ended: 'Why I not offered important but hazardous assignment?' A sober light of day brought London's reply, telling me, 'It's all yours.'

'Why I not offered important but hazardous assignment?'

You need two hands to work a parachute, so they assigned me to a glider. The troops called those WACO CG4A gliders 'cardboard coffins'.

NO ONE SLEPT MUCH at our eve-of-battle rendezvous near Paris. Someone put on the wireless to hear Radio Berlin as it blared: 'Allied airborne landings on a large scale to establish bridgeheads east of the Rhine must be expected. We are prepared.' Another station said Eisenhower had seen a secret German High Command document ordering the execution of Allied airborne soldiers. We were roused soon after 05.00 for the usual American pre-combat breakfast of bacon and eggs, pancakes and syrup, peaches and cream. Condemned men are fed a hearty last meal!

My good arm rested on a box of grenades as I sat, squashed with three companions in a Jeep that was harnessed to the floor of Glider 39. 'Chattanooga' was its name and the pilot said he'd never carried such a heavy a load. Someone else observed that a shift of a mere inch or so of the cargo would tilt us in a terminal nosedive.

But it was exciting as we cavorted in the slipstream of the plane that towed us, flying over the rubble of a devastated Europe towards Germany and proud to be up there with America's crack 17th Airborne in the biggest one-day air landing of the war.

Near the Rhine, we were unhooked and it was as thick with smoke as a London 'pea-soup' fog. Bullets gave the glider convulsions as they ripped its wings. In a weird and fatalistic moment I almost hoped a German 88-mm shell or flak would hit the box of grenades and blow me to Kingdom Come before I knew it, thus sparing me the indignity of a helpless tumble in the back of a Jeep down two thousand feet of nothing.

Then there was an opening in the German-laid smog and the pilot committed Chattanooga to a final dive at almost 100 mph, with no way to adjust the descent or use the rudder. Ahead lay a wire fence, then a stone barn with white walls. The pilot knew – and so did I – that if he caught the fence we had a hope.

He just caught the top of it. The glider lurched to a halt, with its nose and much of the fuselage smashed, but we were alive and already scrambling out, as the craft behind us came in, missed the fence, hit the barn and exploded.

Other gliders plunged like blazing torches, disgorging men and machines in mid-air. Gliders hurdled ditches, wrestled with telephone wires – still coming in to land as the mortars and machine-guns opened fire on those of us on the ground.

We made it to a ditch that was already full of American troops.

'Say, son where d'yah reckon we are?' asked a young officer who was trying to read a silk-handkerchief map.

'Up creek, *sans* paddle,' I replied.

Wounded were being carried to that ditch. A medic used a trench knife for instant surgery.

'Get outta there! Get up and away, you so-and-so's!' That was the voice of General Matthew Ridgway, as he strode from a wood and led the way along a shell-shattered road, exhorting his men to take their noses out of the dirt. We got out in one piece. But Reuters colleague Seaghan Maynes, who had dropped by parachute, beat me by 24 hours with a despatch from the Rhine crossing.

THEN THERE WAS BELSEN – the ultimate depravity, the most evil atrocity I have ever witnessed in five different wars. 'You have actually to see Belsen to realize fully the things that went on.' So wrote Montgomery to an English friend soon after British troops began to liberate the concentration camp on 15 April 1945.

War correspondents first heard about it two days later from the senior medical officer of General Dempsey's Second Army, when he spoke about a camp near Bremen that was 'the most horrible frightful place' he had ever seen. He told us of a heap, more than 60 yards long, of the naked bodies of women within sight of hundreds of children. Gutters had blocked with rotting dead. When I got there I could only write:

**War seems almost wholesome compared with the black spot beyond the big red and white 'Danger – Typhus' notices strung along the road for more than three miles from the main entrance to the compound. Men and women I saw here will be dead by the time you read this copy. In one hut I found about fifty, crammed together almost sore to sore... one was trying to bite rotten wood, another pitifully throwing coal dust into his mouth; and yet another dipped a hard crust in a filthy puddle, because he could only swallow slops. With all their pain and weakness, they tried to smile, to extend withered arms. Most just welcomed us with a certain look in their eyes – an unspoken yet eloquent language.**

Many were professional people, among them teachers, lawyers, doctors, architects, managers, industrialists. A German doctor was there for being rude about Hitler. It was not always a good thing to get a gift parcel, because then you were more likely to be murdered.

I spoke to the camp commandant, Josef Kramer – the 'Beast of Belsen' – his ankles shackled as he sat and brooded on a short three-legged stool.

'I was worried about conditions in the camp,' he said. 'But thousands of prisoners kept flooding in – from fifteen to more than forty thousand – with no increase in food or accommodation. It all got out of hand.'

Half a century later, the German ZDF television channel invited me back there. News and camera crews who were too young to know the reality of Nazi rule wished me to bear witness to the bestiality. I told them how I had written on 20 April 1945: 'War seems almost wholesome.' Those acres of infamy are now a carpet of heather. But you could never forget that beneath this bleak moorland were buried more than 100 000 human beings.

WORLD WAR II WAS ALMOST OVER. Stalin's Red Army swept toward Berlin as we advanced from the west. One crazy day I drove past thousands of armed Germans to enter the disintegrating Reich's second city of Hamburg, three hours ahead of the first Allied soldier. They gaped. On the burgomaster's desk a portrait of Hitler stood among daffodils.

'You are not supposed to be here yet,' said the burgomaster.

Dozens of police scuttled about, still giving the Hitler salute. One had a blanket over his shoulder and a loaf of bread under his arm.

The day before the final unconditional Nazi surrender, I was at the little Baltic town of Wismar, where British and Soviet troops had linked up to see Monty meet Red Army Marshal Konstantin Rokossovsky, who drove up in a black limousine. Three inches taller than the peppery Englishman, he looked more like a benevolent philosopher than the legendary defender of Moscow. They met in a cobbled lane in front of a paratroop guard of honour for a handshake that lasted 90 seconds. As Rokossovsky beamed, his gold fillings glinted in the sun. Then he drowned Monty's opening words with a torrent of rhetoric, hailing him as 'a great soldier of the war'.

I spoke to the camp commandant, Josef Kramer – the 'Beast of Belsen' – his ankles shackled as he sat and brooded on a short three-legged stool.

# DEATH BEFORE NOON

RONALD BEDFORD

FRONTLINES 2

## DEATH BEFORE NOON | RONALD BEDFORD

# For millions of wartime Londoners,

Thursday 8 March 1945 was to be just another dreary winter day of struggling
to work and home again or queuing in the food shops. Allied armies had taken
Cologne, but not even a starry-eyed optimist dreamed that Germany would
surrender within 60 days. For me, from the moment at 4 am when I tumbled out of
bed, it would be a day I would never forget. I was a 23-year-old reporter who, only
a few weeks earlier, had come to London from the provinces to join Reuters.
I had been kept out of the forces, because I was blind in one eye from birth and
had poor sight in the other. My task for the day was to cover an execution.
Before noon I would witness another horrible kind of death that fell as a bolt from
the blue – a strike on London by one of Hitler's V 2 missiles.

**Wartime London: St Paul's Cathedral during the Blitz. This photograph was used as a propaganda shot by both Britain and Germany**
31 December 1940

© Hulton Getty

I TRUDGED THROUGH ILL-LIT STREETS to be outside the grimy walls of His Majesty's Pentonville Gaol by 6 am, which was three hours before the time that had been set for US Army paratrooper Karl Gustav Hulten to be hanged on the gallows for the murder of a London taxi driver. It was a case of some notoriety, which was known as the 'Cleft Chin Murder' because of a description of the victim issued by the Metropolitan Police.

The assignment had come to me because I had earlier written for Reuters a pen profile of a famous campaigner against the death penalty of that time. She was Mrs Violet van der Elst or the 'Woman in Black', as she was everywhere called. She was a millionaire in her own right, a self-made entrepreneur who specialized in perfumes and toiletries, and who introduced the British male chin to the value of brushless shaving cream. She was in full measure a character. She dressed all in black and travelled in a black Rolls-Royce. Her motley army of supporters included genuine abolitionists, as well as the morbidly curious of all ages, and others who were simply attracted as moths to a flame by the sight of a crowd.

Even without Mrs van der Elst, the day's story had the ingredients of a thriller. Hulten and his moll, a Welsh-born 18-year-old blonde dancer called Elizabeth (Betty) Jones, were a Bonnie and Clyde duo who rampaged across the London area in an orgy of robbery, often at gunpoint. Their trial for murder at the Old Bailey was the first in which an American soldier and a British girl had been jointly charged in a British court and the first time, since the 1922 Thompson–Bywaters case, that a man and a woman had been sentenced to death together.

Hulten was the first American GI to be hanged by the British, and his execution was set for his twenty-third birthday. His blonde accomplice missed dying at the end of a rope because Home Secretary Herbert Morrison reprieved her some 48 hours before she was to do so. She would spend ten years in gaol.

There was plenty of activity outside Pentonville. Mrs van der Elst marshalled her forces from her black Rolls, which she used as a mobile HQ outside every gaol in Britain where executions were carried out. Hangings would go on until 1965, when the House of Commons voted for abolition.

Three hours before sentence was carried out, the Woman in Black was already haranguing the crowd on a loudhailer, powered by the car's battery, to expound her reasons why the death penalty should be scrapped. Men with sandwich-boards, whom she hired on such occasions, paraded her slogans and a brass band, also hired, was tuning up for the moment of the execution, when it would strike up the hymn, 'Abide with Me'.

When 9 am came, Mrs van der Elst's ragged army, by this time several hundreds – maybe even a thousand – strong, suddenly decided to rush the gaol gate. What they hoped to achieve was never clear to me, but as I ran across the road to keep up with the action I was hurled to the ground, striking my back on the kerb and almost passing out.

By the time I picked myself up, the official Notice of Execution had been posted, and Mrs van der Elst had been arrested with some of her followers. Although in considerable pain, I filed my story before returning to Reuters headquarters at 85 Fleet Street, feeling that I had had enough excitement for one day. But it was not to be so.

CHIEF NEWS EDITOR SID MASON insisted that I go immediately to the nearest hospital, St Bartholomew's, to make sure that no bones had been broken. Things were fairly quiet at Bart's when I arrived, and it was not long before I was being examined by a young doctor, who gently poked and prodded my spinal area. He told me that he did not think anything had been broken, but he wanted me to go for X-ray to be absolutely certain. By this time it was ten past eleven. I was stripped to the waist and he had his white coat on, when there was an almighty bang, the building shuddered, and we were showered with the dirt that had accumulated in the almost eight-and-a-half centuries during which Bart's (established in 1123) had been caring for the sick. We looked at each other and burst out laughing. We might have been a couple of miners coming off-shift in the days before pithead baths were introduced.

'What the hell was that?' I asked.

The doctor did not know. It was only minutes before we found out, as the ambulances started to arrive with dead and wounded.

… a brass band, also hired, was tuning up for the moment of the execution, when it would strike up the hymn, 'Abide with Me'.

A V 2 rocket had hit Smithfield, London's meat market, a few hundred yards away. Meat porters, shop assistants and customers, many of them women, were the victims of the horror of the missile strike that came without any warning from the grey sky. All told, 110 people had been killed and 123 injured, many seriously, in the twinkling of an eye.

The young doctor who had examined me had no time for niceties. As he rushed away to help cope with the dead and the dying that were now pouring in, he told me, 'If you are in severe pain this time tomorrow, come back for that X-ray.' I did not return.

Outside the hospital, the scene was one of absolute horror. Rescue workers were already scrabbling amid great chunks of masonry and ironwork, to try to pull free those trapped beneath a mountain of debris. The warhead had exploded in the railway loading bays close to the Circle Line of the Underground. At ground level, twisted girders and a sea of broken glass showed the severity of the blast.

This was to prove, however, to be almost the end of the terror assault by V 2 rockets on British civilians. The V 2 was the precursor of the intercontinental ballistic missiles of the nuclear age. Unlike its V 1 predecessor or 'doodlebug', which was a flying bomb, it was a silent killer. You could hear the putt-putt of the V 1 engine; no sound heralded the approach of the rocket. George Orwell summed up this life-or-death difference when he wrote that the V 1 at least gave Londoners a chance to dive under the table.

THOSE WHO SURVIVED A V 2 ATTACK almost always said that they heard nothing. Many remembered just an awful draught that preceded the explosion. The V 2s were launched mostly from mobile ramps, usually in Holland, Belgium or France. Weighing 12.7 tons, each carried a one-ton warhead of high explosive and smashed down at up to 4000 mph from a height of around fifty miles. Of 1115 V 2s that reached Britain, 501 fell in the London Civil Defence area, killing 2724 people and injuring 6476 more.

> Those who survived a V 2 attack almost always said that they heard nothing.

There was an ironic twist for me to that day of 8 March 1945. The man largely responsible for the development of the V 2 was the German rocket scientist, Wernher von Braun. He went on to mastermind the gigantic Saturn 5 rocket, which put a total of 12 Americans on the moon. I reported the Space Age for the *Daily Mirror* from the first earth orbit by Russia's robot Sputnik in 1957 until my retirement in 1985, and met von Braun often at Cape Canaveral and at Mission Control in Houston during the exciting days of the US Apollo men-to-the-moon programme.

## 'THE POWER OF THE SUN'

A DEADPAN COMMUNIQUÉ that America had dropped an atom bomb on 6 August 1945 didn't quite say that mankind now knew how to wipe out the planet, or that it had caused 140 000 deaths, nor could it be known that the Nagasaki bomb three days later would kill some 75 000 more people. But as details emerged, amid wartime secrecy, the news tickers began to hint at the enormity of the event.

GUAM – T ATOMIC BOMB WIPED OUT OVER FOUR SQUARE MILES OR 60 PER CENT OF HIROSHIMA, IT WAS ANNOUNCED FROM GENRL SPAATZ'S HQ TODAY. REUTER MF 0500

'The men aboard with me gasped, "My God!" And what had been Hiroshima was a mountain of smoke like a giant mushroom.' The late Jack Smyth of Reuters had that quote from US Navy Captain William Parsons, an observer in the Superfortress 'Enola Gay' – named for the pilot's mother – that bombed Hiroshima. A headline writer on another report also found words to signal how science was rewriting history.

'POWER OF THE SUN' HURLED AT JAPAN
ATOM BOMB NO. 1, THE WORLDS MOST SOUGHT-AFTER AND MOST DEVASTATING MISSILE, WAS DROPPED BY A US PLANE ON T JAPANESE CITY OF HIROSHIMA TODAY. T BOMB, WHI HAS THE POWER OF 20 000 TONS OF TNT, WS MADE IN SECRET FACTORIES IN AMERICA BY BRITISH AND AMERICAN SCIENTISTS AFTER YEARS OF RESEARCH, SAYS REUTER. ITS EXISTENCE WAS DISCLOSED BY PRESIDENT TRUMAN ON HIS RETURN TO WASHINGTON FM THE BIG THREE CONFERENCE TODAY IN THESE WORDS:
'SIXTEEN HOURS AGO AN AMERICAN AEROPLANE DROPPED ONE BOMB ON HIROSHIMA, AN IMPORTANT JAPANESE ARMY BASE. TT BOMB HAD MORE THAN 2000 TIMES T BLAST POWER OF T BRITISH GRAND SLAM WH IS T LARGEST BOMB EVER YET USED IN T HISTORY OF WARFARE'. REUTER MF

Japan surrendered on 14 August, ending World War II. Winston Churchill spoke of 'God's mercy' that Nazi Germany failed to acquire a nuclear weapon and Stalin put secret police chief Lavrenti Beria in charge of the Soviet bid to catch up with the West. A 'balance of terror' would mark the new Cold War. Nuclear warheads were placed on upgrades of the Nazi V 2 rocket, to create the Intercontinental Ballistic Missile. France and China joined the nuclear club and late entries included India and Pakistan – President Clinton called Kashmir one of the most dangerous places on earth. After the Cold War, security of the formerly Soviet arsenal would be a new worry.

**The devastation of Hiroshima after the first
atom bomb, named 'Little Boy', was dropped,
6 August 1945**
01 April 1946

©AP photo

# WHO, WHAT, WHEN, WHERE AND WHY?

DEREK JAMESON

FRONTLINES 3

## WHO, WHAT, WHEN, WHERE AND WHY?  |  DEREK JAMESON

# Few people know that Derek Jameson,

the slum kid who became a national celebrity as editor and broadcaster, began his career at Reuters. Spurred on by gaining first prize in a wartime essay competition, he climbed aboard a No. 6 bus at Hackney Wick, jumped off before 85 Fleet Street and went inside to land a job as messenger boy. It was January 1944 and he had just left school, aged 14. Two years later Walton A. Cole, the agency's editor and presiding genius, spotted his potential and made him a trainee reporter.

**Derek Jameson (right) begins his career in journalism**
Easter 1946

© Ronald Bedford

OBVIOUSLY TONY COLE WAS VERY TAKEN with my Cockney cheek. He was a Scotsman of awesome proportions who tended to issue orders in a kind of mid-Atlantic Scots drawl. Well over six feet tall and weighing some eighteen stone, he put the wind up most of those who came under his steely gaze. Lowly messengers kept well away, especially as he invariably wanted cigarettes. That meant tramping the streets of wartime London to find a tobacconist with some rare supplies and join the inevitable queue.

A piece of cardboard labelled 'Editor' and shaped like a bell would jiggle back and forth over the messenger desk when the big man rang. Groans all round until someone decided to respond. Usually me. The day came when he demanded brusquely, 'Why is it, every time I ring the bell, you appear, laddie?'

What gratitude. I didn't hesitate. 'Because all the other lads say, "Let the old bastard wait – he only wants fags."'

He loved that and roared with laughter. I was taken on there and then as his personal messenger. To me he was unfailingly kind and generous. Mr Cole – I never call him anything else – lived for Reuters, sitting at his desk some 13 hours a day when not travelling on business. In those austere days at the end of World War II, he more or less took charge of my life. How was I getting on? Was I keeping up night school, as he had commanded? How was my shorthand? What about spelling? His devoted secretary, Joyce Hewlett, was always ready with her dictionary with a word he had chosen for me to learn.

On occasion, editor and messenger boy would chat in low tones, usually at eventide by the light of a single desk lamp at the far end of the fourth floor editorial.

'You won't earn much, but you'll learn to be a journalist in the best school of all.'

It was during one of these exchanges that I told him the time had come for me to leave. I was desperate to become a journalist and would have to find work as a trainee in the provinces.

'You can't do that,' he said. 'Aren't you giving money at home? You can't afford to go to the provinces and still send money to your mother.' He thought hard, weighing me up behind his thick spectacles, and came to a quick decision.

'We'll train you here. There's no reason why not. You won't earn much, but you'll learn to be a journalist in the best school of all.'

And so it came to pass. At 16, Fleet Street's youngest trainee of all time. It meant a seven-year apprenticeship, because the National Union of Journalists didn't recognize anyone in Fleet Street as a trained journalist below the age of 23. Nevertheless, I was on my way.

I LEARNED MY CRAFT under the chief reporter, Ronald G. Bedford, one of Fleet Street's best-loved characters, who went on to spend more than 30 years as the *Daily Mirror* science editor. Just about everything I know is down to this feisty little Yorkshireman.

Who, what, when, where and why? Five honest servants and the essence of good journalism. Ronnie drummed the mantra into my head. Remember, too, that truth is everything. Always be fair, balanced and objective. A lifetime later I cannot read a newspaper or listen to a news bulletin without noting whether or not its reporters are up to scratch.

We all recall our first story. Ronnie insisted I should find my own. It turned out to be a good human situation on the banks of the Thames alongside Tower Bridge. The Port of London Authority proposed to abolish a stretch of sand dumped there, the only kind of beach many East End kids like myself had ever known.

He made me rewrite it 14 times. That's right – 14. Who says the beach is dangerous to shipping, how did it get there in the first place, how many kids use it, what do the locals say, where are quotes from the Port Authority? And so on until he was satisfied it was complete and of some interest to Reuters subscribers across the world.

It took about a week to produce and in the process teach me to be true to the best Reuters traditions. 'Fine, fine,' Ronnie finally concurred. 'Put it on the wire.' Would you believe, it was actually published. A cutting turned up months later from a paper in Java. As for the beach, it disappeared never to be heard of again.

WE WERE PART OF THE UK DESK that put together a British news file serving adjoining regional desks. Their role was to edit global dispatches for their own areas of interest – Europe, South America, North America, Africa, India, the Far East and Australasia. Hub of the operation was the General Desk, later renamed 'Central Desk', where the world's news flowed in by cable, radio, telephone and teleprinter.

Tony Cole was the human dynamo who took Reuters from a dull Empire-driven agency, rooted in the past, to the highly professional outfit that became news centre of the world through the war years. One reason for its success was that it remained a neutral observer, never a participant.

By the time peace arrived, Reuters had a staff of nearly 2000, operating in 40 countries. Some correspondents found themselves with no war left to report, while others had been displaced in the political turmoil of the post-war years. Thus it was that chief reporter Ronnie Bedford became mother hen to a bunch of odds and sods, each with a large question mark hanging over his future. I was the gawky kid happy to sit at the feet of these exiles, who had been through six years of war and knew most of the answers. Men like Monty Radulovic, a tall powerful Yugoslav who escaped invading Nazi forces by stealing a submarine and sailing it to Alexandria. He had never been in a sub before. Now he had been forced to flee his country yet again by Marshal Tito, its new communist ruler. Then there was Alfonso Mauri, a fiery Spaniard who had fled Franco's fascist regime for Argentina, only to be exiled yet again by dictator Juan Peron.

Here they were side by side, communist and royalist, professional friends and political enemies. They would go at each other hammer and tongs in halting English, while the rest of us fell about.

'Monty spit on communists!' he would roar and look as if he were about to do just that.

'Monty, you very silly person,' came back the curly-haired Spaniard. 'I think you nice man. In the head? Nussink!'

These two were good for laughs, but my favourite was a quiet Irishman named Jack Smyth, a hero to us messengers during the war when he parachuted into Arnhem with British airborne forces and was captured by the Germans.

Held prisoner for nine months, he was tortured by the Gestapo. They wanted to know how many Allied paratroopers were under training back in Britain.

'There was I, a neutral Irishman, demanding to see the nearest Irish ambassador,' he told us. 'Well, they were having none of that. They gave me a hell of a pasting. "Jaysus," I'd tell 'em, "if I knew the answer, wouldn't I be telling? It's not worth losing my teeth for. I'm an Irishman."'

Liberated by Allied forces, Jack immediately volunteered to cover the end of the war in the Far East. In August 1945 he was the first to give the world an eyewitness description of the atomic bomb on Hiroshima.

Now he was in London with the rest of us, kicking his heels and wondering what was coming next. Our first major peacetime story was the protracted negotiations leading to independence for India and the creation of Pakistan. Jack, with his Irish charm, usually managed to outshine the rest of us. It didn't take long to work out that his mysterious female contact on the telephone every day was Countess Mountbatten, wife of the Viceroy of India.

MY BEAT WAS MOHAMMED ALI JINNAH, founder of Pakistan, whose rip-roaring speeches may have inspired his Moslem followers, but left me in desperate straits. He never finished a sentence, which played hell with my rookie's Gregg shorthand. I feared getting a quote wrong and pouring fuel on the flames about to devour the Indian subcontinent.

'Don't worry, old boy,' said my fellow reporter, Monty Taylor. 'Just get the context. Long as it sounds right they'll never know the difference.' I took unflappable Monty at his word. He had famously sent some of the first dispatches from the D-Day invasion using a carrier pigeon. He told me later it was just as well that his unit found a relatively quiet sector, because otherwise his feathered friend, Gustave, might never have got through with the news: 'First assault troops landed 07.50.'

Poor Ronnie Bedford had to make sense of us lot. He would stoop over the typewriter, his eyes inches from the keys, knocking our reports into shape before they went on the

*Ronnie Bedford became mother hen to a bunch of odds and sods, each with a large question mark hanging over his future.*

wire. 'You've written this with the left boot,' he would grumble, though he always forgave our errors and omissions.

Otherwise, God help us, we might fall foul of Sidney J. Mason, a belt-and-braces former docker in charge of all correspondents. Sid, as everyone called him, had been poached from a rival agency by Tony Cole and made chief news editor. There was no pleasing him where I was concerned. Every word of mine seemed to come in for harsh criticism. I assumed he objected to a Cockney waif like himself daring to follow his footsteps, though in later years he confessed he had been less than fair.

'You've written this with the left boot,' he would grumble ...

Whatever the merits of Tony Cole's decision to play Pygmalion in my case, never again would any 16-year-old Reuters London messenger be given the same opportunity.

In the 1950s the agency recruited a handful of Oxbridge trainees, though most ultimately left to seek richer pastures elsewhere. Notable exception was Cambridge graduate Gerald Long, who was to succeed Cole as general manager after his premature death in 1963 – overwork and overeating had taken their toll. He was only 51. David Chipp, first Western correspondent to report Communist China, was another varsity entrant. Eventually he became boss of the Press Association, Reuters domestic sister.

At one time the three of us beginners shared a table at the far end of the Central Desk as we got to grips with the art of sub-editing. We liked to josh each other about who would make it in journalism. In the event, each was to earn a place in Fleet Street's turbulent history. After all, as Tony Cole said, didn't we learn our craft in the best school of all?

# A TYRANT AND HIS BIRTHDAY BALLOON

DON DALLAS

FRONTLINES 4

**A TYRANT AND HIS BIRTHDAY BALLOON** | DON DALLAS

# In 1947 Joseph Stalin was at the height

of his power. The world was in the icy grip of the Cold War. I had not been assigned abroad before, but when Reuters surprised me with the offer of a post in Moscow I jumped at the one in a thousand chance of penetating to the heart of the Iron Curtain. A precious Soviet visa in my passport, I said goodbye to the subs' desk in Fleet Street…

**Joseph Stalin**
c.1947

© Hulton Getty

I SET OFF ON MY FIRST FOREIGN ASSIGNMENT for Reuters with a sense of expectation and a spirit of enquiry – a spirit rather confounded when, on my arrival in Moscow, the Russians immediately placed me in the Golden Cage reserved for correspondents and diplomats.

What sort of cage? Travel was barred to approximately 95 per cent of the Soviet Union. Effectively correspondents were confined to Moscow, with an occasional trip to Leningrad after approval by the authorities. Our rooms and offices were bugged. We were constantly denounced in the press as imperialist spies and even more significantly, every word we wrote was subject to censorship. We were in a cage with clipped wings and partly muted. Contact with ordinary Russians (those without special permission to mix with foreigners, the 'trusties') was non-existent and could have been dangerous for them.

**We were in a cage with clipped wings and partly muted.**

The Metropole Hotel in the centre of Moscow, where I lived and had my office, was the hub of the Golden Cage. Most of the Western correspondents during World War II had lived there and a few remained. From the Russian viewpoint, it had excellent facilities for a close watch on activities of foreign residents.

The golden side? In fact we lived the high life, mixing constantly with top diplomats at innumerable receptions held on the national days of the states concerned, sometimes champagne and caviar affairs. The authorities allowed correspondents to import duty-free food, drink and cigarettes, a boon in an austere society where toilet rolls were like gold dust. But, more important, we had privileged access to the finest Russian culture. Tickets were always available for the Bolshoi Theatre for its best opera and ballet performances and to national institutions like the Moscow Arts Theatre with its Stanislavsky associations and its magnificent stagings of the great Chekhov plays, probably the finest in the world.

Top Russian orchestras performed in the concert halls, concentrating particularly on the Russian nineteenth-century composers. Many works by Prokofiev and Shostakovich were played until a 1948 music decree damned several of their works. No Stravinsky of course. He was vilified as an *émigré* who had sold his soul to the West.

To obtain theatre tickets at short notice, it was necessary to write a letter in Russian on a Reuters letterhead and – absolutely mandatory – stamp it with the big Reuters rubber stamp, then deliver it by messenger. No Russian bureaucrat could afford to ignore a request from the privileged owner of a big red rubber stamp. More a traditional Russian approach than a by-product of Communism.

SO WE LIVED ON TWO LEVELS, with compensations balancing frustrations. It soon became clear why Reuters had said a command of Russian was not a prerequisite for the job. The need was for a competent secretary-translator who would painstakingly plough through the often indigestible columns of *Pravda*, *Izvestia* and other publications and monitor Moscow radio.

The accepted aim of national day receptions is to cultivate relations with leading nationals of the countries concerned. But in Moscow so few Russians could be persuaded to attend that the diplomats ended up entertaining themselves – and us. A kind of diplomatic incest forced on them by circumstances beyond their control, but certainly making no contribution towards ending the Cold War.

English was the language of communication at the diplomatic parties. An ambassador from an Asian country remarked to me, 'If I had known how much English was spoken in Moscow, I would have brought along with me one of my English-speaking wives'.

STALIN WAS THE MAN WE NEVER MET although he dominated the scene in a Big Brother way. Everywhere there were portraits and statues of Stalin and Lenin, normally linked together. We saw Stalin only at a distance, reviewing big military and civilian parades on May Day and 7 November, anniversary of the Bolshevik Revolution, when he stood with his closest colleagues on top of the Lenin Mausoleum in Red Square, wearing his marshal's uniform. He was never available for an interview, even with Soviet journalists, and made no public speech during my period in Moscow. He was no rabble-rousing orator and spoke Russian with a pronounced Georgian accent.

Stalin's 70th birthday (23 December 1949) provided a graphic illustration of the fact that Soviet Russia was a country of the bizarre, escalating at times into sheer surrealism in the Magritte style.

*Pravda's* front page had been monopolized for days by fulsome tributes to Stalin, work pledges by factories and farms and reports of gifts from foreign potentates. Andrei Vyshinsky, then foreign minister, gave a birthday reception for the diplomatic corps to which correspondents were also invited. With me, as we drove across Red Square that evening, were Andy Steiger, an American who was about to take over as the Reuters man, and Harrison E. Salisbury of the *New York Times*.

> Stalin was floating above the Kremlin and there was no sign of God.

'Isn't this a ridiculous situation?' I said. 'All this hullabaloo on Stalin's birthday and yet we, correspondents reporting to the entire world, don't even know where he is tonight. Is he in the Kremlin or in one of his *dachas* (country residences) in the south or some place else? We just don't have a clue and it's a sure bet he won't be at the Vyshinsky reception.'

'But there he is,' cried Andy.

'Where?'

'Up there, above the Kremlin.'

I looked up and saw an enormous balloon with, attached to it a giant effigy of the dictator, picked out by powerful searchlights. There is an old Russian saying that there is nothing above Moscow but the Kremlin (an ancient fortress on a hill) and nothing above the Kremlin but God. That night Stalin was floating above the Kremlin and there was no sign of God.

Frankie, my wife, and I left Moscow a few days after Stalin's birthday, travelling overnight by train to Leningrad and then on to Helsinki. At the Finnish border the train stopped for a customs check. A few miles further on, when we assumed we were safely in Finland, there was another stop. Then we heard a clank, clank, clanking noise, coming all the way down the train and suddenly our compartment was plunged into darkness, as iron shutters came down over each window. Now we really knew what the Iron Curtain was all about.

The explanation: at the end of the brief Russo-Finnish war in 1940, the Russians established a naval base at Porkkala, overlooking the Gulf of Finland, about 20 miles from Helsinki. Our train stopped at the approach to the base. The Finnish driver left the train and was replaced by a Russian driver, and the shutters came down, then the train set off again. The Iron Curtain ordeal lasted for the longest 15 minutes of my life. Then the shutters went up and glorious sunshine streamed into our compartment, lighting up a Christmas card scene of snow, ice and forest. We heard later that the driver got off at the second stop and was replaced by another Finnish driver.

From the symbolic Golden Cage to a very real, very solid, iron curtain. The story of my 900 days in Russia.

BACK IN LONDON, when Stalin died on 5 March 1953, I wrote an obituary. I said he would pass into history leaving a question mark behind him: around the world millions revered and millions reviled him.

Three years later Nikita Khrushchev, so lavish in his praise of Stalin in his lifetime, branded him a tyrant and blood-stained executioner. Western historians now put the total of Stalin's victim's (excluding the many millions killed during World War II) at approximately 20 million. In our cocooned existence during my Moscow days, how little we really knew. In that iceberg society, only the thinnest tip of the iceberg was visible – and sometimes even that disappeared from sight.

# ASCENT OF EVEREST

PETER JACKSON AND ADRIENNE FARRELL

FRONTLINES 5

## ASCENT OF EVEREST | PETER JACKSON AND ADRIENNE FARRELL

# In 1953, an expedition set out

for Mount Everest. Twelve earlier attempts on the world's highest mountain had failed. This new British bid, from Nepal, to reach the 26 028-foot (8848-metre) summit was financed by *The Times* of London, which had sent a correspondent with the expedition, and the challenge for other journalists was to break through a wall of secrecy that was created to protect its 'investment'. Adrienne Farrell was Reuters correspondent in New Delhi, responsible for India and Nepal, and Peter Jackson was the staff man in Pakistan.

**Sherpa Tenzing Norgay (left)
and Sir Edmund Hillary
photographed by Peter Jackson
after their ascent of Everest,
seen behind them**
06 June 1953

© Peter Jackson

ADRIENNE

As the British prepared to set out, I suggested to Reuters in London that our only hope of getting news was to send a reporter to Everest. I volunteered myself. Being small, I thought I could be carried in a traditional way over the mountains, in a basket on the back of a Nepali porter. But I added that, if they did not think I could get there, they should send their nearest man. There was no immediate reply to this hare-brained idea and I set off instead for the Naga Hills in eastern India, where a revolt was brewing. Then Reuters suddenly decided the idea was not so hare-brained after all and sent a cable to Peter in Pakistan that would lead to a great scoop and change both our lives forever.

PETER

On 31 March 1953, I was startled to get a cable from London, which said simply: 'You assigned cover British Everest expedition get ready leave soonest.' It was a formidable challenge. Apart from some mountain walking in Norway, I had no climbing experience. To reach the base camp on Everest would mean going up to 18 000 feet (5490 metres), far higher than Europe's Mont Blanc. I cabled London to air freight my mountain boots and flew immediately to Delhi to arrange a visa for Nepal.

ADRIENNE

Meanwhile, I raced back to Delhi to help Peter prepare for a three-month expedition. It was an amateur enterprise, as we had no proper mountaineering equipment. We improvised a sleeping bag out of chicken feathers and filled old kerosene tins with sugar, tea, coffee, rice, tinned meat, cheese, dried fruits and emergency medical supplies. We bought a portable radio receiver so bulky that it needed one man to carry it with its spare batteries. There were no transistors then. We found a foot-long pair of Army binoculars that must have dated from the Boer War. We also added an umbrella in case of monsoon rains; this proved to be also a valuable sunshade and aid to Himalayan trekking.

As communications would have to be by runner, taking more than a week to reach Kathmandu from Everest, we devised a scheme for Peter to fill little plastic bags with messages, in case of a British success, and drop them in the Kosi river, hoping they would carry the news to the Indian plains from Everest in a few hours.

PETER

After anxious days, my visa finally came through and I flew to Nepal on 21 April. Adrienne remained in Delhi as anchor to secure my communications. British and Indian reporters were gathering in Kathmandu, creating an atmosphere of intrigue, conspiracy, double-cross and bribery, all too reminiscent of Evelyn Waugh's classic novel, *Scoop*. There was little confidentiality in the telegraph office and cables were surreptitiously shown to anyone with the right connections or money. My plan for a lone expedition to Everest was a source of much hilarity among my colleagues.

> My plan for a lone expedition to Everest was a source of much hilarity among my colleagues.

Sherpa Da Tseri, sent by the Himalayan Club from Darjeeling, helped me to choose my porters and, at the bank, I sat on the floor with clerks filling a chest with silver coins, as no one in the mountains trusted paper. On 1 May, a Jeep dropped me off at the end of the Kathmandu valley and I set off with Da Tseri and my team of 10 porters, each carrying a load weighing 50 lbs (22 kg).

For the next two weeks we trekked over six increasingly high passes, moving up a succession of pine-clad slopes, above terraced fields of rice and over swaying rope bridges, against a snowy backdrop of the Himalayas. As we climbed, we entered an eerie world. Mists shrouded the gnarled branches of the rhododendrons. Leeches clung to the wet rocks and overhanging twigs, waving their bodies about, looking for succulent morsels. Unwilling to be one, I knocked them off my boots and pulled them from the back of my neck.

At Namche Bazaar, the Sherpa village below Everest, I recruited four local porters and set off for the expedition's base camp. For three days we struggled over the desolate moraine of the Khumbhu glacier. Although by now I was beginning to become acclimatized, I could sense the height, at 18 000 feet, by the audible thumping of my heart, while my head ached from lack of oxygen. We headed straight for the icefall, a formidable barrier sweeping down from the Western Cwm, where the expedition's leader, John Hunt, was camped with the main team.

We were soon slithering over the snow and trying to avoid crashing through the thin ice into one of the myriad torrents pouring through the glacier, but, in the end, we reached a point above the base camp – then, as I had no climbing equipment or experienced companions to go on with, we headed lower again. That startled *The Times'* correspondent, James Morris, as we seemed to him to be coming down the mountain. He hospitably gave me tea and a piece of tinned fruitcake, but no vital information.

I was not equipped to camp on the glacier and retreated to the Thyangboche monastery, on a green saddle facing Everest, where the friendly Buddhist abbot took me in. For the next few days I sat on the meadow typing news stories and features about the Sherpas, Tibetan Buddhism, the Abominable Snowman and the problems of climbing Everest, pausing to gaze at the massive pyramid towering at the end of a corridor of snow-clad peaks. Sturdy Sherpas hurried over the mountains for more than a week to deliver my stories to my colleague in Kathmandu and so on, via Adrienne, to London.

On 30 May, I went down to Namche Bazaar, where an Indian security officer had a secret radio connection with Kathmandu – a Morse key powered by a bicycle generator. He showed me a message he had received from Morris, for whom he had agreed to radio just one short despatch. It said: 'Snow conditions bad stop advanced base abandoned yesterday full story follows by runner stop john hunt.'

The officer was willing to send a message for me too, but Hunt's cable struck me as highly suspicious, and probably meant to mislead anyone reading it, as indeed it was. I declined the offer. As I returned to Thyangboche, I met Morris, tight-lipped as ever, hurrying down the trail to distant Kathmandu.

Three days later, on the morning of 2 June, I switched on my radio and heard the dramatic words: 'Mount Everest has been conquered.' That Morris message had been in code, telling *The Times* that the New Zealander Edmund Hillary and Sherpa Tenzing Norgay had reached the summit on 29 May. I hurried down to Namche Bazaar, where I announced the news to a notably indifferent and sceptical Sherpa audience. There was no excitement or rejoicing – just doubts that the haven of the gods could have been trespassed upon. But the Indian security policeman repeated his offer to radio a short message for me, and this meagre reaction was all I had.

There had been little risk of Morris's dispatch from Namche Bazaar leaking in Kathmandu. It was received at the Indian embassy and passed to the British embassy for transmission by diplomatic radio to the Foreign Office in London for forwarding to *The Times*. The newspaper published a special edition on the evening of 1 June, as crowds gathered in readiness for the coronation of Queen Elizabeth II on the next day.

I had – like everyone else – had to concede the newsbreak. But Morris, naturally anxious to ensure that the great news got through, had left for Kathmandu after sending only a brief account of the climb and without meeting or interviewing the climbers. That prize was left for me. I sent a note of congratulations by runner to John Hunt, who replied with a courteous invitation for me to meet the expedition, as they felt they had now fulfilled their obligations to *The Times*. At Thyangboche, Hunt described the climb and gave me freedom to interview the climbers.

'I felt damn good at the top,' Hillary told me. He actually said 'bloody good', but in those days that was unlikely to be published and so I changed it. Even so, he told me later, his mother had been cross that he had said 'damn'.

Tenzing smiled and said, 'I was very happy and not particularly tired.'

I asked if he would like to climb Everest again. 'No, no – not again.

There, amid the peaceful rhododendron forests below the Himalayan peaks, far from any competition, I was able to write up the full accounts of the momentous climb. I found a young Sherpa willing to race to Kathmandu. He tucked my precious despatches into his gown and headed off down the trail. I doubled my usual payment of 20 rupees for the 160-mile trek. A week later, as I trudged back to Kathmandu, I heard my story on the radio and knew that he, and I, had made it. The interviews

> 'I felt damn good at the top,' Hillary told me.

were splashed around the world with banner headlines and there was special satisfaction when I learned that they were also published in *The Times*.

Mystery remains as to whether or not Everest had been climbed before. In 1924, British mountaineers George Mallory and Andrew Irvine were glimpsed through cloud at 28 000 feet (8540 metres), climbing towards the summit with only 1000 feet (300 metres) to go. They never came back. Mallory's body was found, locked in the ice, in 1999 by an American expedition. A broken leg and a frayed rope suggested he had fallen to his death. As I write, Irvine's body has not been found, nor does anyone know if they reached the top.

ADRIENNE

For us, Everest had a happy ending. Peter and I were married the next year and we now have four children and nine grandchildren. Also, on the way to Everest, Peter spotted a large bird soaring, as on the cover of the bird book he was carrying, till then unopened. This fortuitous identification of a Himalayan black eagle sparked an interest in birds, then in all animals, especially the tiger, and led him to a second successful career after Reuters in wildlife conservation.

# RUSSIAN SECRETS AND SPIES

SIDNEY WEILAND

FRONTLINES 6

**RUSSIAN SECRETS AND SPIES** | SIDNEY WEILAND

# When Joseph Stalin died

on 5 March 1953, after 29 years in power, Russians hoped for a better life. World War II had killed 20 million people in the Soviet Union. About as many again were in the despot's *gulags*. The new Cold War had worsened as America and Russia massed troops and raced to build up their nuclear arsenals. The late Sidney Weiland reported from Moscow in the early 1950s on how a new collective leadership, led by Nikita Khrushchev, tried to come to terms with Stalinism and thaw relations with the West. Hardly anyone believed it then, Weiland recalled, but the communist system, scarred by tyranny and mired in the past, was already showing early signs of disintegration. In this article, which he had drafted just before he died, and which was edited by his wife Rosemarie and son David, he remembers his notable scoops – Khrushchev's denunciation of Stalin and the day he found the British diplomats, Guy Burgess and Donald Maclean, whose defection to Moscow was the sensational spy scandal of the era.

**Joseph Stalin lying in state in Moscow**
12 March 1953

© Hulton Getty

TO ARRIVE FOR THE FIRST TIME IN MOSCOW, following the death of Joseph Stalin, cast a visitor into a weird atmosphere of fear. The midsummer sun was warm and sultry, but there was always suspicion on people's faces. The tension was palpable, withering and there was a cold unease as Muscovites turned away from each other as they hurried across the city.

A brief taste of East European Communism did nothing to help prepare for Moscow, the citadel of Communism. Prague and Warsaw were part of old historic Europe, even if immured in an unyielding Soviet camp, but there was still a sense of hope. Moscow, though, was a more awesome experience, a bizarre unreal holdover from Byzantium. In Moscow, after Stalin's death, there was also hope, but it flickered only dimly because hope had so long been suppressed.

Moscow, dominated by the surreal golden domes of the Kremlin's Orthodox churches, was a city at the far edge of Europe. Beyond were Siberia and central Asia, the remote outposts of the Russian Empire. It resembled no other city, neither in Europe, nor Asia. Red Square, in the heart of Moscow, was dominated by the Kremlin. It was hushed and eerie, especially in winter when the snow covered the cobblestones and the Kremlin's crenellated red brick walls. Red stars shone atop the Kremlin towers, providing the only bit of cheer.

BIG BLACK RUSSIAN ZIS LIMOUSINES swept out of the Spassky gate every few minutes, waved on by grim sharp-eyed militiamen. No other traffic was allowed in Red Square. Streets were drab, grey, shabby and unpainted; on the rare occasion when paint could be spared, doors and window frames became uniformly brown – chocolate colour. This seemed to be the only shade available. It was brutally cold in winter, unbearably hot in summer. The pavements were cracked, there were large potholes in the roads, and chunks of masonry often fell from dilapidated and crumbly buildings, frequently killing hapless passers-by.

I had been sent to Moscow as correspondent for Reuters, aged 25, with no preparation and virtually no Russian. It was a hurried posting, I was sent to reopen the Reuters bureau; my predecessor was an American journalist who had looked after the interests of Reuters part-time. His Russian wife, after years of anxious waiting, had finally received an exit visa following Stalin's death and both were eager to leave. Of the handful of Western correspondents in Moscow, almost all had Russian wives and had been forced to stay because of punitive Stalinist edicts. My lack of knowledge of Russia and its language was no reflection on Reuters. It was the way it was done at the time – you were thrown in at the deep end, you learned on the job. Some survived!

The job was made harder by the harsh restrictions the Russians placed on a foreign correspondent based in Moscow.

CENSORSHIP WAS THE BIGGEST FRUSTRATION. Every scrap of copy had to be taken to an office in the Central Telegraph Building to be handed to an unsmiling clerk through a small window, behind which the unseen and anonymous censor worked. He only removed words with a thick black pencil. He never made any corrections or additions. The resulting truncated story was not open for negotiation or correction. The censor despatched it and the correspondent did not see his often-distorted story until hours or days later. Sometimes he never saw it again at all, the censor having conveniently mislaid it. It was a constant battle of wits and resourcefulness.

For the average Russian, life in the last years of Stalin had been a nightmare. Nobody was immune. Everyone felt insecure. Russians brought up to distrust each other distrusted foreigners even more, especially Westerners. There was always somebody watching or listening. It was never safe to talk, hardly safe to smile. Even the trees on the grand boulevards were said to be wired.

It was never safe to talk, hardly safe to smile. Even the trees on the grand boulevards were said to be wired.

Soviet society was fixated on security. Every citizen was viewed as a potential traitor. Every foreign diplomat or journalist was regarded as a spy, to be kept under surveillance. It was better to stay out of trouble and away from suspicion. Few foreigners had Russian friends or even acquaintances. Some Russians, such as selected journalists or officials, were licensed to attend foreign cocktail parties or diplomatic receptions, but never alone. Afterwards, they were called in to report on what happened and on each other.

In seven years in Russia, the only Russian friends – the word is used advisedly – that I had were journalists. In all these cases the friendship was severely limited; I was invited only to three Russian homes; two of the journalists were known KGB operatives, one was a journalist who had worked in the US for TASS, the Soviet news agency. He may have been an informant. I like to think I was invited because they rated my conversation highly or felt a need to repay hospitality – all had been guests in my apartment. Although these and other Russians gave me useful insights into Soviet life and Soviet thinking, none told me anything that would not have come out in normal conversation in the West.

We lived at arm's length from the people of the country we were supposed to report on, and they from us. There were no official briefings or press conferences. There was little access of any kind to government or party officials and there was no one to answer questions unless authorized to do so. We relished every crumb of information. We scoured all the newspapers for snippets. We kept card-index files on Soviet officials, so that a brief reference in a provincial newspaper might reveal a new assignment, which could disclose a policy shift. There were no announcements of assignments, promotions or, more significantly, demotions.

MAJOR SHIFTS OF POLICY could sometimes be detected in a very roundabout way. For the traditional May Day Parade of 1954, Khrushchev appeared atop the Lenin–Stalin mausoleum in a distinctive white linen jacket, when his colleagues wore dark suits. Absurd as it seems, diplomats and journalists deemed this of significance. Officially, at that time, he was a member of the collective leadership. The next day *Pravda* appeared with a photograph of the scene across half its front page. It showed, not only Khrushchev in his white linen jacket, but also with his arm aloft waving at the marchers in Red Square below him. He had been First Secretary of the Communist Party for eight months. *Pravda* was the newspaper of the Party. Thus, it was subtly demonstrated that Khrushchev

> Thus, it was subtly demonstrated that Khrushchev was a rapidly rising star, with his tentacles spread widely within the apparatus.

was a rapidly rising star, with his tentacles spread widely within the apparatus.

Khrushchev had been a close associate of Stalin, but he decided at the beginning of 1956 that the time had come to explain to the Russian people why the collective leadership of the Communist Party Presidium was superior to a leadership based on the practice of a cult of personality, which was how Stalin had ruled.

Therefore the forthcoming Twentieth Party Congress generated great interest and anticipation. It was the first post-Stalin Party congress and expected to be a great historic event. Khrushchev claims in his memoirs to have urged his colleagues to make a clean breast to the delegates about the conduct of the Party leadership during the years in question. He meant the Stalin years.

Officially the Moscow foreign journalists had no information about the Party congress. Rumours of it had been picked up through contacts with the embassies. Phone calls to the press department of the foreign ministry elicited the usual equivocal reply: 'The necessary arrangements will be announced in due time.' Later we were informed that we were not to be admitted to the Kremlin. So the few Western journalists waited at the Central Telegraph Office for a delivery of texts. But the most significant story of the Party congress meeting was not in the texts.

The correspondents were not aware that a special secret closed session had been convened, from which foreign communist guests were barred. It was at this secret session that Nikita Khrushchev denounced Stalin and accused him of numerous crimes, misdeeds and errors. His secret speech changed the shape of Communism.

I heard of the denunciation in a whispered conversation 15 days after the party congress. Moving slowly around the buffet table at a Finnish embassy reception, a friendly communist journalist gave me a few scant details – enough to show that the speech was political dynamite. Khrushchev had called Stalin a mass murderer and a military incompetent. All press dispatches out of Russia were still subject to heavy censorship at that time, but my first guarded cable got through, possibly even the censors were unaware of its significance. It was so circumspect that it attracted little attention. However, minutes after the first message was transmitted, the censors clamped down. All further cables about the speech were suppressed.

The details I had were meagre and we set about to get more. John Rettie, also a Reuters correspondent, obtained a graphic and full account from a Russian friend, adding to the first report. We did not discuss the story in the office, even with the radio blaring or a water tap full on – which were devices we sometimes resorted to – but instead we walked the deserted snow-covered streets at midnight, comparing notes and discussing how best to handle the news.

During the next four days, all attempts to get the story past the censors were blocked. As Rettie was due for leave, we decided he should fly to Stockholm and break the news from there. Once there, he assembled a vivid story from his notes and telephoned it to London. To protect his position when he returned to Moscow, it was decided to route the report through Germany and publish it under a Bonn dateline, attributed to reliable communist sources. Three days later, the censor allowed me to transmit a much-cut dispatch, in which I reported that 30 million Russians have now heard about the denunciation of Stalin, mostly at secret Party cell meetings. Most of our details came from an ordinary young Russian, who heard them indirectly through a briefing session. Later we found out he had been rigorously interrogated by the KGB.

The repercussions were immediate. Our Russian girl secretary suddenly disappeared, officially sick, the tapping of our telephones became more obvious and surveillance of our movements increased. To replace our secretary, the Soviet government agency, which supplied office workers, sent a translator who took a closer interest in our dispatches and how we obtained our information. She was later identified as a KGB contact.

The attack on Stalin created deep confusion and questioning in communist Eastern Europe. The disarray unleashed by Kremlin propagandists startled the communist world. Thousands of Party members in the West resigned in disgust, riots broke out in Poland, and in Hungary the Khrushchev speech played a major role in events that led to the Budapest uprising later in 1956.

WHEN I RETURNED TO RUSSIA IN 1964 for a second tour as Reuters correspondent, Soviet friends told me the authorities had been horrified by the Khrushchev scoop. This historic speech was only officially published in April 1989!

From time to time, national interests dictated that events just had to be publicized.

Russia kept silent for five years on the fate of Guy Burgess and Donald Maclean, two British Foreign Office diplomats, turned spies and traitors, who defected to Moscow in a typical sensational Cold War adventure in 1951. They finally showed up in Moscow's National Hotel in a spectacularly staged media event in 1956. Why? Because Khrushchev and his prime minister, Marshal Nikolai Bulganin, were due to pay a state visit to Britain. Inevitably, the Russians realized, questions would be asked about the missing diplomats. The affair was an outstanding embarrassment in relations towards Britain. It was time to come clean. They could no longer deny the presence of the diplomats in Russia, nor divert official enquiries with the usual Soviet answer, 'I don't know anything about it.'

AS BUREAU CHIEF OF REUTERS, I was invited to the bizarre reappearance of Burgess and Maclean, together with Richard Hughes, a visiting correspondent of *The Sunday Times*. The incident was another example of the Byzantine ways of the Soviets.

> As bureau chief of Reuters, I was invited to the bizarre reappearance of Burgess and Maclean ...

I was in my office in Moscow's Savoy Hotel, a few steps from KGB headquarters in the Lubyanka, when the telephone rang at 6 pm on a Saturday night. A man's voice, ostensibly from the Soviet TASS news agency, asked if I could meet a deputy director-general of the official news agency at 8 pm. The request was unusual. Could I meet him in the National Hotel? Why not? Where? Room 101. That seemed very strange.

At 8 pm I was in the dim light of the dilapidated baroque hotel on Red Square, where Lenin stayed before he moved in to the Kremlin in 1918, and climbing a curved staircase to Room 101. A hand broke free from the heavy dark velvet drapes at either side of the entrance to the room.

'I'm Burgess,' said a voice as a figure emerged from the gloom.

'I'm Maclean,' said another voice from the other side of the drapes, as hands were proffered in greeting. It was uncanny, to say the least – the sort of incident that had been staged in Russia since medieval times.

Even in Russian terms, the reappearance of the diplomats was extraordinary. Two British reporters – myself and Hughes – joined by two Russian colleagues, had a few minutes with Burgess and Maclean – not more than five. We were handed prepared statements, and the two men made it clear they would answer no questions.

As journalists, Hughes and I were trained in extracting information.

'How are you?' we asked.

'Fine. Great.'

'Where have you been these five years?'

No answer.

'What have you been doing, what work do you have?'

No answer.

'What about your families?'

'Give my best to my mother,' said Maclean.

By then, we were on Gorky Street, outside the hotel, walking with the two men. It was clear they were not prepared to engage in any kind of conversation. I had a story to file.

# B AND K

JOHN EARLE

FRONTLINES 7

**B AND K** | JOHN EARLE

# In May 1955 a wider world

had its first glimpse of the new Kremlin rulers who'd succeeded Stalin, led by Nikita Khrushchev and Marshal Nikolai Bulganin, when they visited Yugoslavia. Russia had now caught up with the Americans and had tested a hydrogen bomb and, in anxious times, everyone was understandably keen to know what these people were like. I'd parachuted into Yugoslavia as a combatant in World War II and now I was leading a team of Reuters correspondents covering their visit. They failed to coerce communist maverick Josip Broz Tito of Yugoslavia back into the Soviet Cominform fold, from which he'd broken away seven years earlier, and my diary records that a final communiqué was pure blather; but both the ebullient Khrushchev, the man who would one day famously bang his shoe in the United Nations, and Bulganin showed us that they were at least human in their fondness for the bottle. Some entries from my diary:

**Bulganin (left) and Khrushchev visit London**
20 April 1956

© Hulton Getty

SATURDAY 14 MAY: In bed with temperature, after infected wisdom tooth removed. The big news of the year broke overnight, from Moscow fortunately. A high-powered Soviet delegation, including Khrushchev, Bulganin and Mikoyan, is to visit Belgrade late this month. This got me out of bed, despite a swollen face and difficulty in speaking.

SUNDAY 15 MAY: A very busy day. Tito made a speech at Pula to commemorate the tenth anniversary of the end of the war. Said the forthcoming talks would be on an equal footing between the two countries and 'we shall let no one meddle in our domestic affairs' – a clear warning to the Russians. The speech was only broadcast at lunchtime, although it was made in the morning. There was also a Scotland v. Yugoslavia football match in the afternoon to be covered. We were still busy with Tito, so could not get to watch it, but had to provide coverage from the radio, a skimpy job.

THURSDAY 26 MAY: The Russians arrived, at 5 pm. We journalists, a hundred of us perhaps, had been shepherded into an imaginary square on the tarmac an hour earlier. Tito came at 4.55 pm, resplendent in his powder-blue marshal's uniform. The Soviet plane, only two-engined not four-, opened its doors and Khrushchev appeared, a small squat waddling creature in baggy creased light-grey suit. He was followed by Bulganin (prime minister), like a German professor with spectacles and goatee beard, and similarly attired. Then Anastas Mikoyan (economic chief), swarthy, Levantine, vaguely sinister and of course wearing similar clothes. The usual clicking of cameras and perfunctory handshakes between Khrushchev and Tito, the latter smiling sardonically at this moment of victory over the past.

... Khrushchev appeared, a small squat waddling creature in baggy creased light-grey suit.

The surprise came a few seconds later, when Tito motioned Khrushchev to the microphone. The Yugoslavs expected a few conventional words of greeting, and had not bothered to have an interpreter present. Instead, Khrushchev shook everybody with a 12-minute speech calling for cooperation between the two countries' Communist Parties and blaming the Cominform dispute on Beria and Abakumov – 'enemies of the people'. Only Tito was unshaken, his eyes steely and his face impassive as a mask. The speech over, Tito did not deign a reply, but motioned Khrushchev curtly to a waiting Rolls-Royce and they drove off. Belgrade was in high excitement that evening, and we ended by sending over the wire to London the whole text of Khrushchev's statement.

FRIDAY 27 MAY: Had to get up early, as the Russians were laying a wreath at Avala – tomb of the unknown soldier, on a hilltop outside town – at 8.30 am. Something went wrong with the security arrangements and we had to argue our way through the barriers; dashed up to Avala just as Khrushchev was clambering up the steps to the monument, with a wreath almost as big as he was being carried in front of him.

Then another dash to the Guards Officers' Club in Topcider on the outskirts of town, where the conference was held. I was one of the few journalists allowed into the opening – just the Belgrade correspondents of news agencies. The conference room had an ornate chandelier; otherwise, not richly furnished. The Yugoslavs and Russians filed in, not wasting words with frivolous conversation, and sat down on each side of a green baize table in a rather frigid atmosphere. The rest of the day was just very busy. There was a press conference in the special press centre – about 150 correspondents present – notable mainly for protests from the French journalists. Why was their language not used alongside Serbo-Croat, English and Russian?

SATURDAY 28 MAY: Lunched with Statskevich of the Soviet embassy. He invited me and took me to the press club, which was of course full of journalists, mostly visitors. We killed the conversation in surrounding tables, as all ears strained in our direction. Despite having to talk in whispers, he gave me quite an interesting little story. Hinted that some of the Party leaders in Moscow are not entirely happy about the visit. Could that be (Vyacheslav) Molotov, former foreign minister and an old hack under Stalin?

In the evening Tito gave a reception at the White Palace. It rained and the 600 guests were very hot, squashed indoors, not in the garden. Tito took the Russians into his usual private room for dinner. Afterwards, foreign ambassadors were called in one by one to be introduced and talk. The Russians also toasted the head of government of each one's country, Khrushchev in fruit juice, Bulganin emptying a glass of champagne. We journalists clustered outside the door, to get some chit-chat from each head of mission as he came out.

*Bulganin, replete with champagne, had got lost in the background. Someone pushed him gently forward and supported him …*

The party did not break up till after midnight. I had a good view of the Russians, two or three feet away, when they paused in the hall while the national anthems were played. Bulganin, replete with champagne, had got lost in the background. Someone pushed him gently forward and supported him in his correct place according to protocol, and there he stayed, swaying and sweating, till the anthems were over.

SUNDAY 29 MAY: A long long drive with John Talbot [a distinguished colleague who had reported from Yugoslavia in World War II and spent six months in solitary confinement as a Gestapo prisoner] up to Pula, to follow the Russians, who left the reception last night to travel by special train on their way to Brioni, Tito's private island off Istria. At Pula, the nearest one could sleep to Brioni, we put up at the Riviera Hotel, said to be the best. A good solid Austrian pile, with large rooms and ornate ceilings, it had had little attention since passing under Yugoslavia. Filthy stair-carpets, laid over but not attached to the stairway. My room, with private bathroom, had no hot water; a lavatory that flushed permanently all night; no means of covering the window, either curtain or shutter, to keep the early morning light out; ants in Indian file on the floor to my suitcase; and one solitary cockroach stood in the centre of the room with upraised antennae, resentful of my presence.

TUESDAY 31 MAY: Tito has stayed on Brioni and let his guests go 'sightseeing' on their own in Slovenia and Croatia. He evidently wants to show he's got other things to do … The Soviet spokesman came out and, in an impromptu press conference about the talks, tried to be witty with heavy-footed Russian proverbs like, 'It does not matter whether the cat is grey or white, as long as there is a cat.' What nonsense.

Afternoon. We followed the Russians to Bled. Enjoyable dinner in the Hotel Toplice – risotto with crayfish and fresh fruit salad. By talking to some Yugoslav journalists, I was able to piece together a story to send. The only difficulty was getting it through. The old night porter in the Toplice was not up to dealing with the international calls of 20 foreign correspondents; and to make matters worse, he managed to snarl up the hotel exchange, so that you could only speak from his phone. So we each in turn dictated our piece, overheard by everyone else, while a series of green lights from hopeful outside callers vainly went on winking and winking. By now fed up with it all, the porter with one fell swoop pulled out all the plugs from their holes; the man from *Unità* [the Italian communist newspaper] was speaking with Rome, being briefed on his Party's line. Inexplicably, he went on speaking.

WEDNESDAY 1 JUNE: Up at 6 am, to Litostroj engineering works in Ljubljana, where we had a good view of the Russians. What warts on Khrushchev's neck! What clumsy shoes; a pneumatic 'squeak, squeak' at every step. To think these men rule the second most powerful country. They had their usual unsmiling faces, though Khrushchev did allow a questioner to approach, then fobbed him off with a meaningless 'life must be lived to the hilt'.

THURSDAY 2 JUNE: The last full day of the Russian visit. Thank goodness; we were feeling tired. The Russians and Yugoslavs had their final talks, again at Topcider on the outskirts of town, and Tito and Bulganin signed the so-called Belgrade Declaration … full of bla-bla; indivisibility of peace, respect for sovereignty, equality between states, peaceful coexistence, non-interference in internal affairs. But the Kremlinologists were agog, as much for what it did not as what it did say.

In the evening came the Russians' reception. Masses of the proverbial vodka and caviar. Also 17 singers and concert artists specially flown from the Soviet Union. Good, though horrible dresses. But the real entertainment was to come. About 1 am Khrushchev emerged, clearly in his cups, extravagantly promising surrounding journalists that he would give us all visas, till, at a sign from Mikoyan, clearly not amused, he was lifted under the armpits by their security men, down the steps to his car.

FRIDAY 3 JUNE: We heaved a sigh of relief when the Russians left. Tito saw them off with correct, if rather frigid, handshakes and waves. No controversial speech from Khrushchev this time. They went to Sofia, on a visit only announced last night. Our Reuters team celebrated with a dinner at the Moskva Hotel. Talbot and I were joined by Ian Fraser who had come in from Bonn, David Jones our Russian speaker and Belgrade man Barney Petrovic. For once the waiter who usually looks after us, fat Charlie, was slow in his service; grumbled about the last few days. I wonder why?

Tito saw them off with correct, if rather frigid, handshakes and waves.

# PARATROOPS AND NECROPHILIA

ALECO JOANNIDES

FRONTLINES 8

**PARATROOPS AND NECROPHILIA** | ALECO JOANNIDES

# On 26 July 1956, the firebrand

Arab nationalist ruler of Egypt, Colonel Gamal Abdel Nasser, nationalized the
Suez Canal. Its British and French owners were flabbergasted. They tried
diplomacy to get it back again, but they were soon girding for war – in collusion
with the Israelis, who wanted to preempt an Arab threat by invading Sinai.
As war loomed, the Egyptians began to expel British and French journalists.
I was a Greek, based in Athens, so it wasn't long before I was in Egypt, checking in
at the Casino Palace Hotel in Port Said at the Mediterranean end of the canal.
It was near the Marconi Post Office. We depended on the public cable in those
days and, although I'd never covered a battle, it seemed to be a good idea not
to have to run too far to send my telegrams.

**The Suez Crisis: a grief-stricken Arab woman dashes through the streets during fighting in Port Said**
08 November 1956

© Hulton Getty

MY FIRST AND LASTING IMPRESSION of Port Said, home then to 150 000 people, was of a toy town that seemed to go to sleep when there were no ships in port and to light up as if by magic, even at midnight, as soon as a liner steamed in. Dozens of small boats gyrated around the incoming vessels. Their crews had curios or oriental sweets for sale, or they chanted invitations to see a belly dance or visit the emporium of Simon Artz, where European passengers sailing to the East or the African colonies bought their sun hats. But now there was a sense of menace. The arcades, under their trellis balconies, were empty a lot of the time. Constantine Chikov, the Russian consul, used a loudspeaker van to broadcast Soviet support for Egypt.

Early in September, Australia's prime minister, Sir Robert Menzies, led a committee representing 18 nations on a peace bid to Cairo. Correspondents felt, however, that the die was cast. Nasser stood by his decision to nationalize the Suez Canal Company – which had originated in 1858 with Frenchman Ferdinand de Lesseps, who built the waterway.

A good contact of mine was the US consul, Anthony Cuomo, with whom, I planned a trip to some archaeological finds on an island in nearby Lake Manzalleh. The trip was planned for 29 October, which was the day the Israeli attack in Sinai began.

'Aleco, sorry –
I don't think we can
go to the island
tomorrow. The war
is on.'

He rang me to say, 'Aleco, sorry – I don't think we can go to the island tomorrow. The war is on.'

Britain and France soon gave Nasser a 12-hour ultimatum that they would intervene, ostensibly to separate the forces of Israel and Egypt. Their bombers pounded Egypt's air force on the ground late on 31 October, and the next day I watched as the Egyptians blocked the Suez Canal. Cranes were towed into the harbour with their lifting forks placed crosswise in an outsize 'out of bounds' sign, then the 3000-ton dredger *Paul Solent* was towed out too. There was a huge explosion and it sank, its bow sticking up above the waves. Several more ships were sunk later, trapping 14 vessels, including a Russian tanker loaded with kerosene, in the canal.

In a few days the Israelis had conquered almost the whole of the Sinai peninsula and, led by General Ariel Sharon, reached Sharm el Sheikh on the Red Sea. On 4 November, the Anglo-French strafing of Port Said began, as a prelude to their invasion and occupation of the Canal Zone. At dawn next day I watched French and British paratroopers drop like bunches of grapes on both sides of the canal, as warships bombarded the beach, where wooden holiday cabins went up in flames.

REUTERS CENTRAL DESK LOG for 5/6 November 1956 said: 'Joannides, filing via New York, got through a Port Said datelined piece describing the landing of the paratroopers. His despatch, the only Port Said dateline sighted in London, suggested that there was fighting in the centre of Port Said. The first of his two cables was despatched at 8.15 local time.'

I had filed to Reuters in New York – America was pressing the British and French to stop the war – as a 'neutral' destination. Maybe telegrams would get there faster. I'd been in the Greek Army during a war but I'd never reported one. Reuters objectivity 'should be beyond criticism,' said my briefing letter from the chief news editor, Sidney Mason. I felt that this clad me in armour.

In a lull in the street battle, I moved from the terrace of the Casino Palace to the better vantage-point of the Messageries Maritimes Building, to see a British fighter-plane rocket an anti-aircraft gun emplacement. Some of the gun crew were killed outright and one hopped on his remaining leg, then fell to the ground. Egyptian soldiers waiting for a ferry were engulfed in flames when an ammunition truck blew up. Oil storage depots blazed for two days.

Later, a local truce was arranged. I remember seeing the Franciscan matron of the French Hospital, accompanied by the chief surgeon and an Arab orderly with a white flag, march through the debris to the American consulate to seek help, as the hospital was filled to the limit with Egyptian wounded. I was the only resident left now at the Casino Palace, besides the Italian owner, Simonini, and his lady partner, and a mentally disturbed Greek telegraphist who had been disembarked ten days earlier by his ship. The telegraphist turned out to be also a necrophiliac and kept darting into the garden and screaming loudly on the discovery of a corpse. This suited Simonini. When they were found, he could have the dead – there were 12 in all – swiftly removed to the hotel cold room.

Exaggerated reports about casualties were bandied about as usual, but I remember that I figured from various sources that the number of killed was about 1300 on the Egyptian side, for 28 dead Britons and Frenchmen. The invaders were under orders to try to avoid causing casualties or too much destruction – confirmed by the British commander, General Sir Hugh Stockwell, when he dropped by the hotel himself and asked how things were there.

'We've had just a few windowpanes blown out,' I said, to which he returned, 'Jolly good show.'

The United Nations imposed a formal ceasefire on 8 November. Russia had threatened London and Paris with mass destruction, but pressure from the United States – which wouldn't help stop a run on the pound sterling – was decisive. Within weeks, UN troops would replace the British and the French in the Canal Zone. Nasser kept the Suez Canal. The British prime minister, Sir Anthony Eden, resigned.

BETWEEN THE TRUCE AND THE FINAL CEASEFIRE, the Egyptians began passive resistance. Dockers refused to unload food ships and the police chief told his men to go home. They discarded their uniforms and went away in their underwear. Amin el Asfoury, secretary-general of the Liberation Party, told me, 'No attacks will ever take place against the British and French troops, but in case they disobey instructions of the UN a merciless war will start.' He said six guerrilla *fedayeen* bands were on alert.

Passive resistance meant that I could no longer send telegrams through the Marconi Post Office. I was lifted aboard a British destroyer on a rope and sent some copy to another navy vessel where, I had heard, there was a press facility. But I was writing into a void. When the war correspondents came ashore, in battledress, they confirmed that my stories had been spiked, as I was not accredited to the forces.

With them was Reuters World War II veteran, Seaghan Maynes, and a personal friend of mine, David Seymour, a gifted Polish-American photo journalist. David, a founder of Magnum Photos, had been with the Israelis in Sinai and he was war weary and upset. He really specialized in warmly human pictures of people and especially children. We met on 9 November and

arranged lunch the next day at a local restaurant I'd persuaded to open in spite of the passive resistance.

'I have done it all, now this is small beer for me,' he said, adding he planned to leave soon.

I waited for him for lunch in vain. That evening we heard that, riding in a Jeep inadvertently across a ceasefire line, he and *Match* reporter, Jean Roy, had been mowed down by Egyptian machine-gun fire. I thought it strange that with so much death around I was so devastated. David missed the beautiful picture of their funeral, organized by the French Army with Gallic pomp and circumstance. The coffins were draped in the Tricolour and the Stars and Stripes, out on a golf links where tall Senegalese buglers in red fezzes, silhouetted against a brilliant blue sky, sounded the last post. French General André Beaufre paid 'profound homage to the often ignored and unsung heroes of the foreign press corps'. We all had tears in our eyes.

French General André Beaufre paid 'profound homage to the often ignored and unsung heroes of the foreign press corps'.

REUTERS MEN IN PORT SAID included Sandy Gall, later to be a television journalist with Independent Television News, and David Sells, who went from the agency to the BBC. Sells endeared himself to me by having the cook of the Ledra Palace hotel in Cyprus work at night, so he could get me a roast chicken on the next shuttle flight to Port Said. On the American side – the Egyptians cheered US journalists because of the American role over the war – by far the most famous was Reynolds Packard of United Press, the author of *The Kansas City Milkman*. The book is a 'must' for anyone in journalism. It takes its title from the mythical character, like the 'Man on the Clapham Omnibus', for whom UP correspondents were urged to write.

Pack, as he was known, now represented the *New York Daily News*. He said UP fired him when, in a flat news period in post-war Shanghai, he filed on the discovery of a 'human-headed spider'. He faced down a torrent of others' denials for a week, then sent what he says was his last UP wire: 'Human-headed spider died today.'

He disliked war, and Port Said, and wished he were back on base in Rome, where it was his dream that he would one day be able to file the headline: 'Pope caught in bed with Sophia Loren'. He never did that, but on his return to Cairo, where we were both soon assigned, he scooped us all by having King Saud of Saudi Arabia leave an Arab Summit early 'because of trouble in the harem with open warfare breaking out between his wives and concubines'. Beat that if you can.

# REVOLT IN HUNGARY

RONALD FARQUHAR

FRONTLINES 9

**REVOLT IN HUNGARY** | RONALD FARQUHAR

# The 1956 Hungarian uprising

was the bloodiest struggle by a satellite nation to free itself from the post-war Soviet domination of Eastern Europe. Nowhere else did students, workers and soldiers unite to battle Red Army tanks in the streets. Western sources put the toll at 4000 dead, including 700 Soviet soldiers, in a revolt that made the communist world quake. It jeopardized efforts by Nikita Khrushchev to relax Stalin's repression and thaw relations with the West. For a few days the issue hung in the balance. The Kremlin seemed to vacillate on Hungarian demands for liberty. I'd been at Reuters for four years, a Glasgow Scot up from the provinces, and I was reporting Poland at the time. Frontiers were being closed. But London cabled me to drive to Hungary.

**Soviet tanks rolled into central Budapest and were used ruthlessly by the USSR in the suppression of the Hungarian uprising**
03 November 1956

© Hulton Getty

I KNEW FROM REPORTS that had reached us in Poland that the crisis in Hungary was brewing up. A rigid communist leadership there had resisted any reform. Then crowds besieged the radio building and demanded that calls for an election be broadcast. Party bosses called in the Red Army. Shots were fired. A battle had begun. London agreed I should try to get in, despite a closed frontier, on a visa readily granted by an anguished Hungarian embassy in Warsaw and in a Czechoslovak Skoda car, I drove 530 miles through fog and rain across the treacherous roads of the East European communist heartland.

Czechoslovakia was quiet, although there were signs of tighter security – but, at the Danube crossing into Hungary, a border guard told me cheerfully, 'No food, no milk, no bread, no trains, no buses, plenty shooting.' After an hour of uncertainty, the barrier swung up and I drove across in the dark.

A curious crowd, all with lapel ribbons in Hungary's red, white and green national colours, then surrounded my car.

> ... a border guard told me cheerfully, 'No food, no milk, no bread, no trains, no buses, plenty shooting.'

Nearby, the ruins of a demolished Soviet war memorial lay across the road. Budapest was about 60 miles away and people warned me not to drive at night so I slept at a workers' hostel, where supper – and breakfast – were bread and dripping, salami, paprika and cold water.

In the morning I set off with five passengers – all Budapest men anxious to go home – and, as we turned into the main street, a truckload of Soviet troops sped past, then a Hungarian tank blocked our way.

'The Russians are fighting with insurgents up the road,' the commander said. He did not say which side he was on. 'But there is a detour that will take you through.'

We turned into a rutted muddy lane across farmland until we met a truck flying a Hungarian flag, with a score of riflemen in civilian clothes aboard who aimed their weapons at our Skoda. Their leader spoke to me in Hungarian. I told him I did not understand. 'Perhaps,' he suggested ominously, 'the gentleman speaks Russian.'

My companions came to my rescue and, after explanations, a search and an identity check, he let us through in convoy with a truck loaded with potatoes for Budapest hospitals.

I wondered afterwards what would have happened if I had indeed been a Russian.

SOVIET TANKS AND TROOP CARRIERS guarded each corner of the Margaret Bridge, as I drove unchallenged across the river to Pest, the other part of the twin capital city, where I dropped my passengers. It was 28 October and the Russians had a tight grip now, after five days of fighting. The rattle and crump of gunfire told where nests of insurgents still resisted in the inner city and the Buda hills.

Shell-pocked buildings, uprooted tram rails and lamp standards, burned out tanks and lorries, dangling overhead cables and lime-covered bodies of Soviet soldiers lying in streets strewn with rubble and splintered glass, all testified to the ferocity of the combat. Open lorries, their sides covered by white sheets with improvised Red Cross markings, rushed with Hungarian doctors and nurses in white coats past Soviet soldiers, many very young, standing, rifles at the ready, at street corners and in doorways.

International telephone and telex were cut, but the Hungarian news agency, MTI, allowed me to file a story on a radio newscast that could be picked up by Reuters monitors at Green End near London. It was a tangled tale.

Imre Nagy, a 60-year-old reform-minded communist who had been swept into power by the revolt, had announced on radio an agreement for Soviet troops to pull out of Budapest. Talks on a full withdrawal from Hungary would follow. Some tanks had already left. But others still pounded the Kilian barracks, a rebel stronghold.

The MTI office was in a hilltop suburb of Buda. Each trip there entailed two Danube crossings and checks by jumpy young Soviet sentries. I learned on my first night that driving after dark was not without hazard. Sefton Delmer of the London *Daily Express* returned to the riverside Duna Hotel, where most reporters were based, with news that the *Daily Mail's* Noel Barber had been shot and wounded in the head, as they were scouting the city by car after curfew.

Reuters had no resident local string correspondent, but I enlisted help from a young English-speaking Hungarian as guide and interpreter. He sported a natty camelhair cavalry-type overcoat, which once earned him the contemptuous epithet 'bourgeois' from a sneering Russian sentry. As his more proletarian-clad driver, I escaped censure.

Some fighting continued next day in heavy rain. But by the following day, 30 October, the bulk of the remaining Russians appeared to be pulling out. Telephone and telex lines reopened. Frontier curbs relaxed and Bill Krasser drove in from Vienna to join me.

BUT THE BLOODSHED WAS NOT OVER. Insurgents hit the streets to hunt down men of the hated AVH security police, who had fought alongside the Russians. Some were shot or beaten to death and hanged from trees and lampposts. The climax was an attack on AVH men at Communist Party headquarters, when French photographer Jean-Pierre Pedrazzini of *Paris-Match* was fatally wounded.

Joyful Hungarians rallied behind a coalition government with non-communists that Nagy had formed with a pledge of free elections. They hoped, as the Soviet tanks withdrew, that they had won.

Joyful Hungarians rallied behind a coalition government ...

Jubilation then turned to disbelief, dismay and anger at the news a day later that British and French bombers had struck Egypt to begin a war to recover the Suez Canal, which President Gamal Abdel Nasser had nationalized.

Hungarians sensed it as a deathblow to their dream of freedom. They had counted on the West for support, but it was now embroiled in an international crisis that made Hungary a sideshow. Khrushchev, who was on Nasser's side, blustered he would drop rockets on London. Hungarians were sure that, in the circumstances, he could not be seen to flinch from them.

The Russians came back. Fresh troops poured over the frontier and encircled Budapest.

Nagy, a professorial figure with pince-nez and flowing moustache, protested vainly to the Soviet ambassador. He was Yuri Andropov, who would later be head of the KGB and then for a brief time the Kremlin ruler. Then Nagy renounced Hungary's membership of the Moscow-led Warsaw Pact and declared his country neutral, appealing to the United Nations and to the great powers for protection. But they were busy with Suez.

AT 5 AM ON 4 NOVEMBER, the capital awoke to a thunder of guns, as the Red Army attacked on three sides. From the windows of the Duna Hotel, I saw gun flashes silhouette the hills and red tracer stab the darkness. By dawn Soviet tanks were in the city. They surrounded parliament and public buildings, and straddled the Danube bridges.

Hotel telephones went dead, so Krasser and I dashed in his Volkswagen to a nearby newspaper office where we had been allowed to use the telex. It was also a headquarters for some rebels, and teemed with armed men, as a radio in the background blared an appeal to the world for help. Miraculously, the telex was not only free but already connected with Reuters

... a radio in the background blared an appeal to the world for help.

in Vienna, where bureau chief Harry Harrison had called the Budapest number on hearing of the Soviet attack and held the line open. Krasser and I took turns to pound out as much copy as we could off the tops of our heads with scant concern for style. When we had finished, Harrison told us, 'London says you should get into a cellar.'

The Russians had imposed a 24-hour curfew and said anyone on the streets could be shot on sight. Krasser sheltered at the Austrian legation and I at the British. Before quitting the hotel we overheard an American newsman tell a colleague, 'Reuters got the story out!'

In Prague in 1968 – incidentally – Krasser would complete a double, with a world scoop on the Soviet-led invasion of Czechoslovakia but, alas, that was not for Reuters, but for the German DPA wire.

Another fugitive in Budapest that November day in 1956 was Cardinal Jozsef Mindszenty, Roman Catholic Primate of Hungary, who sought asylum at the US legation. He had been free only three-and-a-half days after eight years of communist detention and would now remain in his new quarters for more than 14 years.

The British took in some 30 refugees, mainly newsmen. We slept on mattresses on the floor and dined from tins, as we followed events as best we could, from the noise of battle outside and transcripts of broadcasts monitored by Hungarian staff. But we could not file. The legation had a radio link with the Foreign

Office in London, but reserved it for diplomatic traffic.

Heavy fighting raged for three days. We could see Soviet artillery firing from a hilltop. Sometimes Ilyushin IL-28 bombers screamed low overhead. Bullets whipped through legation windows, apparently ricochets from a sniper across a nearby square, when a Soviet tank column rumbled past.

By the night of 6 November the city was quieter and the battle appeared to be moving south. My notes recorded: 'Firing died down after dark. In Pest occasional crumps of mortar bombs, flares, sporadic crackle of machine-gun and rifle fire. Tanks patrolling the streets in steady rain. In Buda very quiet, isolated spurts of small-arms fire. Some occasional gunfire in the distance. Looks like the finish.'

A week later the Russians had crushed the last resistance. They installed a new communist regime under Janos Kadar, a 44-year-old defector from the Nagy government who had been freed from a Stalinist prison only two-and-a-half years earlier. He denounced Nagy, now in the Yugoslav embassy, as a man who allowed 'reactionaries and fascists' to exploit legitimate anger over past errors.

We ventured out in the battle debris. Shell holes yawned in battered buildings. The Duna had suffered three hits. A corpse lay on the pavement. People queued for hours in bitter cold outside food shops amid rubble and the wreck of barricades.

A frustrated Western press corps organized a road convoy to Austria, because international links were not yet restored, but they made slow progress through Soviet lines and had not got to Vienna when, next day, the communications in Budapest reopened. So I filed ahead of the pack – with the help of Gizi, Lonci and Maria, the formidable middle-aged sisters who operated the Duna switchboard.

HUNGARY'S MOOD NOW WAS BITTER, disillusioned and fearful. Reports told of people being rounded up and deported in railway wagons – the government acknowledged arrests of 'criminals, armed gangs, counter-revolutionary elements, terrorist and anti-social instigators', but denied that any had been transported out of the

**Hungary's mood now was bitter, disillusioned and fearful.**

country. Hungarians felt abandoned by the West and by a United Nations that had been preoccupied with Suez.

As a Briton I was a target for wrath over Suez.

'Our compliments to Sir Anthony Eden,' said a steelworker in an ironic jibe at the British prime minister. 'He stabbed the Hungarian revolution in the back!'

But there was light relief too. Hungarians spread stories that the Russians thought they had been sent to Egypt and that the Danube was the Suez Canal. Once, as a Soviet officer checked my passport at a roadblock, a passing Hungarian carrying a precious loaf of bread leaned over his shoulder to peer at the document.

Turning to me he said cheerfully in English, 'I heard your name on the BBC last night.' Then he walked on.

Leaflets called a one-hour 'silent strike' on 23 November; a month to the day after street demonstrations had ignited the revolt. Traffic stopped and people vanished indoors. Soviet tanks appeared again, but took no action. Unexpectedly the official radio signalled the end of the silence with the national anthem, 'God bless the Hungarians'. As the music echoed in hushed streets, I remember a small schoolgirl standing in a doorway singing the words straight into the muzzle of the gun on a Red Army tank.

That evening Nagy and some of his associates left their refuge in the Yugoslav embassy, on what they thought was a safe conduct to their homes, negotiated between Kadar and the Yugoslavs, but a bus they boarded was seized by Soviet troops and they were exiled to Romania.

Kadar then said Nagy could not go home, as he might be murdered by 'counter-revolutionaries' – a comment that would ring hollow when, in 1958, he was returned to Budapest to be tried in secret and executed for treason.

THE MAGYARS PAID DEARLY FOR THEIR VALOUR. Western sources put the death toll at nearly 4000 in the revolt itself and scores of others were sentenced to death for counter-revolutionary crimes. Around 200 000 Hungarians, mostly young, fled abroad.

Other satellite countries would later incur the Kremlin's wrath. In 1968 Warsaw Pact troops invaded Czechoslovakia to snuff out the 'Prague Spring', when a reforming Communist Party leader, Alexander Dubcek, tried to introduce 'socialism with a human face'.

A Reuters man who was there, Mark Meredith, recalls the courage of one of his Prague contacts, a passionate reformer who used to meet him in a Jewish graveyard or a public lavatory to hand over documents from secret Party hearings. To protect his source, he'd cross the frontier to file reports. He also remembers how important reliable contacts were in an atmosphere charged with wild rumour. A fiction that Soviet soldiers had executed some Czech students drew one of few cautions ever issued by Reuters to its clients, advising against using a story. Reports of that kind might have led the Russians to expel the Western press and they risked inflaming the situation in Prague.

Elsewhere in the Eastern Bloc, General Wojciech Jaruzelski declared martial law in Poland in 1981 and arrested Lech Walesa, who led the Solidarity trade union in challenging communist power there. The Roman Catholic Church – which the communists never succeeded in undermining – urged Poles not to start a civil war.

The Hungarians never rebelled again, but in 1989, when Mikhail Gorbachev relaxed the Kremlin grip, they punched a hole in the Iron Curtain. They tore down the barbed wire on the frontier with Austria and let thousands of East German 'visitors' pour through to the West, months before the fall of the Berlin Wall and the end of the Cold War.

# THE DAY I STEPPED ON MAO'S TOES

DAVID CHIPP

FRONTLINES 10

## THE DAY I STEPPED ON MAO'S TOES | DAVID CHIPP

# 'Peking, Sunday 7 October 1956:

Lovely autumn day, beginning to get crisp but with a clear sky. Finished off a piece for the *New York Times* … Sino-Nepalese treaty signing probably worth covering.'
Thus the bare facts about what looked like a routine day – from a diary I had kept since I arrived in Peking, as we old China hands still call it, earlier that year.
A 29-year-old bachelor, I was the first non-communist resident correspondent since Mao Tse Tung led the communists to power in 1949.

**Mao Tse Tung**
c. 1956

© Hulton Getty

THERE WERE NOT, I REMEMBER, any direct flights to Peking (Beijing) in the mid-1950s, except from Moscow, so I'd travelled up there to start my assignment from Hong Kong, taking with me into the unknown a vast amount of luggage, including a typewriter, office supplies, a radio and a record-player. For this last I had a sort of *Desert Island Discs* selection. I still have one or two of them and I tell credulous guests that the imperfections are caused by the dust of the Gobi Desert. Visitors replenished the stock from time to time and, briefed by the incomparable Dick Hughes, the doyen of Hong Kong correspondents, brought me pork sausages and kippers as a treat.

I was installed by the China Travel Service in a large room (Number 271) in the Hsin Chiao Hotel, which was close by Hata Men, sometimes known as the Noble and Refined Gate, one of the ancient and great routes from the Mongol to the Chinese City – and there I was to stay for two years, partly because of its convenience and partly due to my own laziness.

It was within walking distance of the city centre – Tiananmen Square, the Peking Hotel, the main shopping street, Wang Fu Ching, and the wonderful covered market, Tung An Shih Chang. The telegraph office was not too far, either, and this was important in the age before telex and fax, e-mail and mobile telephones. There were no international telephone links with China, and so I filed my stories by cable or airmail. Unlike in Moscow, at the time there was no censor.

The disadvantage of staying in the hotel was that I had to have the teleprinter of the Chinese *Hsinhua* news agency in the bathroom, where it clattered away producing a spate of news items 24 hours a day. Luckily, I am a good sleeper and it did not worry me; but I thought it might annoy the great Russian pianist, Sviatoslav Richter. He was living for a few days in the next room. So as not to disturb him – and so that I could listen to him practise through the wall – I switched it off for a time. Rather unprofessional, I suppose, but good friends at *Hsinhua* promised that they would tip me off on any big news breaks. They did not let me down.

That Sunday – in a non-Christian country a normal working day – seemed like any other in Peking. The information department of the foreign ministry, responsible for the foreign press, had told me about the routine formal signing of a treaty of friendship with Nepal. I decided to go to it after attending the Anglican service in the British compound, conducted as usual by John Addis, a considerable and eccentric Chinese scholar who was number two in the office of the British chargé d'affaires.

It was worth going to every event, however unpromising a story, because there was always a chance of meeting some leading figure, or at least being able to identify a future contact. Premier Chou En-lai would often have a word or two with any journalist who might be present at such occasions, or at the many diplomatic receptions and banquets – informally he spoke to us in excellent English, unless we began to ask questions on the record, when he would call over his interpreter. But I had never been really close to Mao Tse-tung or the head of state, Liu Shao-ch'i.

There was another reason for going to that Sunday's treaty signing. It was taking place in Tsong Nan Hai, adjoining the Forbidden City to the south-west. This area is entered by an inconspicuous unmarked gate, guarded by soldiers, which was once the entrance to the Tower of Yearning, where the Emperor Chien Lung's Fragrant Concubine, the homesick Ke Fei, climbed each day to look at the Mongol market and dream of home. Now it is called the Gate of New China and leads to the place where party and government leaders live. In my explorations of Peking, I had never been there.

IT WAS SUCH A LOVELY DAY that I had not bothered to take my car. So, after the service, I turned left out of the compound that the British legation had occupied since the middle of the nineteenth century and walked north towards the Forbidden City.

Wang, who always seemed to be around with his pedicab, was waiting outside and I told him where to meet me later. Pedicabs are bicycle rickshaws propelled by sturdy independent rascals with great knowledge and a taste for gossip. Political correctness meant that pedalling these vehicles was considered demeaning. They were taken off the streets for a time and the drivers, who had no other means of support, were, like millions of others, sent to the countryside for re-education by labour. But they had

I had to have the teleprinter of the Chinese Hsinhua news agency in the bathroom ...

always served a need and, after a time, they reappeared, with the drivers looking just as villainous and raffish as before.

The guards seemed surprised when I arrived on foot. This, it seemed, was just not done. After making enquiries, they put me in a car to take me on a five-minute drive, passing tranquil lakes and old and modern buildings, to the place where the treaty was to be signed. It was one of many beautifully restored pavilions used for formal occasions. When I asked where the leaders lived, my foreign ministry minder answered with the typical Chinese response, 'I am not quite clear about that.'

*The guards seemed surprised when I arrived on foot.*

He herded the few Chinese journalists and myself to the back of the room just before the proceedings started. It seemed to me that almost the whole of the Chinese leadership was there, lined up behind the long table where the foreign ministers were to sign. There were brief speeches and then the signatures. Handshakes all round and everyone trooped out, leaving me thinking I could just as well have relied on picking up the basic facts of the story from the *Hsinhua* ticker in my bathroom.

I tried to identify where I was from my guidebook and wandered in to an adjoining courtyard. As I was studying a rather large piece of what looked like jade, I saw Liu Shao-ch'i walking towards me. I stepped back with a bow straight on to someone's toes. I heard a 'Ho, ho, ho' and turned to find to my horror that it was Mao.

With Liu looking on, laughing and saying a couple of times, 'Chi Da-wei', I stammered in my shaky Mandarin, 'Hello, Chairman Mao. I am Chi Da-wei.' It was my Chinese name, given me by Premier Chou and meaning 'Lacquered Defender of Morals'. 'I am Reuters correspondent,' I added. The Chairman looked suitably bemused and, although obviously this encounter was not the reason, a few weeks later it was reported that, at 63, he had decided to learn English!

I SAW BEFORE ME A SOLID-LOOKING MAN, taller than I had expected and with blackened teeth, stained by the strong Hunanese tea that he had drunk since childhood. They were always air-brushed to appear clean in photographs. Mao was wearing a smart tunic and was bare-headed. He looked slightly surprised and definitely amused at the appearance of this strange stumbling foreigner, probably the first he had met in such informal circumstances since those long-gone campaigning days in the caves of Yenan. He held out his hand and smiled, and said he hoped I was liking China. I replied that I was.

I had seen him a few days earlier, high up on the Gate of Heavenly Peace, as he took the salute at a national day parade; being mobbed by the cast of a musical evening; and across a ballroom at a state reception. In each case, he was received with adulation that bordered on hysteria.

Now I was face to face and, even after almost half a century, that first impression remains. Here was a great man. He had an aura, much more than charisma, and the presence of absolute assured certainty. Here was someone who had changed the course of history. His presence mesmerized me and I felt lucky indeed to have met him; even though he was certainly a tyrant and responsible for many deaths – and was to cause millions more to die of starvation during the Great Leap Forward.

Before I could ask him any questions through the foreign ministry man who, understandably alarmed, had rushed up, Mao moved on. On reflection, when asked why I had not managed to interview him, I felt that I might have replied, like Dr Johnson after he was presented to King George III, 'Sir, it was not for me to bandy civilities with my Sovereign.'

THERE WAS NO STORY TO FILE. Who in the world would care that Chipp and Mao had shaken hands and said 'hello' to one another? Certainly not Reuters with cable rates as high as they were. So I got in Wang's pedicab and he took me to the telegraph office, where I sent a report on the Sino-Nepalese treaty and added that Mao and Liu were present. My meeting with the Great Helmsman would have to wait for my memoirs, but I am still known among my friends in China as 'the Englishman who stepped on Chairman Mao's toes and lived to tell the tale'.

*Who in the world would care that Chipp and Mao had shaken hands and said 'hello' to one another?*

Meanwhile I would go to the Black Cat, the only remaining bar in Peking, and boast about it.

# GLOBETROTTING WITH THE PRESIDENT

JOHN HEFFERNAN

FRONTLINES 11

**GLOBETROTTING WITH THE PRESIDENT** | JOHN HEFFERNAN

# Dwight Eisenhower was the President

when, in February 1957, I began almost 20 years as Reuters chief correspondent in Washington – that 'sleepy southern city' as people used to call it. It was so sleepy then that Sidney Gampbell, our top financial writer, complained to me that nobody could find him the latest exchange rate for sterling against the dollar. We would soon awake, however, to the New Frontier days of John Fitzgerald Kennedy, then mourn his assassination and report the emotion-charged induction to office of the tall Texan, Lyndon Baines Johnson. The Vietnam War made its catastrophic way into history. Then came Richard Nixon's historic visit to mend fences with China and his downfall over the 'third-rate burglary' known as Watergate. If there was a thread through this era for me, I think it was Air Force One. Besides starring in a movie, the famous airplane that, with a 'pool' of reporters, flew successive presidents around the world, became a symbol of the post-war ascendancy of the United States and the hurt that often attended that.

**Lyndon Johnson, with Jackie Kennedy beside him, is sworn in as US President aboard Air Force One as it takes the body of JFK from Dallas to Washington**
22 November 1963

© Hulton Getty

DWIGHT DAVID EISENHOWER had many titles: General of the Army, Supreme Allied Commander in Europe in World War II, President of Columbia University in New York and twice-elected President of the United States. You could add 'Jet-Setter'. It was he who acquired a Boeing 707 that, in the late 1950s, became Air Force One. President Harry S. Truman had used an airplane in an earlier decade, but that was a nonentity compared with this sleek – and in those days novel – jetliner at Ike's disposal round the clock. The Republican Party rallying cry throughout his electoral campaigns was: 'I like Ike.' With the advent of Air Force One, the word soon spread that: 'Ike likes flying.' He found that swift safe air travel gave him a potent new foreign-policy tool and he used it to the full. Air Force One was waiting to take him anywhere he needed, to bring his personal touch to the job of steadying his Cold War allies across the world.

> With the advent of Air Force One, the word soon spread that: 'Ike likes flying.'

The White House decided that, wherever Ike flew, he should be accompanied on the aircraft, not only by staff and Secret Service officers, but also by a press pool. I flew often with Eisenhower, not so much with John F. Kennedy, but with greater frequency than ever with Lyndon B. Johnson. A chartered jet flew in company for reporters who were not in the pool. One Eisenhower trip was to 11 countries on 4 continents in 14 days. It embraced Rome, Ankara, Karachi, Kabul, New Delhi, Tehran, Athens, Tunis, Paris, Madrid and Casablanca.

A leader we met then who made a big impression on the press corps, I remember, was Pope John XXIII, who granted us a special audience, speaking in Italian with an Irish monsignor as interpreter. Jovial and loquacious, the Pope obviously had a great time himself, often rocking with laughter at his own sallies. I'm afraid the Irish monsignor missed much of it, but he did get clearly the farewell message: 'You are the modern Mark, Matthew, Luke and John. God bless you all.'

Another experience for Ike and for us was to be driven into Tehran, then ruled by the Shah, over a mile of Persian carpets. The story is told, perhaps apocryphally, that there was so much haste in taking off from Tehran airport at the end of a five-hour visit that a barrel of caviar intended for the press plane was left behind on the tarmac.

THE CONFIGURATION ON AIR FORCE ONE in those days was, one presumes, largely the same as now. It provided daytime space for the President and his spouse, with a conference table, a bedroom and shower, all up front. The mid-section was for staff and security personnel, with correspondents at the rear. The comfort was undoubtedly a consideration in Eisenhower's decision to undertake a gruelling world itinerary, despite an earlier heart attack, a bout with ileitis and a small stroke.

In New Delhi, he was almost overwhelmed by the boisterously happy Indian crowds, numbered conservatively by the authorities at more than two million. His open car was piled high with clumps of fresh flowers that were thrown at it. It was a welcome fit for a king or a maharaja and was reported then to be the greatest outpouring of affection for anyone anywhere. But a laconic Ike could only say, 'That was sumthin', wasn't it.'

Next day, Prime Minister Pandit Nehru took him to a ceremony just outside the capital and told him, 'This will give you the opportunity to see what a million people, close together, looks like.'

> 'This will give you the opportunity to see what a million people, close together, looks like.'

The President muttered, 'My goodness. This is unbelievable.'

Another Eisenhower trip was to Scotland to take up residence at Culzean Castle, in Ayrshire, where the Scottish people had honoured him with the lifetime gift of an apartment for his wartime leadership. On a flight from Paris to Prestwick in Scotland, Ike telephoned one of his corporate golfing friends in New York and jovially ordered him to be on the first tee at the nearby Open Championship course of Turnberry, ready to play, the next morning. The friend obliged.

BESIDES AIR FORCE ONE, Ike took delivery of a White House helicopter fleet. Late in 1959, when Kremlin leader Nikita Khrushchev came on a visit, he showed off one of the helicopters by taking him on a flight over Washington in the rush hour. The Russian was so impressed that he told his staff, 'I want one of these for myself.'

Early on that tour, trading invective for insult, Khrushchev threatened to pack his bags, but the visit ended with cordial talks at the presidential retreat of Camp David. The atmosphere was so good that headlines proclaimed 'The spirit of Camp David', suggesting a thaw in the Cold War. But that was not to last.

In the spring of 1960, a summit of allied leaders with Khrushchev blew up in Ike's face, when the Soviet leader angrily backed out because of the downing of an American U-2 spy-plane over Russia. Days earlier the President had allowed the State Department to deny that any flights had been made over Soviet territory. The lie was exposed when Russia produced captured pilot, Gary Powers.

It came to something of a climax a few months later at the United Nations General Assembly. Ike stayed away, leaving British Prime Minister Harold Macmillan as the West's chief spokesman – and it was during his speech that Khrushchev created uproar by banging his shoe on the table. That same UN meeting also gave the new Cuban leader, Fidel Castro, the opportunity to visit the United States amid reports, almost certainly false, that he and his followers were cooking chickens in the hallways of their hotel.

In mid-1960 Ike was off to South America, leaving behind the presidential election campaign between his vice-president, Richard Nixon – who lost narrowly but would run again and win in 1968 – and John F. Kennedy. Air Force One had to make an unplanned descent, at Surinam, when it developed a snag. A back-up aircraft, which always follows the President, picked him up there.

A PERSONAL NOTE ON KENNEDY. About three months into his presidency I was asked, with others, to appear on a television talk show, hosted by David Susskind, to discuss the new administration. A *New York Times* reviewer did not think much of the show, but praised my 'geniality'. A month or so later, Kennedy was at Key West, Florida, greeting Macmillan. He asked reporters to line up to be presented and, when it came to me, he added in an aside, 'I hear you're very good on television.' He did not miss much.

Kennedy flew in Air Force One to Paris in 1961 and then on to Vienna for his only meeting with Khrushchev, still angry over the U-2. France gave a big welcome to the President and his wife Jackie, including a sumptuous white-tie banquet at Versailles, hosted by Charles de Gaulle, and a foreign press lunch, where the President said he thought it appropriate to introduce himself as 'the man who accompanied Jackie Kennedy to Paris'. On trips in South America, incidentally, Jackie translated to Spanish for him, winning a rapturous welcome.

... 'the man who accompanied Jackie Kennedy to Paris'.

In contrast with the warmth of Paris, Kennedy found himself almost in a shouting match with Khrushchev in Vienna. Relationships with the Soviet Union worsened and the Cold War became more and more chilling until, in 1962, he demanded that Khrushchev withdraw Soviet missiles from Cuba and, before the Russians eventually backed down, Washington prepared for the absolute worst – an exchange of nuclear weapons.

ONE GREAT MOMENT of Walton Cole's tenure as the head of Reuters was to come to Washington to witness the installation of the Reuters news ticker, graciously received by Kennedy, at the White House. None of us guessed how valuable it would be to the administration. Press Secretary Pierre Salinger said afterwards that, during the Cuba crisis, US embassy cables from Moscow were terribly slow and the White House used texts taken off Reuters of Soviet statements. This led soon to the so-called 'hot line' between Washington and Moscow.

Another innovation, so long ago now that it is almost forgotten, was the introduction of television into presidential press conferences. It happened during Kennedy's tenure and was announced by Salinger, amid complaints by news agency correspondents.

'It is only an experiment,' he commented. 'It probably won't last long.'

It would be a political asset to Kennedy – and later to Hollywood actor turned president Ronald Reagan – but not to others, such as Lyndon Johnson.

TO AIR FORCE ONE FELL THE TRAGIC DUTY of bringing Kennedy's body to Washington hours after his assassination in Dallas on 22 November 1963. With Jackie, her pink suit spattered with her husband's blood, beside him, Vice-President Johnson was sworn in as his successor aboard the airplane.

I was not in the pool that day, but within a week my wife and I were invited to his private quarters in the White House for a drink and informal chat. We came away with an impression that this man of Texas, who, because of his career in the House of Representatives and as majority leader in the Senate, was more identified with domestic matters, was determined to assure the world that foreign affairs remained in competent hands. Unfortunately for him, it was his conduct of the Vietnam War and the escalation there of the US military force to half a million men, together with the large loss of life, that later led him neither to seek nor accept a second four-year term.

LBJ changed press secretaries three times. His second was Bill Moyers, a Texan and an ordained minister, who later became a distinguished newspaper editor and television personality. Bill gave out hot news more frequently than his predecessor – too much, so LBJ was said to think. Bill tells the story of how they were at the President's ranch in Texas. Bill came out to see the reporters and the following ensued.

'What is the President doing?'

'He's down at the lake.'

'Is he boating?'

'No, he's taking a walk.'

The inference that he was walking on water was just too much for the press corps and, presumably, the President, because soon afterwards Bill moved on.

AN EPIC 1967 LBJ TRIP was to attend a memorial service in Melbourne for Australian Prime Minister Harold Holt, who was lost in a swimming accident. It eventually entailed going around the world in four-and-a-half days, with one night in bed. The journey was planned in utmost secrecy. Nobody ever knew the next stop. This annoyed some of the correspondents, and Hugh Sidney of *Time Magazine* had the guts to tell the President firmly that he regarded the whole affair as absurd. LBJ took it all very calmly and explained that he could not say beforehand whether we would fly from Karachi either to Rome or Madrid. The Italian capital was preferred, but he did not want to make a premature announcement and give the 'commies' the opportunity to stage

a Vietnam War protest. Eventually he put down in Rome to confer with Pope Paul VI and issue a Vietnam peace declaration. To make the trip from the airport to the Vatican in the darkness of eventide, we were all flown in a posse of six or seven helicopters. The press corps landed in St Peter's Square and LBJ in the Vatican garden.

*… we were all flown in a posse of six or seven helicopters. The press corps landed in St Peter's Square and LBJ in the Vatican garden.*

ONCE, I DELAYED THE TAKE-OFF of Air Force One. After I explained that I'd kept him waiting on the tarmac because I had to dictate my copy, LBJ invited me up front for an off-the-record chat until the next stop. Vietnam tarnished his presidency, but he compiled a historic domestic legacy, which included legislation such as the 1964 Civil Rights Act, medical care for the poor and the Head Start programme for pre-school-age children – all still very much in being.

Richard Nixon, too, although remembered for Watergate, left a record of achievement as he jetted round the globe. He ushered an era of East–West *détente* by making historic visits to Moscow and Beijing and as he also withdrew US troops from Vietnam. Reuters White House man, Ralph Harris, wrote eloquently on 9 August 1974, when Nixon resigned over Watergate: 'The scandal assumed the elements of a Greek tragedy … not even his dazzling foreign policy successes could save him.'

After Watergate, Gerald Ford declared the nation's nightmare over, then Jimmy Carter became mired in a new crisis, involving militant Islam, when Iranian supporters of Ayatollah Ruhollah Khomeini held Americans hostage in the US embassy in Tehran. They'd be freed only as Ronald Reagan became the fortieth President of the United States on 20 January 1981.

THERE WERE OTHER STORIES in Washington away from the White House. One of the most interesting assignments I had ever had took me in 1953 with Sir Winston Churchill, newly installed as British prime minister a second time, who sped off after talks with Ike to a holiday in Jamaica – where the islanders all seemed to have perfected his famous 'V for Victory' salute.

The four reporters were invited to talk with him, as he sat in a familiar-looking set of overalls and a wide-brimmed straw hat, with his artist's easel by his side. We drank a deliciously spiked punch and he had a Scotch and soda. The talk was off-the-record, but it can be told at this late date that he did explain to us, in response to questions, how he had come by the V for Victory sign. It was during the bombing of London, when he followed the example of the King and Queen and went out in the blitzed areas to cheer the people. Royalty traditionally waved the right hand in a circular motion. Sir Winston proposed that he hold up the first two fingers with the palm inwards. Then, he explained, advisers thought that might be misinterpreted, so he turned the hand around and people apparently liked it.

## 'THEY SHOOT LIKE PIGS'

BASIL CHAPMAN

FRONTLINES 12

**'THEY SHOOT LIKE PIGS'** | BASIL CHAPMAN

# It was a sunny spring on the Riviera

and, as a correspondent based in Paris, I was lucky to have been assigned to report the 1958 Cannes Film Festival and the Monaco Grand Prix. Politics seemed remote. The top story would anyhow be covered by Reuters legendary chief correspondent in Paris, Harold King – or *'mon cher 'Arold'*, as de Gaulle once famously addressed him in public. But Paris was in a ferment, fearing a *coup d'état* or even a civil war. Orders to return swiftly to base came with the roar of Formula One exhausts in my ears. Soon I was in Paris, hearing General Charles de Gaulle say that he was ready to take power.

**Charles de Gaulle**
May 1958

© Hulton Getty

FRANCE TEETERED ON THE BRINK of disaster in May 1958, when leaders of its large army in Algeria joined a popular uprising there by the *pieds-noirs* – the European settlers – who were afraid that the politicians in Paris might be ready to negotiate an end to colonial rule with Moslem rebels. Amid a general strike, demonstrators took over the government building in Algiers to deliver inflammatory speeches from the balcony and form a Committee of Public Safety to take charge of affairs. Their choice of a paratrooper general to lead their committee fuelled the fears of a *coup d'état* in Paris, spearheaded by airborne forces from Algeria. France needed a strong man with both military and civilian support to end the revolt, and a strong hint was given on who this might be when the commander-in-chief in Algeria, General Raoul Salan, ended a speech to the crowds with a cry of: '*Vive de Gaulle.*'

De Gaulle enjoyed the prestige of having led Free French forces during the Nazi occupation of France in World War II and he had headed a provisional government when the war ended. But he had then resigned, declaring himself disillusioned with the fractious politics of the Fourth Republic, in a belief that, in its hour of need, France would one day call on him to return. Now, from his country house at Colombey-les-deux-Eglises, he let it be known that he was ready to answer such a call and, fearing that delay might be dangerous, he called a news conference in Paris for 19 May.

The venue was an hotel on a site where, today, art lovers queue to enter the Musée d'Orsay. That renowned museum was then a railway station with the hotel beside it. Armoured cars lined both banks of the River Seine on that afternoon. Traffic was diverted. Demonstrations were banned. But the authorities took care to mark their esteem. The 40 policemen who guarded the door of the hotel wore white gloves.

De Gaulle strode in on the dot of the announced time of 3 pm in a dark suit, not uniform, and looking solemn. He sat down and gave the photographers a moment to snap the famous haughty patrician profile, then he made his declaration, 'If the people wish, I am ready to assume the government of the republic.'

Besides, however, a strong hint that he sought more powers than usual for a head of government, he rejected dictatorship or a coup. He had never suppressed civil liberties, he said, and if someone assumed power it should be because it had been delegated by the republic. 'Why do you think I should begin a career as a dictator at the age of 67?' he asked.

'Why do you think I should begin a career as a dictator at the age of 67?'

King, as chief correspondent, reported the press conference. I was there with other colleagues to help him. In the event, it was the first of many close-up encounters that I would have with the man who was to rule France for the next ten years and decisively change its policies at home and abroad.

WHILE AN EFFERVESCENT ALGIERS AWAITED the next step, secret talks went forward in a cloak-and-dagger atmosphere. Journalists – given false clues by officials – raced to a château in a village to the east of Paris to cover a crucial session between de Gaulle and Prime Minister Pierre Pflimlin, only to discover that they had met in a discreet private home on the opposite side of the city. Finally, President Réné Coty intervened with a message to parliament saying that he had decided to call on 'the most illustrious of Frenchmen' and that he would resign unless de Gaulle became prime minister.

Within three days de Gaulle was head of government. Six months later he would be president. The change was dramatic. In his 12 years out of office, called by supporters his 'crossing of the desert', there had been 25 governments – average life about six months. After de Gaulle became president, France had only two prime ministers in just under a decade and but one head of government. That was de Gaulle himself, who, unlike previous presidents, chaired the cabinet. The currency, after repeated devaluation, stabilized and, after conversion to a 'new franc' was freed from exchange control.

De Gaulle was by nature authoritarian, apparently more through absolute conviction that he was right than any other motive, and he worked hard to get his facts straight before any decision. A man of iron self-discipline himself, he imposed discipline on subordinates. One minister deemed to have behaved incorrectly was forbidden to re-enter his ministry, even to collect his belongings. But dire predictions of dictatorship, fanned by the left, failed to materialize and were eventually forgotten, except by de Gaulle. They fed his mistrust of politicians and dislike of the press.

The ordinary citizens of France pictured de Gaulle as a remote austere person who unbent only on his frequent meet-the-people trips around the country, designed to bypass the political parties while he tested local opinion. Large crowds turned out to cheer him and he relished this popular adulation, plunging into the crowds to shake hands, regardless of the apprehensions of his security men, who feared that his imposing figure, well over six feet tall, made him an easy target. Like army camps awaiting an inspection, towns and villages smartened up for those visits. One municipal council raised the height of the town-hall toilet doors. De Gaulle would meet local notables and ask, 'Alors, M. le maire, what are the people saying here?' He'd listen to a lecture on the need for a fast train to Paris or a lament about a disastrous drop, perhaps, in the price of artichokes.

FRANCE PROSPERED under its newly found stability – but in the crisis over Algeria, which had toppled successive governments in Paris and inspired the return of de Gaulle, four painful and bloodstained years lay ahead.

Within four days of his investiture as prime minister, de Gaulle was in Algiers. On the balcony where activists and army leaders had delivered their inflammatory rhetoric, he flung his arms above his head and called out in ringing tones, 'Je vous ai compris.' 'I have understood you.' It was pure theatre. The crowd in the forum responded with wild acclaim, taking him to mean that he agreed with them that Algeria must remain French. He calmed the insurrectional fever among the Europeans for the time being, but then adjusted his policy, step by step, until in four years' time Algeria was an independent Arab state. A gradual realization that this was his goal was the source of much violence, with the formation in Algiers of a Secret Army Organization (OAS), several attempts to assassinate de Gaulle and two more European uprisings in Algeria.

One was a putsch by four generals, who quickly began to attract support, so that it became the biggest test yet for de Gaulle and for his controversial Article 16 in the new constitution, which accorded him full powers in any national emergency. He gave the occasion his typically theatrical treatment. Dressed in his general's uniform he appeared, stern-faced, on television to condemn a 'quateron' of generals and invoke Article 16. Then he went on, fiercely, raising his voice, 'I forbid any Frenchman, and above all any soldier, to execute any of their orders.'

It was remarkably effective. The generals found support for their enterprise crumbling and within three days either disappeared or gave themselves up. De Gaulle had won.

His choice of the word 'quateron', which was not in common use, caused a small problem of translation. Dictionaries were not much help. They suggested a platoon of 25 Roman soldiers or a 25-kilo measure of grain. Later publications opt for 'a small group' used pejoratively.

THE UNIFORMED TELEVISION APPEARANCE, and his earlier performance at the Algiers forum, gave de Gaulle a reputation as an actor. He certainly played his part impeccably in whatever role circumstances placed him – usually as the aloof fount of wisdom and presidential guidance, except when he was taking his 'crowd bath' among cheering admirers.

He did not give interviews to journalists and his contacts with those accompanying him on his many trips around France, Algeria and abroad were anything but intimate. The few who enjoyed his confidence knew that the slightest indiscretion would end that situation. His most important policy announcements came in speeches on television – which de Gaulle considered should be the political preserve of the state – or at news conferences. He wrote his own speeches with great care and committed them to memory, speaking without notes. His memory was astonishing. When journalists had an advance text, they could confirm that his delivery was word perfect.

On provincial tours so many speeches were required that he would have either to repeat himself or extemporize. In Calais he once achieved a single sentence of 234 words with 23 subsidiary clauses, so impressing the staff of a local newspaper that, pitilessly, they printed it in full. If style had suffered somewhat, the grammar was impeccable.

In Calais he once achieved a single sentence of 234 words with 23 subsidiary clauses …

In another unusual manifestation of style, de Gaulle would sometimes refer to himself in the third person, as if seeing himself through the eyes of an observer. Was this just reluctance to use 'I' or 'me'? Another peculiarity, in conversation, was a habit of pronouncing the final syllable of the word '*politiciens*' as if it were '*chiens*'. Those dogs!

News conferences were staged set pieces, with the entire cabinet in attendance. De Gaulle prepared what he wished to say, as well as replies to predictable questions. Those he especially wanted to answer were farmed out by his press secretary to journalists who were willing to cooperate and they would be answered first. If a question he wished to deal with was not raised, he would say, amid much amusement, that, 'I think that someone has asked me about so-and-so.'

FRANCE'S FINAL WITHDRAWAL from Algeria was attended by chaos and violence there amid bitter resentment. Nearly one million Europeans fled, as safeguards for their future under an independence agreement proved unworkable.

... the two most determined attempts – among several – to kill de Gaulle came within a hair's breadth of success

In France itself the two most determined attempts – among several – to kill de Gaulle came within a hair's breadth of success. One enveloped his car in a blinding flash of flame, as he and his wife Yvonne drove from Paris towards their home at Colombey-les-deux-Eglises. Powerful explosives hidden in a roadside heap of sand had failed to explode completely. 'Blunderers,' said de Gaulle, when he was sure no one was hurt.

The next attempt, soon after Algerian independence, was a machine-gun ambush at Petit Clamart on the Paris outskirts.

About 150 bullets were fired and 14 struck the presidential car, which kept going and reached its goal of a nearby airfield, with de Gaulle, his wife and two other occupants unhurt. De Gaulle's comment, 'They shoot like pigs.'

Madame de Gaulle played no active part in politics and preferred their creeper-clad home, La Boisserie, at Colombey-les-deux-Eglises to the Elysée Palace in Paris. She was popularly known throughout France as '*Tante Yvonne*', after a journalist discovered in 1958 that she was so called by no fewer than 17 nephews and nieces.

De Gaulle was unfailingly called '*le général*' by his entourage and by those who were described as his companions, who had joined him with the Free French in London when France was occupied by Hitler's Germany. You could guess at loyalties by the formula that people used. The semi-jocular '*le grand Charles*' was non-committal, but usually meant less-than-enthusiastic support. '*Grand*' can mean 'great' or else just 'big' or 'tall'.

DE GAULLE SOUGHT TO RAISE France's international status and emphasize its independence in the face of what he considered an Anglo-American hegemony in the Western world. He championed an independent French nuclear deterrent and kept the British out of the European Common Market, while taking the initiative in a reconciliation with Germany. He resigned in 1969 – refusing a pension – when '*Non*'-voters gained a small majority in a referendum on his plan for regional and senate reforms. He died a year later, aged nearly 80 and halfway through writing his memoirs. A towering granite Cross of Lorraine, symbol of the Free French, stands as a monument to his memory on a hilltop overlooking Colombey-les-deux-Eglises. His Fifth Republic endured.

# PRIVATE PRESLEY

PETER B. JOHNSON

FRONTLINES 13

**PRIVATE PRESLEY** | PETER B. JOHNSON

# Reporting in Germany for Reuters

in the late 1950s was quite a slog. The file was busy. Money was tight. We were short-handed. Mieke, the Dutch wife of our dedicated news editor, John Bush, laughed at a party that it was the only time they'd been out to dance in five years of marriage. We needed something to brighten up the file in those dark days of the Cold War and one day we got it. Elvis Presley, drafted into the US Army, arrived in Germany. My diary tells the story.

**Private Presley
at Friedberg barracks,
Germany. Peter Johnson is
in the background**
October 1958

© AP photo

1 OCTOBER 1958: To Friedberg, small town near Frankfurt, Main, to report on the arrival of the United States' best-known soldier, Private Elvis Presley, 23, star of rock-and-roll music, which he performs with much hip-waggling while playing a guitar. 'Just a sex symbol,' said one of my colleagues. Elvis was a country lad, a truck driver I believe, when he sprang to fame a few years ago.

> Elvis was a country lad, a truck driver I believe, when he sprang to fame a few years ago.

One of his records sold six million copies; he's made several films and is worth several hundred thousand dollars. But now, since he was drafted some months ago, he's a private with army pay of about a hundred dollars a month. Teenage girls swoon at the sight and sound of him. There were a few hundred waiting at Friedberg's old railway station tonight, in sweaters and jeans, but the army disappointed them by having Elvis, and 200 other men, arrive at an army siding some distance away. Several teenagers, including three I took in my car, managed to get to the siding where Elvis, in trim grey-green uniform and peaked cap, emerged from a railway carriage in the glare of floodlights, behind a fat military policeman.

I was surprised to see that he is really a pleasant-looking lad, a little Italianate, with shapely hands. He waved rather effeminately, and a sapphire ring worth 1500 dollars flashed on the little finger of his left hand. He picked up his kitbag, like the other men arriving, and walked along the platform through a milling crowd of pressmen, with the fat MP by his side. As he was getting into a bus, photographers called to him, so he grabbed three of the girl teenagers, put his arm round a couple of them, smiled nicely and posed for pictures. That was all we had of him tonight.

2 OCTOBER 1958: Elvis – reveille for him at 05.30 – was paraded at a press conference at 09.00, answering questions for an hour or so, until too many journalists started asking for autographs. He answered simply, in a friendly way, without side. He said he had not got into trouble in the army, didn't play crap (dice) because he did not want his teenagers to stop admiring him.

4 OCTOBER 1958: Although the press has been kept out of Presley's barracks since yesterday, a sharp Italian photographer, Manlio Lucentini, talked his way in and I was able to accompany him. At Presley's barrack block we were told he was out, but Lucentini spotted him hiding behind a bed. He stood up rather shamefacedly, but let the Italian take some pictures.

Later Presley went to a hotel in Bad Homburg, some 12 miles from his base, where his father and grandfather were staying. Presley at first refused to pose for pictures with a guitar, which Lucentini – of course – had borrowed from a waiter. But Elvis later relented, when assured it was not against the code of military discipline.

> At Presley's barrack block we were told he was out, but Lucentini spotted him hiding behind a bed.

Lucentini and another Italian had me laughing my head off with their antics in adjusting Presley for shots, shoving his arm a little one way, gabbling at him in Italian and saying, 'See me!' when they meant, 'Look at me!' I admired the way Elvis, who was dog-tired by now, stood up to it all. He'll be a good advert for the United States, that lad.

Lucentini told me that he (Lucentini) is shortly to be tried for sacrilege. He and a colleague found out the whereabouts of Mussolini's grave, beneath an altar, and dug it up.

# AT GUNPOINT IN AFRICA

SANDY GALL

FRONTLINES 14

## AT GUNPOINT IN AFRICA | SANDY GALL

# It all started, as these things

usually did, with a telex message in the time-honoured Reuters formula: 'How you placed proceed soonest Bakwanga where government troops reported fighting Kalonji forces?'

I did not know much about Bakwanga – now called Mbuji-Mayi – except that it was in the Congolese province of Kasai, and the site of the world's largest industrial diamond mine. I was in the next-door province, Katanga (Shaba), and soon after the panicky Belgian government thrust independence on the Congo in 1960, both Katanga and Kasai, one rich in copper and uranium, the other in diamonds, seceded. The first to leave the sinking ship was Moise Tshombe of Katanga, the Belgian-educated son of a millionaire businessman, to be followed almost immediately by the self-styled 'King' Albert Kalonji of Kasai.

**Idi Amin: correspondent Sandy Gall survived arrest in the Congo only to find himself in jail again a decade later in Amin's Uganda**
c. 1972

© Hulton Getty

DID THESE TWO DEFECTIONS HERALD the break-up of Africa's newest, and vastly wealthy, independent state? That was the question which alarmed the United Nations as it tried to keep the peace in the Congo and which Reuters wanted answered. For some reason the roulette wheel stopped on my number. So, one sunny morning in August, I found myself taking off from Elisabethville (Lubumbashi) the Katanga capital, in the company of George Gale of the *Daily Express*, with his naughty boy's face and mop of ginger hair; Dickie Williams, of the BBC, small, witty and honey-voiced; and of course the pilot, Alan Kearns, a large and unflappable Rhodesian. I was the Reuters man in southern Africa, based in Johannesburg, and the least experienced of the three. We climbed above Elisabethville's colonial bungalows with their Day-Glo gardens, and flew north-west across the grey-green bush of Katanga. To find out who was really in charge in Bakwanga – Kalonji's forces or central government troops – Dickie and I had called the day before on the Belgian head of the Katanga Army, ominously named Major Crevecoeur, which means 'Breakheart'. He assured us, citing radio messages from Kasai, that after a recent battle Bakwanga was in 'friendly hands'.

Half asleep, lulled by the reassuring roar of the Cessna engine, I jerked awake to hear Alan say that we should be over Bakwanga. I looked down. Nothing broke the endless carpet of bush. We began to circle, Alan muttering, 'I'll give it one more go.' Then almost immediately he shouted, 'There it is,' and neat rows of mine houses appeared as if by magic, surrounded by the sprawl of the *cité indigène*. 'Control tower doesn't answer,' Alan announced, flying low over the runway to have a look, and then dropping the little plane down in a perfect landing. We climbed out and, to my surprise, another British journalist appeared and greeted George, who introduced him as Tom Stacey of *The Sunday Times*. He said there had been a big battle two days before and that the Congolese Army, a rough mutinous bunch, were now in charge. Where had we come from? Tom asked.

... the Congolese Army, a rough mutinous bunch, were now in charge.

'Elisabethville,' we replied.

'God, don't tell them that on any account,' Tom said.

At that point, an arrogant-looking figure in camouflage uniform came striding towards us. 'Who are you and where have you come from?' he demanded in French.

Ignoring the second part of the question, I said politely, 'We're British journalists,' and we all handed him our passports. He did not seem particularly interested, flicking impatiently through the pages. Apart from his hostile manner, the most noticeable thing about him was his ingrowing beard, a mass of tiny black ringlets which covered his chin and throat, and seemed embedded in the skin. It looked painful. No wonder he seemed irritable. Looking up suspiciously, he repeated, 'Where have you come from now, in your plane?'

I took the plunge. 'Leopoldville,' I said, which was partly true. It was the Congolese capital, later known as Kinshasa.

'Leopoldville?' he repeated disbelievingly. 'Where is your *laissez-passer* then?'

'We don't have one,' I said. 'Nobody said we needed one.'

'If you came from Leopoldville, you must have come through Luluabourg (a provincial capital) and you need a permit to enter this area,' he said in a checkmate tone of voice.

We said nothing.

'I don't believe you came from Luluabourg,' he said finally. 'I am going to check with them now. I hope for your sake you're right.'

KNOWING HOW INEFFICIENT COMMUNICATIONS were in the Congo, we guessed it would take all day or longer to receive a reply. If we left that afternoon, we might get away with it. As we stood on the tarmac, rather at a loss, there appeared another soldier, wearing smartly pressed battledress with the blue and white United Nations badge on his shoulder. This was Lieutenant Ali Trabelsi of the Tunisian Army, the UN commander in Bakwanga, who offered to show us round. As we climbed gratefully into his white UN Jeep, he unslung his Stirling sub-machine-gun, gave it a pat, and said, '*Ca, c'est ma bible.*'

'Are things that difficult?' I asked.

'Yes,' he said, 'very difficult indeed.'

As we drove into the little town, he described how Russian Antonovs had flown in a battalion of Congolese government troops a week before, and how, after a lot of wild shooting, they had captured the town and the airport. Some of the Kalonji troops had taken refuge in a mission school on the top of a hill, which the government forces had attacked with everything they had: mortars, bazookas, machine-guns and rifles. When some missionaries finally entered the building, they found no soldiers, but a large group of terrified civilians, including women and children, and about a dozen dead. One old man, with six gunshot wounds, lay in an empty bath, miraculously still alive.

As we drove past the Belgian houses, I realized they were empty. 'Where are all the Belgians?' I asked.

'Come and see,' Trabelsi answered.

We drove to the Belgian Club, to find 200 or 300 nervous mine staff and their wives under house arrest. An hour later, we were back at the airport, to be met by an anxious Alan Kearns. 'Bad news,' he began. 'They won't refuel the plane.'

At that point, Ingrowing Beard arrived, looking angry. 'You lied,' he shouted. 'I have checked with Luluabourg and they have no knowledge of your plane. You are under arrest.' His voice rose, 'You are Belgian spies. You will be taken to Luluabourg and shot.' I protested, '*Non, non, nous sommes des journalistes anglais.*' He had seen our passports. He waved this away. 'Your plane is from Rhodesia. Your pilot is Rhodesian. You are spies. The penalty for espionage is execution by firing squad.' He turned to some waiting soldiers, and snapped, 'Take them away.'

> 'You are Belgian spies. You will be taken to Luluabourg and shot.'

AS WE WERE BUNDLED INTO A LAND ROVER, I saw Lieutenant Trabelsi out of the corner of my eye, and then we were bumping off down the road with the soldiers aiming their rifles at us, as they do in bad films. Our destination was an army camp on the outskirts of Bakwanga. It was Saturday afternoon. Off-duty soldiers, drifting about and drinking beer, glared at us. It did not look very promising.

We stopped at the orderly room and were marched inside at rifle point. The Beard spoke to the orderly corporal, and then repeated his speech that we were Belgian spies, his voice carrying through the open door to the soldiers standing outside. All of them understood French. After he left there was a lull while we discussed our predicament in low voices. Suddenly the

corporal shouted, 'Silence,' got up from his desk and advanced, furiously shaking a soda bottle and then spraying the contents over us. I felt it splash over my face and drip on to my shirt. Harmless in itself, the act was somehow full of violence.

Outside the crowd was growing. A soldier stepped into the room, gripping his rifle. Another followed. Then a third. We waited. The soldiers outside began to shout to the ones inside. The heat and noise were overpowering. More soldiers forced their way into the room. Suddenly they were all confronting us, menacingly, a mass of faces, angry, shouting. One soldier ripped my gold Rolex off my wrist. Another grabbed George's wallet. One brawny man, face shining with sweat, and wearing dark glasses, brought a stick down as hard as he could on Alan's head. We were forced back against the wall. Someone tore off my shoes. '*A genoux!*' they shouted. 'On your knees!'

Fighting to stay upright, the scene froze on my retina like a breaking wave caught by the camera shutter. During that fraction of a second, as we waited for the all-out attack, the kicking, punching and the rifle butts, an extraordinary thing happened.

Through the open doorway, making a passage for himself, came an almost venerable figure, a grey-haired military police officer. He said something in Lingala – I imagine the equivalent of a British bobby's 'Hullo, hullo, what's goin' on 'ere, then?' Everything stopped. In the long silence that followed, two huge young military police with red-and-white-striped steel helmets followed him into the room. Then the soldiers, who had been pressing so close to us that I could smell their sweat, stepped back silently and began to melt away, like ice in a sudden thaw. In ten seconds the room was empty.

'Are you all right?' the captain asked, rather bewildered.

'I think you came just in time,' I said.

He shook his head in sympathy, adding , 'I've come to take you to the UN.'

THE CONGO WAS not the only country in Africa where independence was followed by tribal conflict and army intervention.

Twelve years later, in 1972, having left Reuters and joined Independent Television News (ITN), I found myself in Kampala, the capital of Uganda, covering the latest antics of Idi Amin, a former sergeant-major in the King's African Rifles, who had deposed the president, Milton Obote, and appointed himself in his place. A figure of fun to readers of *Punch* – he declared himself Conqueror of the British Empire, even offered to be the King of Scotland – but not to the unfortunate people of Uganda, Amin was busy deporting 40 000 Asians with British passports and taking over their businesses. Less well publicized was his purge of tribal opponents in the army and elsewhere, most of whom ended up in Lake Victoria.

I HAD COMPLETED THE ASSIGNMENT, and was on the point of flying home, when I found myself caught up in the middle of an invasion by Obote supporters from neighbouring Tanzania. Amin declared an emergency, and ordered the arrest of the 'many British spies' he claimed were in the country, among whom he included about a dozen British journalists, and one American.

I was arrested by a Special Branch man, who like Idi himself, was British-trained.

> I was arrested by a Special Branch man who like Idi himself was British-trained.

As we left the hotel, he tried to hustle me out through the back door, but I made a point of ostentatiously leaving my key at the desk. Outside, as I was pushed into the back of a white Peugeot, I tripped on something hidden under a newspaper: it turned out to be a black sub-machine-gun. There was only one other occupant in the back – a young Reuters correspondent called Nick Moore. While we introduced ourselves politely, the driver gunned his engine and raced up the hill, past the old British houses, wreathed in bougainvillea, finally swerving through a gateway with the sign: 'Makindye Military Police Barracks'.

In the guardroom there were no formal proceedings. 'Sit down,' barked the big corporal. I looked round. There was nowhere to sit. Nick put it in words, whereupon a private behind the desk stood up, leaned past me and struck Nick a stinging blow with his truncheon.

Shorn of our personal belongings, including shoes and socks, we were taken outside on to a small lawn shaded by trees. A tall soldier came forward, carrying an FN, the heavy NATO automatic rifle. He shouted in Swahili.

'He wants us to run,' said Nick.

'Where?'

I got the answer in my back, a terrific jab from the FN. We started to run, rather slowly up the hill, and the soldier gave me another vicious blow in the back.

'He wants us to run faster,' Nick said.

Halfway up the hill, he hit me again, and I gasped with pain. The fourth time, I knew what to expect, but it did not help. 'You bastard,' I thought.

Someone was coming towards us, swinging a club. We stopped panting in front of him. I saw he was a major.

'Sit down,' he said, waving the soldier away.

I started to talk fast. 'We're British journalists – my friend works for Reuters, I work for Independent Television News in London.'

'Television?' he interrupted. 'How long have you been in Uganda?'

'A week,' I said.

He told us to get up, and gestured to a row of cells. After some hesitation, the major indicated one, numbered C19. The door clanged shut. It was a long hut with a smooth concrete floor. Half a dozen frightened-looking Africans sat near the door. We walked to the end and sat down with our backs to the wall. I inspected our surroundings. They were not particularly reassuring. Behind us, a bullet had made a two-inch hole. To our right, a line of bullets – it looked like a burst – climbed the wall. My eyes went to the ceiling. It was splashed with blood.

> I inspected our surroundings. They were not particularly reassuring.

I recalled the murder of two young Americans who had been investigating reports of killings by Amin's men at Mbarara barracks, in the south, a year before. At one point the door opened and a guard came in, followed by four prisoners carrying a fifth man. When they dumped him on the floor, I saw his shirt was covered in blood. He groaned. The guard looked up, saw us watching, and ordered the prisoners to take the injured man out again, one of them returning with a brush and pail to clean up the blood.

The door was locked again, and a minute or two later we heard a curious thumping sound, like a hammer or a club hitting something soft, followed by the ringing sound a shovel makes on hard ground. I was told later by Bob Astles, a Briton married to a Ugandan, who had also been arrested, that it was common practice for prisoners in Makindye to be beaten to death by 28-pound hammers.

At dusk, the cell door opened again, and several officers and half a dozen armed soldiers came in. They were laughing and talking as if they had been drinking. Eventually, after they had doused a prisoner under the shower and then kicked him back to his corner, one officer saw us through the gloom. 'Who are you?' he asked.

I explained. He looked surprised and made us write down our names and organizations. He then disappeared, returning an hour later. It was now dark. Boots scraped on the cement and torches zigzagged towards us. 'You two. Come with me.'

WE STOOD OUTSIDE IN OUR BARE FEET, in the warm dark. Inside I had felt relatively safe, now we were vulnerable again. I wondered apprehensively what was going to happen. The major pointed down the hill. We walked down, stopping by a hut silhouetted against the perimeter lights. After much rattling of keys, the major said, 'Go inside.' They were the sweetest words I had heard all day.

Two Africans were reading the Bible by the door, and inside half a dozen people sat in a dimly lit circle.

'Hey, Sandy! When did they pick you up?' asked the familiar voice of photographer Don McCullin, then working for *The Sunday Times*.

Someone pushed a cup of tea into our hands. It was Astles, who had originally worked as an information officer for Obote, and later became close to Amin. 'Where have you come from?' he asked. I told him. 'C19?' Astles repeated. 'Why, that's the execution cell. You're bloody lucky, mate, to come out of there alive. You'll be all right here. This is the VIP cell.'

'C19?' Astles repeated. 'Why, that's the execution cell. You're bloody lucky, mate, to come out of there alive.'

We probably were lucky, much luckier certainly than the many thousands of Ugandans who were bludgeoned to death, or fed to the crocodiles during Amin's reign of terror. Among his victims were some of the country's leading citizens, including Anglican Archbishop Luwum, Chief Justice Benedicto Kiwanuka and ironically, Mr A. C. K. Oboth-Ufumbi, the interior minister who signed our deportation orders. He was killed in a 'car crash', on Amin's orders.

# ORANGES IN GORKY STREET

ROBERT ELPHICK

FRONTLINES 15

## ORANGES IN GORKY STREET | ROBERT ELPHICK

# In the early 1960s, the Soviet Union

seemed to ride the crest of a wave. Ebullient Communist Party boss Nikita Khrushchev believed that he had the edge over the West. He'd seen off Dwight Eisenhower by having an American U-2 spy-plane shot down over Russia and in Moscow, where I had arrived as a correspondent in 1958, the word was that he had little more than contempt for the new President, John F. Kennedy. In April of 1961, I returned from a trip to Helsinki where Eve, my wife, had given birth to our first child, Sarah Louise, and we were getting ready to celebrate her first month of life. But there was a sense in the air that Khrushchev had another card up his sleeve to keep us busy in the office.

**Yuri Gagarin**
April 1961

© Hulton Getty

WE JOURNALISTS WERE A SMALL BAND in Moscow at the time, just the main wire services, a few staff men from London, New York and the European capitals. A couple of weeks before, we had all been dependent on the whims of the official censor, who was housed at the Central Telegraph Office just off Gorky Street. But censorship had been lifted. The censors packed their anonymous bags and vanished into the dark history of the Stalinism that Khrushchev was now denouncing, and we got used to the novelty of just dictating copy on the telephone.

On 11 April 1961, my Reuters colleague John Miller, and I, and the two Russian girls, Alla and Lena who helped us run the tiny office in Sadovo Samotochnaya on the inner ring road, sat and listened to Moscow radio and sifted the latest rumours. Then the loudspeakers on the lampposts were all turned on to play very loud patriotic music. An announcement must be imminent. Our driver, Grisha, warmed up the engine on the office Humber in case we needed to go somewhere in a hurry.

The first untoward happening, though, was the arrival of the Russian woman who helped clean our flat and look after the baby. In great excitement, Tonya called my wife to announce, 'It's fantastic! There are oranges in Gorky Street. If you're quick, you can get some for Sarah.'

This was news indeed. Nobody could remember seeing oranges in the austere world of post-war communist Moscow at all, let alone on sale in Gorky Street. Eve dashed off to try her luck.

That, I recall, was just when state radio interrupted the jaunty patriotic airs and peasant songs to declare that the Soviet Union had put a man in space. The announcer was the character who had always been used during World War II to proclaim Red Army victories. He had a style that could only be called portentous.

> Nobody could remember seeing oranges in the austere world of post-war communist Moscow at all, let alone on sale in Gorky Street.

AN AIR FORCE OFFICER CALLED YURI GAGARIN had been sent up in a rocket in an elaborate operation from the Soviet space centre – he informed us – proving beyond doubt the triumphant superiority of the Soviet system over all others, especially the capitalist one.

It was left to us to try to fill in a lot of the detail that had got lost in the rhetoric.

The Russians did announce the times when Gagarin had been blasted off and when he came back to earth – but we had to work out that he had done just a single orbit. John and I actually made the calculation by long division – no computers in those days – and scored a world beat over the other wire services with that information.

My wife, meanwhile, was struggling to keep her place in the queue of women on Gorky Street. The announcements on the Gagarin story followed one another with rising urgency, but all the women's eyes were on that dwindling mound of oranges that had miraculously appeared in the Soviet capital. They were being rationed to a kilo per person. Eve got hers and returned just in time to hear the radio report that a big welcome was being prepared in Moscow for Gagarin.

> The announcements on the Gagarin story followed one another with rising urgency, but all the women's eyes were on that dwindling mound of oranges …

Khrushchev turned out at Vnukovo Airport with the entire Party and government leadership on a crowded podium, watched by a few privileged foreigners, including journalists like ourselves.

As Gagarin, in full uniform and a brand new overcoat, stepped from the aircraft that had brought him from the space station out in the steppes, I noticed that one of his shoelaces was trailing. It was heart stopping. I wondered if a second or two of carelessness as he had dressed that morning might send him tumbling on his face in front of the Soviet élite and a world that would watch on television. It did not – and the joy was unconfined all the way from the airport to the huge crowd massed in Red Square.

We were quite used to the telephone ringing with the news that there would be a 'spontaneous demonstration' by workers to protest at some or another new act of oppression by Western imperialism. Our informants would then give us a precise time and location – mostly outside the US or the British embassies. But this was the one occasion when I witnessed real spontaneity from ordinary Russians in my time in Moscow.

I MET GAGARIN THAT EVENING at the glittering Kremlin reception in his honour. He was quite small in stature with a cheeky grin and the 'wizard-prang' attitude to life of a fighter pilot – shrugging off his historic flight as the kind of job that a Soviet aviator was expected to take in his stride. I shared a toast in Kremlin vodka and tasted the caviar.

*He was quite small in stature with a cheeky grin and the 'wizard-prang' attitude to life of a fighter pilot …*

The horizon would soon cloud for Khrushchev. He'd have to build a wall across Berlin to stop East Germans fleeing to the West, then, in 1962, Kennedy – who vowed that America would beat the Russians to the moon – called his nuclear bluff to force him to dismantle Soviet missile bases in Cuba. In 1964 he was ousted in a Kremlin palace coup by Leonid Brezhnev. I never saw oranges in Gorky Street again.

# 'DIE GRENZE IST GESCHLOSSEN'

ADAM KELLETT-LONG

FRONTLINES 16

## 'DIE GRENZE IST GESCHLOSSEN' | ADAM KELLETT-LONG

# In the early hours of Sunday

13 August 1961, I felt very much alone as I drove down Unter den Linden, the deserted main thoroughfare of what was then the communist Eastern sector of Berlin. As I approached the towering mass of the Brandenburg Gate, the usual road crossing between the Soviet and Western sectors of the city, a red torch flickered like a firefly in the darkness ahead of me. It was in the hands of a uniformed border guard. I opened the car window to ask him what was going on, and he leaned over and told me that I could not go any further. *'Die Grenze ist geschlossen.'* 'The border is closed.' I was 26, on my first foreign assignment, and I'd just heard some of the most momentous words in Europe's post-war history.

**East German soldiers construct the Berlin Wall. The sign reads, 'Road blocked due to the Wall of Shame'**
1961

© Hulton Getty

I TURNED REUTERS little red Wartburg car round and set off at speed for my flat, which was also my office, a couple of miles away to send the story, but I didn't get very far before I was stopped again, this time at the edge of the huge Marx Engels Platz, the square where the communists staged their ceremonial parades. Another uniformed figure with a red torch. Then a seemingly endless column of trucks filled with police and what seemed to me to be troops – actually, most were factory fighting guards, members of the 'Home Guard' militia – thundered out of the darkness across the square and on down towards the Brandenburg Gate. Some lorries pulled what appeared to be small field guns, although in the daylight of a few hours later I saw that in reality they had been the stovepipes of field kitchens.

As the last lorry passed and the guard disappeared into the shadows, I had a brief debate with myself. Should I return and see whether they had stopped at the Brandenburg Gate? Perhaps they'd rumbled on into West Berlin. Or should I continue to the office to file the crucial information that was already in my possession, that the communist rulers had reacted to an exodus of East Germans to the West by sealing off their side of the divided city.

Common sense won – I would probably have been detained if I'd gone back just then – and I continued on to the office. Mary, my 22-year-old bride of just under two years, was waiting for me. In her diary, she recorded that I was 'white to the lips'. I described to her in a few words what I had seen and told her to go to bed and not wait up for me. Fat chance! I then sat down at the teleprinter and typed an urgent story that began: 'Berlin Eastern Sector Aug 13 Reuters – The East/West Berlin border was closed early today.'

*... this was the first hard news to reach the outside world of what was to become the building of the Berlin Wall ...*

I didn't know it then, but this was the first hard news to reach the outside world of what was to become the building of the Berlin Wall – one of the most hated symbols of the Cold War.

Looking back, I marvel that I was only 'white to the lips'. I'd been the correspondent in East Berlin for eight months,

but before my assignment there I'd only just ended two years as a graduate trainee. I was astonished to have been given the posting – I had a rather spurious claim to speak German after I'd briefly learned it at school – and Reuters was the only non-communist news organization to have a correspondent in East Berlin. It had a lot of Eastmarks in an otherwise blocked account in the East German State Bank that it needed to use up.

For my first few weeks in Berlin, nothing much had happened, so at least I'd brushed up on my German, but it was soon evident that a swelling flow of East Germans through the open border to West Berlin, in quest of a new life, was becoming an unbearable burden on an ailing East German economy and a painful embarrassment to the Soviet Union. Something had to happen to stop or slow the exodus from the East. But what?

In June, Walter Ulbricht, the goatee-bearded veteran East German communist leader, held his first press conference for international journalists for many years, delivering a familiar tirade against West Berlin as a centre of espionage and subversion and against its 'slave trade' – jargon for the refugees – but when someone did actually suggest building a wall to him, he was scathing. How could such a thing be done? 'No one intends to build a wall.' I, for one, took this reply at face value.

Tension mounted during August. The flow of refugees increased dramatically, as people who had intended to leave at some time panicked, believing that if they didn't go now they might never have the chance. The tone of East German propaganda grew more strident and Ulbricht paid a supposedly secret visit to Moscow – secret until he was spotted at a football match by Reuters correspondent John Miller – before, on 11 August, the *Volkskammer* (parliament) passed a resolution authorizing his government to take any measures that it deemed necessary.

ON THE WAY OUT of that special session, I ran into Horst Sindermann, at that time head of the communist SED Party's agitprop (agitation and propaganda) department. I had got to know Sindermann, who later became prime minister, fairly well and at his instigation we met from time to time for dinner and 'background chats' at the Foreign Press Club. I asked him now to explain the resolution. He did not reply directly, but he looked me in the eye and said, 'If I were you and I had plans to spend this weekend away from Berlin, I wouldn't.'

I took my cue from that and, on the Saturday morning,

> 'If I were you and I had plans to spend this weekend away from Berlin, I wouldn't.'

12 August, as the heatwave drove Berliners to the lakes and swimming pools, I sent out a story that began: 'Berlin is holding its breath this sunny summer weekend waiting for as yet unspecified measures to halt the flow of East Germans seeking a new life in the West.'

Later that day Brian Horton, the news editor for Germany, flew in from Bonn and pointed out that I'd put Reuters out on a limb. What if nothing happened? I could only tell him that I was sure it would, and he was somewhat, but not entirely, mollified when I privately told him my source.

At around 9 pm I drove to the Ostbahnhof, at that time the main railway station in East Berlin, to pick up a copy of the Party newspaper, *Neues Deutschland*. I had an 'arrangement' with an official in the stationmaster's office whereby, for a fairly substantial sum of West German marks, I was handed one of the copies of the newspaper that were destined to be taken by train to the provinces. Numbers of black-uniformed railway policemen were arriving at the station, but that was the only unusual sign and, when I opened the newspaper, there was no word of any decree announcing drastic measures. What I did not know was that, at that very moment, a hand-picked skeleton staff was preparing a special edition!

Dejected, I returned to my office and tried to prepare a story for the next morning explaining why Berlin was still holding its breath – or, rather, had stopped holding it. By midnight, the wastepaper basket was almost overflowing with discarded attempts. All was silence, except for the Reuters ticker at the other end of the office. I felt very isolated. There were no other Western journalists in East Berlin with whom I could compare notes, no diplomats, no businessmen, no one at all. Finally at around two in the morning, I decided to give in and get some sleep, but just as I was switching off the office light my telephone rang and a voice said in German, 'I strongly advise you not to go to bed tonight.'

The caller put down the telephone without identifying

himself and, to this day, I do not know who it was, though I suspect it was a duty editor at the East German ADN news agency. The best thing to do, I decided, after another check on the teleprinters was to go out again and see what was happening. Everything seemed normal. The sultry streets were deserted, except for the occasional couple embracing in a doorway. Then I got to the Brandenburg Gate, where the man with the red torch uttered those historic words: *'Die Grenze ist geschlossen'*, and I could stop holding my breath and set to work.

BACK IN THE OFFICE AGAIN, as I transmitted my urgent story, the ADN ticker was now issuing a spate of decrees, the gist of them being that all links between the two parts of the city were being cut and people could not cross the divide, but that these measures were only temporary – a blatant lie presumably designed to keep the population calm. The decrees were also read on radio, interspersed with spells of soothing jazz, a very unusual sound on the state broadcasting media. Mary sat at the teleprinter in a pink dressing-gown transmitting my fresh copy, as the story evolved, to Reuters.

At around seven, a furious Erdmute Behrendt, our invaluable East German office assistant, burst in, protesting with some reason that I hadn't called her much earlier, and before long I was able to take advantage of a pause in the torrent of decrees to drive out again to see for myself the cordons of border police who now surrounded the Brandenburg Gate, as militiamen

> … militiamen formed a temporary human wall and coils of barbed wire were unloaded from Army trucks …

formed a temporary human wall and coils of barbed wire were unloaded from army trucks to start building a permanent one.

Reports out of West Berlin said, meanwhile, that the Russians had deployed at least two army divisions just outside the city, reinforcing an impression that they were deadly serious and ready to respond if the West contemplated military action.

Ivan Shishkin, my regular Soviet contact, telephoned to 'reassure' me. 'If things get really serious,' he said. 'We will get Mary home through Prague.'

Shishkin was officially a second secretary (press) in the vast Soviet embassy in Unter den Linden, but I'd learn later that he was in fact a KGB colonel-general in charge of counter-intelligence, who outranked his ambassador on all security matters. An outwardly genial man who spoke excellent English and acted very much the Anglophile, he had proved a useful source. When he said, 'I think', he meant, 'I know', and I thought it was therefore safe to attribute what he'd said to 'reliable Soviet sources'.

THE REACTION FROM THE POPULATION, at least in our part of East Berlin, was muted. There was little they could do. The police and militia had formed an unbreakable 'human chain' that I watched inch forward – in from the actual border – as the day progressed. Behind them, East Berliners, some surly, some just curious, stood about three deep in shattered silence. Police fired teargas to disperse about a thousand people who gathered near our office, when, the officer in charge said, they were judged to have been 'getting a little provocative', but that was

the last I saw of any popular reaction. The aim of the operation, as it transpired, was to create a second border some hundreds of yards inside the real one, so that in the days, weeks and months to come the building of the Berlin Wall could proceed away from the gaze of the East German people.

When we watched it go up, we could not yet imagine the full scale of the personal tragedy – mothers and fathers who would never see their sons and daughters again, lifelong friends who would become strangers, the deaths of daring young men trying to escape into what they believed was a free and just society. On Christmas Day 1961, I went to the crowded morning service at East Berlin's huge Marienkirche and listened to one of the most moving sermons I've ever heard, preached by a visiting priest from a small provincial town. His theme was: 'Father, forgive them for they know what they do.' I have always wondered what happened to him.

# SWANS, SPIES AND A GREENHORN WITH RED GLOVES

ANNETTE VON BROECKER

FRONTLINES 17

## SWANS, SPIES AND A GREENHORN WITH RED GLOVES | ANNETTE VON BROECKER

# I was a 19-year-old blonde who

Reuters hired as an editorial assistant in West Berlin in October 1959 and I'd
probably never have become a journalist at all, had it not been for a dramatic
story that unfolded before my eyes at a moment when history was being made –
and, of course, because my mother desperately wanted to get me out of
the house.

**Annette von Broecker at work in the Reuters Berlin office with bureau chief Alfred Kluehs (left)**
Spring 1962

© author

BERLIN, CAPITAL OF THE COLD WAR, 14 years after the defeat of Hitler's Germany. There were still a lot of ruins. The Four Powers who occupied the city had divided it up and they stumbled from crisis to crisis, unable to agree on a peace settlement. Russia threatened to swallow the Western sectors, which were held by the United States, Britain and France. Berliners were often scared. Many left.

The first Russian I had met was a soldier who entered our home in 1945 and took off his boots, then he saw that we had Tolstoy and Turgenev on our bookshelf and he burst out crying. We lived in the British sector near the Olympic Stadium, where our neighbours were 'Tommies' and their families. 'Billy has the ball' was the first English sentence I learned, at the age of ten. I still remember my excitement as the words tumbled over my lips.

My bureau chief, the late Alfred Kluehs, was on holiday on the Italian Riviera when I reported for work on 15 October. I did not know that and I had chosen my outfit very carefully. A pair of red leather gloves, I thought, would lend me an air of authority and divert attention from my too apparent professional shortcomings.

I could do shorthand in English and German, could decipher the punch holes on a teleprinter tape and type with ten fingers. That was about it. The equipment in the Berlin newsroom was truly antiquated. Most of the teleprinters, typewriters and telex machines were Nazi leftovers and one had an SS rune on the keyboard. The dictionary, with 50 lost pages, was from the Weimar Republic.

THE NEWS FILE SOON GOT BUSY. In 1960 Nikita Khrushchev wrecked a Four-Power peace conference in Paris, leaving before it began, because Eisenhower refused to apologize for sending a U-2 Dragon Lady spy-plane across the Soviet Union. It had been shot down near Sverdlovsk and the pilot, Francis Gary Powers, was serving a ten-year sentence as a spy when Khrushchev, his wrath unabated, sanctioned East Germany's plan to build a wall in Berlin.

Thousands of East Germans had fled to the West each day. That needed to be stopped. The communists began the grisly job on 13 August 1961, when our colleague in the East, Adam Kellett-Long, broke the news that the border had been closed at the Brandenburg Gate. It was a Sunday. I stood there soon after midnight, watching East German soldiers drill holes in the pavement and throw coils of barbed wire on the square. Searchlights lit the ghostly scene.

'Note all this down, barbed wire and so on,' came a somewhat stern order from just behind me. This was our news editor, Brian Horton, who had flown from Bonn to stand in for Alfred Kluehs, who was once more sunbathing in Italy. 'Has he forgotten his pencil?' I asked myself. I felt humiliated. But this was Reuters. A news editor is an exalted being.

I was scared that war would break out at any minute, but it wasn't the job of an editorial assistant to mastermind the analysis. 'Go to the airport and find out what Willy Brandt has to say,' said the news editor. I obeyed, flew there in a taxi, and heard Mayor Brandt of West Berlin voice my fears for me. He thought Berliners might storm the border and he spoke of the 'imminent danger of civil war'. It was six o'clock in the morning.

The Western Allies were not to be contacted on a Sunday. Kennedy, who had succeeded Ike, was sailing. Harold Macmillan, the British prime minister, was hunting. De Gaulle was at his weekend resort. The news editor, a cool and rational New Zealander, decided for an early lunch to mull things over with a French journalist but, before they withdrew, he sent me off to a refugee camp to interview those lucky East Germans who had managed to escape at the last moment. There were more than 10 000 people there.

**The Western Allies were not to be contacted on a Sunday.**

THE WALL DID NOT TRIGGER WORLD WAR III. It simply cemented the *status quo* in Europe and put relations between capitalism and socialism in a deep freeze, where they stayed for 28 years. The frosty news editor returned to Bonn without speaking to me again and I was sure now that I would never make it to the top in journalism. No one took me seriously.

The months to follow were, however, exciting. There were shootings and dramatic escapes. Ordinary people, besides the CIA and the KGB, dug tunnels under the wall. Soviet and US tanks trained their gun barrels at each other at Checkpoint Charlie, which was now the usual place where foreigners went through the wall to cross between East and West. Berlin was full of spies. It was the heyday of espionage and spy rumours were a big part of our everyday life in the bureau.

Now it is 10 February 1962 and sources in both Washington and Moscow speak of an imminent 'spy swap' to help create a better atmosphere, as Kennedy and Khrushchev try to ease tension.

WE GATHERED SOON AFTER DAWN in our office on Savigny Platz. Alfred Kluehs, the chief, was already into his second pot of black instant coffee as he spoke to the bureau. Correspondents from radio and the newspapers who shared our building had dropped by too. Everyone had picked up the same rumour: the imprisoned U-2 pilot Francis Gary Powers and a KGB colonel called Rudolph Abel, the most important Soviet agent ever caught in the United States, would be exchanged today presumably at Checkpoint Charlie.

A big story needs the right people in the right place. Our two correspondents were sent off to Checkpoint Charlie to staff both sides of the border crossing, along with our man in East Berlin and all the big shots from the international press who had hurried to Berlin. In a world that teetered on the brink of nuclear war, and loved spy thrillers, this was a very big story indeed. Alfred would stay in the office as Reuters anchorman. I was earmarked to take copy off the telephone and punch tapes in the wireroom.

*A big story needs the right people in the right place.*

I did not really want to be mean, but I felt somewhat mischievous. When they'd all left, I sat down opposite Alfred and stared at a big map of Berlin that was hanging on the wall behind his desk. He sat with his back to it. My eyes wandered about. I looked at all the coloured pins that Alfred had stuck on the map to mark important sites, such as border crossings.

They stopped suddenly, in the southwest corner of Berlin. There was a border. There was a bridge. It spanned the River Havel and connected the American sector of Berlin with the East German town of Potsdam. That was where the Western allies used to have their military liaison missions, which were

attached to the Soviet headquarters in East Germany. Only Allied military personnel were allowed to cross the Glienicker Bridge there, an elegant iron structure in two sets of concave bows across the Havel, some 150 yards wide.

I said nothing for a while. But then I could not hold back. 'Herr Kluehs,' I coughed. 'What about Glienicker Brücke?'

Alfred looked around, then a bolt of lightning seemed to hit him. 'Woman, if you have nothing else to do than make funny suggestions, why the hell don't you get there immediately?' He made a few frantic calls, got ambiguous replies and spurred me to find a taxi. How different if there had been mobile telephones in those days. Perhaps he might have reassigned someone from Checkpoint Charlie. Who knows?

IT WAS A LONG JOURNEY through the streets of Berlin, through the Grunewald forest and past the Wannsee lake. I actually felt silly for losing control, over my jealousy of the 'grown-up' correspondents, and the risk I'd taken of making a fool of myself.

The sun pushed through the late morning clouds over the River Havel and its rays fell on the Glienicker Bridge, illuminating an assembly of men standing motionless in the middle of it. Two swans glided gently from the East to the West, their dazzling white feathers unruffled by a cold wind that seemed to blow straight from the North Pole.

West Berlin border guards stood at a discreet distance. Some American military people also waited at the Western end of the bridge. Half a dozen cars were there too. It was a peaceful scene, static and unreal. The men, wrapped in winter coats, who stood on the bridge, were in two groups, divided by a white line that was brushed across the tarmac to declare that here was the Iron Curtain.

*Two swans glided gently from the East to the West, their dazzling white feathers unruffled by a cold wind …*

As I arrived, the men were set in motion. One group walked Eastwards, the other West, vanishing behind closed curtains in the waiting limousines. They took off like rockets – Abel never to be seen again and Powers on his way to a secret flight out of Berlin.

I was in a near panic. I had just caught a glimpse of the exchange of perhaps the most famous of the Cold War spies, but only the tail end of it. I couldn't even be sure beyond all shadow of doubt that it was indeed the spy swap that I'd seen.

What to do?

I looked around and saw a new set of US military policemen take up their posts. The others had raced off in the motorcade. The West Berlin border guards were also ordered to go home. Their replacements were already at hand. Only the mute swans were allowed to stay, innocent of what had just happened.

I ran after a young fair-haired policeman sporting a fluffy moustache, a briefcase and a Thermos flask under his arm. 'Please don't leave yet. You must help me. Please.' I told him that I was the youngest of all the reporters who had been sent out to cover the spy story and that I had never had – nor would I possibly ever have – a chance such as I had now.

**I pulled out my notebook and I said, 'Tell me.' And he did.**

'I cannot talk about this. We are under instructions not to talk to anyone,' he answered politely. But I had already begun to tug his sleeve and drag him behind a screen of evergreen bushes, where no one could see us. I pulled out my notebook and I said, 'Tell me.' And he did.

HE GAVE ME THE STORY, every detail he had observed. He confirmed that Abel was escorted across the bridge from the West, and it was Powers who came back. That was after an agonizing 20 minutes waiting out there for a radio signal to confirm that other parts of the deal were in place. Powers wore a woollen hat and a dark winter coat, and he looked pale. It was the only eyewitness account that day, and that week, and it was my first scoop. I was so excited when I stumbled into a telephone booth I could hardly speak. 'I have got it. I have got it all.'

'Woman, calm down.' The controlled grown-up voice on the other end of the line belonged to Alfred Kluehs. 'You have a great story there, just keep telling me.'

I was glad it was him, my tutor and mentor. I began to dictate. 'And please Herr Kluehs, don't forget to put the swans in,' I asked him when I had finished. I remembered that someone had said that a flash of colour sells a story. He did not forget.

Back in Savigny Platz, I invited my somewhat disgruntled colleagues to a hot cup of chocolate with whipped cream, as they came back from a cold and futile vigil at Checkpoint Charlie. I couldn't think of anything more exotic to offer. One day I'd be Reuters editor for Germany with a host of other big stories to remember, like the Iranian revolution or the death vigil of Josip Tito – or the day I wore white, riding a press Jeep in Africa just behind that rock of a man, Pope John Paul II. All the tribal chiefs thought I was his wife and cheered madly. But back then, despite my scoop, I was still a greenhorn.

And the swans, yes the swans kept sailing between the East and the West bank of the Havel under Glienicker Brücke in many another story that would be written about Francis Gary Powers; even that of his tragic death 15 years later, in the crash of a helicopter that he was flying as a reporter for a Los Angeles television station.

# THE HAMMARSKJOELD MYSTERY

GERRY RATZIN

FRONTLINES 18

## THE HAMMARSKJOELD MYSTERY | GERRY RATZIN

# Post-colonial Africa soon became

a pawn in the Cold War. Many in the West regarded Moise Tshombe, who led the secession by the mineral-rich Congolese province of Katanga, as a bulwark against communism, while the Soviet Union called him an imperialist lackey. In September 1961, fighting broke out between UN troops who were trying to restore order in the Congo and Tshombe's forces, who included white mercenaries. My assignment was to cover a meeting between the Katangese leader and the UN Secretary-General, Dag Hammarskjoeld, about a ceasefire. Instead, I found myself reporting the mystery plane crash that killed Hammarskjoeld in the African bush – one of those bittersweet moments in a journalist's life when a tragedy is also a scoop.

**Investigators sift through the wreckage of the plane that
crashed, killing UN Secretary General Dag Hammarskjoeld**
20 September 1961

© Hulton Getty

COMMUNICATIONS IN AFRICA were a lottery, but by some miracle Reuters found me, with a telegram, in a hotel in Gabon on the West Coast. They wanted me to fly at once to Ndola in Northern Rhodesia – it is now Zambia – where Tshombe and Hammarskjoeld were going to meet. By chance, an Air France flight was leaving an hour later for Brazzaville – there wasn't another for three days – and I managed to reach Ndola, some 1500 miles away, by taking a ferry across the Congo river and two more flights, the next night.

I soon found myself with a crowd of other reporters who were staking out Ndola airport – not much more than a landing strip – where Hammarskjoeld, an enigmatic 56-year-old Swedish bachelor who'd been in charge of the UN since 1953, was awaited at any moment. Troops and police kept us away from the tarmac, so, over some beers – there was always beer in British colonial Africa – we swapped yarns and compared notes.

**... you had to bribe the telex operator at the bat-infested post office to send your story.**

Few hadn't got a story to tell about a year when so much of Africa was moving so abruptly from colonialism to self rule. I'd already done my own stint in the Congo, arriving in 1960, soon after its hastily conceded independence from Belgium and, for an ex-university trainee at the beginning of a Reuters career, it was a rough debut. The day after my arrival, I remember, an American correspondent was killed in fighting in the interior. Unruly troops roamed the capital, Leopoldville, now called Kinshasa, and you had to bribe the telex operator at the bat-infested post office to send your story. The Belgian colonial rulers left the Congo, a country of 30 million people, with no trained engineer, doctor or senior army officer. Amid the chaos, the prime minister used a Reuters flat to brief the foreign press. Up-country troops arrested me twice, once as a suspected Tshombe adviser and another time for driving a car with no lights that had been loaned by a provincial president.

Now, back with the Congo story again, I caught up on events as we waited for Hammarskjoeld at Ndola airport.

PATRICE LUMUMBA, the Moscow-backed Congolese prime minister, had been overthrown and then smuggled to Katanga, where he was murdered, early in 1961, amid worldwide horror, when Hammarskjoeld won a Security Council mandate to use force to halt a drift to civil war and to expel foreign, especially Belgian, military personnel. The mercenaries who were in the pay of Tshombe in Katanga, however, showed no sign of leaving, so Conor Cruise O'Brien, the Irish diplomat who headed the UN there, began a military operation codenamed 'Rumpunch' to try to round them up.

Tshombe claimed that the UN was plotting to arrest him, in league with the central government – it now included an army strongman called Joseph Mobutu – and this was when fighting broke out between Indian troops of the UN and Tshombe's gendarmes in his capital at Elisabethville. The Soviet Union had accused Hammarskjoeld of complicity in Lumumba's death. Now the UN role drew diplomatic fire from Britain and Belgium. Sir Roy Welensky, the prime minister of Rhodesia, which was then a British colony, moved troops to his border with Katanga on a pretext that his security was threatened.

HAMMARSKJOELD, already on a routine trip to the Congo, decided that he must see Tshombe to seek a ceasefire, choosing Ndola in Rhodesia, just beyond the Katanga frontier, as a secure place to meet. So began a peace mission that took him on a cloak-and-dagger escapade across the Congolese jungle to his death in an air crash.

He left Ndjili airport in Leopoldville at 16.51 on Sunday 17 September aboard a UN DC-6 aircraft, named the Albertina, with a Swedish crew. The same aircraft had brought General Sean McKeown, the UN commander, from Katanga the previous day. It had been fired on, presumably by a Fouga Magister jet that had been acquired by Tshombe's mercenaries, but damage was slight and quickly repaired. The doors of the DC-6 had been locked overnight, but there were no special security precautions at the airport.

Concerned about the Fouga, however, Captain Per Hallonquist decided to maintain radio silence and he filed a flight plan to a town in the Congo, Luluabourg, so as not to reveal his true destination.

At Ndola airport we knew none of this, nor that Tshombe had already arrived by some mysterious means and then left late in the evening when Hammarskjoeld did not turn up. Suddenly, the hot tedious wait was interrupted. It was dark, but we could hear an airplane land. No one in a position to know was prepared to tell us who had arrived.

I had certainly not seen anyone who was definitely Hammarskjoeld and I did not send a story to say that he had arrived. I recall that Cyril Ainsley of the *Daily Express*, much more experienced than I was, came to the same decision and that made me feel better about it. There is an old adage that it's good to be exclusive, but not so good to be too exclusive for too long.

> I had certainly not seen anyone who was definitely Hammarskjoeld and I did not send a story to say that he'd arrived.

Other correspondents, assuming it was Hammarskjoeld, reported his arrival. Reuters, indeed, unknown to me, picked up that story from the South African Press Association and distributed it – then 'killed' it after Friedel Ungeheuer, a correspondent in Leopoldville who knew when the Albertina had left there, pointed out that it could not yet have reached Ndola. In fact, the aircraft that we had heard land was carrying a British minister, Lord Lansdowne, who'd helped arrange the talks.

After a nail-biting wait, I returned to my hotel towards midnight, as we had been told there would be no further landings that night. We did not know what had happened to Hammarskjoeld – but in fact his aircraft was close by at that time, apparently having flown due east across the Congo then south down Lake Tanganyika.

Captain Hallonquist ordered a break in radio silence to announce that he was due to land at Ndola at 00.35 local time. Shortly after midnight the Albertina reported seeing the runway lights and told the control tower that it was descending. The tower told it to call again when it had come down to 6000 feet. The Albertina acknowledged the message and that was the last that was heard from it.

AT DAWN THERE WAS STILL NO NEWS and reporters fanned out around Ndola in a frantic search. Not really knowing what to do, I used a roadside telephone box to call the Rhodesian government information officer in Ndola and he told me that the DC-6 had crashed and that Hammarskjoeld was dead. He hadn't been able to tell anyone else yet, so I had a world beat.

The bodies of Hammarskjoeld and 14 others were found 10 miles west of Ndola airport. A lone survivor died in hospital. The aircraft, wheels and flaps lowered, had cut the tree tops, its port wing had touched the ground and then it had flipped over and burst into flames. In the wreckage of the DC-6 were the contents of Hammarskjoeld's briefcase. They included a copy of the UN Charter, an English version of the New Testament, poems by Rainer Maria Rilke and a map of New York State with areas near Brewster marked as suitable for walks – walks that he'd never take.

> In the wreckage of the DC-6 were the contents of Hammarskjoeld's briefcase.

Investigators reached no conclusion on what caused the crash. Speculation ranged from sabotage or shooting down by the Fouga, to technical failure or simply error by a tired crew. A UN inquiry criticized the Rhodesians for taking more than 12 hours to find the wreckage and, as late as 1998, letters presented to the Truth and Reconciliation Commission in South Africa implicated British, American and South African agents – allegations rejected by all three governments.

The Katanga secession soon ended and Tshombe briefly served as prime minister in a Congolese coalition before being driven into exile, then kidnapped to Algiers, where he died. The UN withdrew in 1964. The Security Council had never placed more than 20 000 troops at Dag Hammarskjoeld's disposal to help the Swedish diplomat try to restore order – and, after the Congo episode, a fractious world community was wary of letting the UN use force to keep the peace in post-colonial Africa.

IT WAS LEFT TO MOBUTU to impose a stability of a sort on the Congo and its mineral-rich provinces, ruling with American and French support as a virtual dictator. But a new civil war attended his own eventual downfall in 1997 and smouldered on into a new millennium, and big power rivalries would exacerbate other African ethnic conflicts.

# THE AMERICAN BOMBER

FREDERICK FORSYTH

## THE AMERICAN BOMBER | FREDERICK FORSYTH

# It seemed a good idea at the time.

It was March 1964 and I was based in East Berlin. It was not an easy posting but, for a 25-year-old on his second overseas tour for Reuters, utterly fascinating. Three years earlier the Berlin Wall had been erected and the Cold War had moved up several gears. That was August 1961.

In October 1962 we had all watched helpless from the sidelines as the Cuban missile crisis unfolded and the world trembled on the brink. November 1963 saw the assassination of John Kennedy – by a communist and former US defector to the USSR.

**Checkpoint Charlie, the main Cold War
crossing point between East and West Berlin**
May 1966

© Hulton Getty

AS I SAY, NERVES WERE AT violin-string tension levels and I had arrived in East Berlin the previous October, just before Dallas. It was a one-man posting and for good reason.

After the building of the Wall the entire West, in the form of all NATO governments, sent East Germany into total ostracism. It was denounced as a non-country, not just a Soviet satellite but Moscow's colony. All East German missions in the West were sent packing and that included the East German news agency, ADN, with which Reuters had a reciprocal arrangement. The ADN representative in London went home for a brief leave in the autumn of 1961 and was promptly prevented from returning there. It looked as if Reuters would be expelled from its East Berlin office.

But the mandarins of Walter Ulbricht's hard-line and pretty brutal regime made no such choice. Believing, quite wrongly, that Reuters had some kind of official status with the British government, and desperate for some kind of spurious 'recognition', it permitted the Reuters office to stay open, with one correspondent and one East German secretary, the redoubtable Erdmute Behrendt.

Still, it was a goldfish-in-a-bowl posting. The secret fuzz, the famous Stasis, were everywhere. Everything was bugged and my car was followed. It was an East German-registered Wartburg banger, in a hideous pink, and belched black smoke.

ONE MORNING IN MID-MARCH I was roused from my slumbers in the wee small hours by the screeching alarm from the office next to my bedroom. This alarm was attached to the telex printer and was only to be used for emergency information.

There were no mobile phones in those days, nor even fax machines. The only link to the West was the telex line, which ran from Warsaw via East and West Berlin to Bonn and London. As I arrived blearily at its side, it was already pumping out the long perforated sheet that would contain the message for me. When I fed it into the playback machine, the message came out in clear.

The US Air Force at Wiesbaden was claiming that one of its aircraft had been shot down over East Germany. Bonn's debonair request was: could I please find it?

The American problem was simple. Under the Four Power Treaty their military mission at Potsdam had the right to send a patrol car anywhere in East Germany they wished, but with one proviso: they had to give the Russians the precise destination they wished to visit. No destination, no permission. And clearly they did not know exactly where their bomber had fallen. Nor did I.

I got back on to Bonn and asked: what was the airplane and where had it gone off the radar screen? There was a long pause while they asked Wiesbaden, and I chafed at the East Berlin end, knowing perfectly well that every communication was monitored by the Stasis. My only hope was that at three in the morning they would have the air brains on duty. While waiting, I threw on some clothes, grabbed a pack of bread, cheese, apples and a flask of coffee and prepared to leave.

After an hour, Bonn came back. The plane was an RB66 and it had gone off the screen near a town called Stendal. Minutes later I was in my car and heading fast for the Wall.

> The plane was an RB66 and it had gone off the screen near a town called Stendal.

I knew I had two tricks up my sleeve, which might work. The Stasi tailing car was already in the rear-view mirror, but it could not get through Checkpoint Charlie. I could. And at the far west of the West Berlin enclave was the crossing point into East Germany proper. With luck and given the bureaucratic sclerosis of the police, I could get there before they could drive round the whole of the Berlin enclave and intercept me. Or before they could report back and whistle up a Stasi car ahead of me. More to the point, they had no idea I was not going to stop in West Berlin and have a full breakfast.

The tail-car slewed to the side of the street as I cruised into the slalom of concrete blocks and sheds that made up 'Charlie'. There was no other traffic; it was 4.30 am and still dark. I was in the Ku'damm in 20 minutes. By the grace of reporters' luck, the West Berlin speed cops were half asleep, for I went through West Berlin like a ferret on skates. Twenty minutes after Charlie, I was at Drei Linden presenting my British passport and claiming I wished to drive through the German Democratic Republic and into West Germany, as was my right.

AS A LINE OF PINK TINGED THE SKY behind me, I headed west down the treaty-protected autobahn, quite legal. At the first exit, I swung off the motorway and into the countryside. Illegal; I should have asked the state press office for permission to vary a route. As I said, it seemed a good idea at the time.

My second trick was that, although I always spoke to the authorities in a silly-billy English accent, I could by then pass for German. So, following tiny rural by-ways, I began to move deeper and deeper into the countryside, always heading west, where my map told me the small town of Stendal lay, north of Magdeburg.

Having been in the RAF, I knew about the RB66. The original B66 was a twinjet bomber, but with the 'R' for Reconnaissance in front, that meant a spy-plane, equipped with long-range cameras. It was clear this particular RB66 had been flying up and down the border, cameras tilted sideways and down, photographing something the 'naughties' were up to on the communist side of the border. It must have strayed well over the line by mistake and either the MiG fighters or the ground batteries had got it. Where had it come down? Was the crew alive or dead?

I skirted Stendal town and found some road workers doing repairs. I thought they might know. I introduced myself as 'from the press in Berlin', but received only surly shakes and no cooperation. I drove on. Some farm workers a mile later were the same. The third time I tried a gamble.

'Good morning,' I said cheerfully to another group of land workers. 'I am from the press in London. Can you help me?'

They gazed at the East German car and listened to the German, then shook their heads again. I produced my passport, the stiff-covered blue-and-gold affair. They passed it round in some wonderment. The words 'Her Britannic Majesty's Secretary of State requests and requires' meant nothing to them, but the gold coat-of-arms did. After that, they were over me like a rash, offering all they knew. So much for communist propaganda.

They knew all about the American plane. One old man had even seen it fall. He recalled the hour of dusk the previous evening; two MiGs screaming upwards to intercept; the launching of rockets at the US bomber high above; the blooming of flame at the wing root; the awful tumbling fall of the doomed aircraft; and the three parachutes that had opened in the sky to the south.

They pointed me south to Magdeburg and thither I went, asking from group to group for more precise information. I was clear it had come down in one of the huge forests that cover that landscape – forest and sandy heath. By 11 am, I discovered what the spy-plane had been photographing.

Columns of Russian tanks began to appear; convoys of mechanized infantry, phalanxes of field guns in tow. I had blundered into a ten-division Soviet war games exercise.

> By 11 am, I discovered what the spy-plane had been photographing.

My last informant was a woodcutter, standing forlorn by a stack of logs, watching another column of tanks roll down the sandy track between the trees. My Wartburg had already been driven off the lane into the verge, so we stood and commiserated. Then I produced my passport and my spiel about being from London.

The woodcutter had a quick look round as the last tank rolled out of sight and pointed to a pinewood about a mile away.

'It's in the middle of that,' he said and was gone. I left the car and walked cross-country. As I approached, I could make out the gleam of metal high among the treetops. The tail of the downed plane.

IT WAS GLOOMY INSIDE THE FOREST, but there was no mistaking the bomber. It was nose-down in the soft mulch between the trees. One wing had been torn right off and was nowhere to be seen. The other was lying close by. The canopy was gone where the pilot and navigator had ejected, and the belly-hatch was missing where the camera-operator had made his escape.

Then I heard voices, but not in Russian, which I spoke haltingly, and certainly not in German. I thought I might have outstayed my welcome. The bracken was four feet high and a man on hands and knees about half that; so I dropped to my knees and began to crawl.

Mistake. After twenty yards, I found myself facing a pair of muddy felt army boots. Above them were a very angry oriental face and a tommy-gun with the catch off. I raised my hands and stood up.

The Russian major was sitting at a folding table when I was marched up by a dozen Mongolian soldiers. He clearly understood their oriental lingo when they reported what they had found. He glared at me and demanded identification. He addressed me in German but not well. I produced my East German press accreditation. He had clearly never seen such before, but he noted the first and second name in Cyrillic script. He had evidently never heard or seen the word 'Reuters' before either.

I felt it better to play the idiot. I was a poor man driving through the forest to visit relatives in Stendal. His tanks had

> I felt it better to play the idiot.

forced me off the road and I had bogged down in soft sand. A local woodcutter had told me there was a farm a mile away that might help me with its tractor. I was walking there when I tripped and stumbled, dropping my car keys among the bracken. (I held them up to show him what car keys were.) That was why I was on my knees when his gallant colleagues found me.

The major was a busy man. He was trying to command a regiment of Mongolians in a complex manoeuvre. The last thing he needed was some East German babbling on about his stuck car. After a conversation on a field telephone with higher authority, he ordered his men to march me back to my car. His instructions to me were plain and clear: get out of this area and stay out. I was profuse in my thanks.

So I drove off and found, eventually, a wayside call-box and rang Erdmute. She called me back and I began to dictate; she typed. It was the way we did things in those days. No laptops or modems. I finished 20 folios of the story when she told me Bonn had been back with another request. Could I find the American aircrew and if possible establish their condition and location? An interview would be nice, for their hometown newspapers.

I informed an East German call-box exactly what I thought of sub-editors in Bonn who asked for interviews with men who, if still alive, were certainly under lock and key in some Soviet HQ. Then I turned round and went back to the forests. As I said, we were young and foolish in those days.

After several more hours of asking around, I found a charcoal burner and had another stroke of luck. He had seen it all. As the parachutes blossomed above him in the dusk the previous evening, he had run to help the men as they landed. Two fell in open country a few hundred yards apart. The third fell into trees and, when found, was lying nursing a broken leg.

As the whole area teemed with Russians, the military were not long in appearing. The wounded man was brought out of the wood, suspended between two soldiers, and the charcoal burner's handcart was commandeered to bring him to the nearest road, where he went off in a Soviet military ambulance. The other two were packed into the rear of a GAZ Jeep and taken away to the Soviet *Kommandantura* in Magdeburg.

'They were not American, they were Dutch,' said the charcoal burner. He described the uniform of the airplane's pilot: flying overalls with the word 'Holland' above the left breast pocket. I realized that was his name, not his nationality.

WITH HINDSIGHT, I should have returned to my car, rediscovered the autobahn and headed back to East Berlin fast, but it had come on to rain hard; I was soaking and cold. Only the story in my head was still hot, and I needed a phone.

By chance, I came across a country inn after driving half a mile. It was almost dark. An inn meant a phone, so I parked and went inside. A log fire burned. It was cheery. Old-style German rather than modern GDR. *Gemütlich*. I yearned for a bath and a meal, to be warm and dry. I had been on the go for 16 hours. I decided to overnight. Mistake.

They had room, they took me for a German from East Berlin and I checked in. Miles away Erdmute took my call and I dictated the second story. This one I kept short, with all the salient details in the first page. The Stasi eavesdroppers in East Berlin had been caught with the earlier story and had been slow to cut the line. This time they would be faster. They were. As Erdmute sent the hole-punched telex tape through to the West at maximum speed, the line was cut at folio four.

I dried out, bathed, dined, went to bed and slept like a baby. Through the night, the Stasi traced the call. The next day I breakfasted, paid up and prepared to leave via the front door.

The scene outside looked like a wedding at the Guards Chapel – one of those affairs where the loving couple walks down a corridor of soldiers with swords drawn to make an arch. There were two lines of People's Police with guns and at the end two men in grey leather coats with expressions on their faces. It was clear they were not happy bunnies. Something had hit the fan, and it was not a lavender tablet.

So off I went to the local secret police headquarters. The interrogation lasted three hours. Then I was left in an office, not a cell, while they all conversed with Berlin. Clearly, they had two options: hardball or softball. Hardball could mean planted spy equipment, a trumped up charge of espionage, a show trial and a stay in one of their less pleasant holiday camps. The Russians might even insist on Siberia.

> So off I went to the local secret police headquarters. The interrogation lasted three hours.

Aware of this, I came absolutely clean, describing everything that had happened since I was woken by the emergency call to my flat. I only left out the helpful workers, the woodcutter and the charcoal burner. Everything that the police could check, texts of telexes from Bonn, my replies to Bonn, phone calls to the office – all was true and I said so.

Hardball would have given them problems and we both knew it. Framing Westerners in the Soviet Bloc had worked quite well until the KGB tried to frame an American academic called Professor Barghoorn; he happened to be a friend of President Kennedy, who kicked up a hell of a fuss. With important trade contracts going down the pan, the Russians back-pedalled and let the professor go.

I WAS HOPING THE EAST GERMANS, still obsessed by their loony idea that the Reuters man was a sort of British government official, would wonder whether it was worth the candle to create a blazing row with London over me.

Unfortunately, I also knew something they did not; that the record of the Foreign Office in protecting British reporters in trouble abroad could fill an entire postage stamp, if written in large script.

By mid-afternoon Berlin made its mind up; I was escorted back to the autobahn and followed all the way home. This time, no West Berlin. I had to drive right round the city and enter by one of the sanctioned police posts on the eastern side. At the police barrier the Berlin heavies took over from the Magdeburg squad and bracketed me all the way back to my flat.

There was a pretty angry interview with a deeply unpleasant government press chief, Kurt Blecha, the next day but after that, the mood seemed to be to forget it all.

The story played very well in the Western papers and was splashed all over America while I was asleep in the forest inn. London sent a note of thanks and, to my surprise, the other (but non-East German and non-Russian) communist correspondents took me out for a slap-up meal. Poles, Hungarians, Czechs and Yugoslavs simply loved to see the East Germans and their Russian bosses given a right seeing-to and they had all got the story off their agency services.

The US mission in Potsdam had an exact description of the wood between Stendal and Magdeburg, and with a huge-scale map worked out exactly which wood it was. Then they could send a prowl car and, under the terms of the treaty, the Russians could not stop them. President Johnson put on some pressure and the airmen were returned without delay.

I have never been back to that forest in the now reunited Germany, but for all I know that bomber, or the bits that remain of it, may still be there!

# MING MING, ME AND CAT-STRANGLER CHI

ANTHONY GREY

FRONTLINES 20

## MING MING, ME AND CAT-STRANGLER CHI | ANTHONY GREY

# In the summer of 1967 in China,

Mao Tse Tung's Great Proletarian Cultural Revolution entered its most violent and chaotic phase. Because I was the sole British journalist resident in Peking (Beijing) at that time, I became arguably the first of a long line of modern political hostages who were taken captive by governments or terrorist groups. Held in solitary confinement for more than two years by Mao's Red Guards, instead of reporting the news, I became the unwitting focus of an international news story myself.

**Ming Ming**
1967

© author

A HORDE OF 200 RED GUARDS stormed my house, close to the vermilion walls of the Forbidden City in the centre of Peking, on the sweltering night of 18 August 1967, yelling, 'Hang Grey! Hang Grey!' But instead of hanging me, the mob hanged, before my face, a fluffy brown-and-white female cat named Ming Ming, which had been sharing my imprisonment with me.

Then they stabbed the cat's lifeless body with a pair of scissors and daubed her blood on the bed-sheets in my newly improvised 'prison cell' – an eight-foot-square ground-floor boxroom with black-painted windows, situated at the rear of the house, which had been used by my Chinese driver to store spares for the car.

I was held in a state of solitary confinement in that noxious 'cell', then in a slightly larger adjoining room, for a period of two years and two months in all. I had been placed under house arrest initially by the foreign ministry in mid-July, as a reprisal for the imprisonment in Hong Kong of a single communist journalist, Hsueh Ping, who had been employed there by China's official Hsinhua news agency.

The chaos in China that summer had inspired the local Chinese communists in the British colony to riot. Eventually some 13 Chinese 'news workers'– people associated in one way or another with communist news organizations in the colony – were jailed for rioting offences. I was released only after the last of the 13 was freed.

In his efforts to transform China, Mao and his supporters devised several arbitrary categories of enemies, ranging from 'revisionists' to 'those taking the capitalist road', to 'bourgeois reactionaries', 'black elements' and 'imperialists'. As representatives of a nation with an anachronistic colony on Chinese soil, British diplomats and myself were seen as 'class enemies' of the very worst kind. I was branded by my Red Guard captors as 'imperialist newsman Grey'.

**I was branded by my Red Guard captors as 'imperialist newsman Grey'.**

FOUR DAYS AFTER MY HOUSE WAS INVADED, 10 000 screaming Red Guards surrounded the British diplomatic compound and, late in the evening, they set it ablaze with the diplomats and their families inside. When the Britons stumbled out through the flames, men and women alike were physically beaten and in some cases sexually abused by the mob of male and female Red Guards.

Irrationality ran wild in this phase of the Cultural Revolution. Throughout China it produced great confusion and chaos, which I am sure Mao intended as part of his demented strategy to destroy those who, in reality or in his imagination, opposed him. People struggled frantically to avoid being targets of the criticism that was now a matter of life or death, and it was against this background that the Red Guard mob smashed their way into my house on that hot August night to subject me to a 'struggle meeting', as they called their kangaroo courts.

On the steps outside the front door I was held bent double until the sweat from my face and upper body formed a pool on the top step close before my eyes. In this puddle I was able dimly to see my own reflection. This posture was widely known as the 'jet-plane position', because a victim's arms were held stiffly out behind him like the backswept wings of a fighter aircraft and he was forced to remain bent over, with head close to the ground, for long periods to discomfit and humiliate him. After my release, I learned that I was treated just like countless Chinese who became political outcasts and were made prisoners in broom cupboards and storerooms at their schools, universities, theatres, factories, farms and offices.

Charges yelled against me that night had been totally surreal and strongly reminiscent of those levelled against Franz Kafka's victim, K, in his famous and baffling novel *The Trial*. The mob was told I had 'despised the paper tiger effigy' that had been strung up by Red Guards above the gateway to my house a few weeks earlier in order to ridicule Britain. I had also 'sneaked around' in my own house during the first month of house arrest, when the Public Security Bureau guards had remained outside in the courtyard and I had access to all rooms and my telephones. Finally I had 'even drunk alcohol in the house'. These successive charges, each more ludicrous than the last, drew demented howls of anger from the crowd, along with calls for retribution to be visited on 'imperialist newsman Grey'.

Ming Ming was drawn into this bizarre trial and hanged on a rope from the balcony above the steps for well-defined reasons, according to Mao's perverted political logic. In fact about a year earlier almost all pets in Peking and other cities throughout China, including goldfish, songbirds, dogs, cats and even tiny caged cicadas, had been ritually slaughtered by rampaging Red Guards. The Maoists had decided that pets were symptomatic of a bourgeois lifestyle not in keeping with the correct philosophy of revolutionary Chinese workers and peasants. Humble people were not allowed to have any love for animals. Ming Ming had escaped this first wave of slaughter, because she lived within the safety of the walled courtyard of the Reuters house, but sadly that August night the Cultural Revolution caught up with her.

*The Maoists had decided that pets were symptomatic of a bourgeois lifestyle ...*

The telephone line to my house was cut that night. Before then, while I was simply under house arrest, it had remained connected and I'd played chess by telephone with John Weston, a friend in the British mission who later became ambassador to the United Nations. Then Ming Ming had often sat endearingly beside the board, dabbing delicately at the pieces with her paw, and I had photographed her doing this.

AFTER MY RELEASE, when the full story of the house invasion could be told, the photographs, which somehow survived the invasion in my camera at the bottom of a wardrobe, were printed and shown around the world on the front pages of newspapers, on television news programmes and in magazines. They appeared, too, in the book *Hostage in Peking*, which I wrote soon after my release.

I had inherited Ming Ming from my Reuters predecessor, Vergil Berger, and his wife Joyanne. During four months of intensive reporting work, after I arrived from East Berlin in February 1967, I had not had too much time for Ming Ming. But once I was under house arrest we had bonded more closely and become regular playmates, particularly enjoying a complicated game with a ping-pong ball, played up and down the stairs.

At the moment of her death among the mob I was suddenly jerked upright from my 'jet-plane' position to find Ming Ming's lifeless body dangling inches from my face on a rope held by Red Guards on the balcony above. Appalled, I stared expressionlessly ahead as they yelled, 'Hang Grey! Hang Grey!'

In all its mindless stupidity and cruelty, the violent death of Ming Ming remains a poignant symbol of the political hysteria and madness that then gripped the world's most populous nation.

In the years that followed my release, faint but persistent echoes of the hanging of the unfortunate Ming Ming continued to reverberate back to me from China in a curious – and dare I say – faintly amusing way. These echoes concerned the officious Chinese diplomat who had been involved in the act of placing me under house arrest. A long-serving official spokesman for the information department of China's foreign ministry, both before and after the Cultural Revolution, he was universally known until then as 'Mr Chi'.

*... the violent death of Ming Ming remains a poignant symbol of the political hysteria and madness that then gripped the world's most populous nation.*

Always immaculately groomed, in his navy blue cadre's tunic buttoned high to the neck, he spoke near-perfect English, enunciated quickly and confidently in an impressively cultivated Oxford accent. In *Hostage in Peking* I described him at our initial meeting on my arrival in Peking as having 'a sharp frozen smile that flickered across his narrow handsome features like the flashes of a faulty neon tube'.

That description perhaps lacked charity, but Mr Chi, who I think was roughly my age or a little older, had spent a considerable time at the London embassy, and therefore appeared to be linguistically very much at ease, not to say condescending, in dealing with English-speaking journalists. He was also the first point of call for Western diplomats at the information department, so his brisk unbending manner and appearance were familiar to an entire generation of Western journalists and embassy people.

Mr Chi was the first link, in a sense, in communication between China and the Western world, or more accurately perhaps, the chief obstacle, since his techniques for avoiding giving out any information at all were legendary, especially in the dangerous and deeply puzzling days of the Cultural Revolution.

'You know the answer to that question very well,' was his standard reply to almost any query conveyed to him in person or by telephone. 'Think it over for yourself ... There is no need for me to answer that question now.'

This evasiveness was obviously official policy, and was grudgingly acknowledged by correspondents to be fair play in the running contest between governments and reporters that goes on everywhere, but it was exasperating. Perhaps that explains why a myth soon began to attach itself to Mr Chi in connection with the hanging of Ming Ming, which has persisted over many years into the present.

I HAVE NO IDEA who first mooted the idea or who coined the nickname, but some wag of a foreign correspondent, I suspect, created the notion that Mr Chi himself had been personally and directly responsible for Ming Ming's death. Somehow or other, he became known among Western journalists and diplomats as 'Cat-Strangler Chi'. It even emerged over time that this title had become known to Mr Chi himself, to his obvious embarrassment. That it sat so uncomfortably upon such an impeccable, fastidious and polished man only added to the relish with which it was used outside his hearing.

During the two years when my incarceration was a big news story, Mr Chi was often referred to in the British press as 'Grey's jailer'. This was because he'd been the official who had summoned me to the information department to place me under house arrest. He telephoned on the afternoon of 18 July and announced abruptly, 'We would like you to come to the ministry at six o'clock.' When I asked why, he added no less brusquely, 'It is about your work.'

I was driven to the foreign ministry by John Weston, through great crowds of chanting Red Guards, who were marching to protest against events in the industrial complex of Wuhan in Central China, where a state of near civil war existed. It was rumoured that Premier Chou En-lai, who flew there to intervene, was under arrest.

I was ushered in to Mr Chi, to find him on this occasion bristling, at least outwardly, with revolutionary outrage. A dowdy female official in a high-buttoned cadre's suit, who was obviously his superior, read a prepared statement in Chinese. Mr Chi, in turn, read a translation from his own sheet of paper, glaring at me between sentences and emphasizing his words

vehemently in a fashion calculated to convey revolutionary antagonism towards the class enemy.

The British authorities in Hong Kong had 'committed fascist atrocities' and 'kidnapped patriotic Chinese correspondents'. As a result 'the freedom of movement of Grey of Reuters in Peking was to be restricted'. I was to remain in my home. Then I was driven back there through the chanting mob in a Public Security Bureau car, flanked in the back seat by uniformed guards.

I did not see Mr Chi again until, in early October 1969, I was summoned from my one-man prison to the ministry. Then he sat beside another superior official, this time a male. Urbane as ever, occasionally flashing that quick 'frozen' smile in my direction, he now explained that the British authorities in Hong Kong had been told many times that my freedom of movement would be restored, if the 'illegal and unjustifiable detention of correspondents in Hong Kong' was ended. As all the Chinese correspondents had now been released, I was now free too. It was as simple as that.

As all the Chinese correspondents had now been released, I was now free too. It was as simple as that.

I DID NOT RETURN TO CHINA until 1988, but over the years I learned from friends that the 'Cat-Strangler' epithet had attached itself ever more firmly to Mr Chi. He was invariably referred to as such in all casual conversations among journalists, with a certain malicious glee, yet in all honesty it was unlikely to have been literally true.

The foreign ministry would certainly have been aware that Red Guards intended to invade my home that night. The saner elements there, who probably included Mr Chi, were not in control. They'd have had to bow to the 'Gang of Four' leaders, who faithfully carried out Mao's instructions and who undoubtedly also used his authority for machinations of their own. They were led by Mao's wife, Chiang Ching, who, after he died, was put on trial and sentenced to death for no less than 30 000 murders.

She was also found guilty of 'unjustly persecuting millions of others' and seemingly one individual among that number was eventually considered to be the British Reuters correspondent of the period.

That was certainly the tone of an apology to me by the Chinese chargé d'affaires over dinner at the Chinese embassy in London in December 1987, shortly before I left for my return to Peking. I was invited to the dinner after applying for a visa to make a documentary film for BBC Television in China, showing how much had changed. At the start of a convivial evening, the Chinese diplomat formally and fulsomely expressed regret at what had happened to me, and when I reached Peking, to my great relief, the red carpet treatment continued.

The New China News Agency, China Television and the foreign ministry all made me very welcome and even presented me with small gifts, including a decorative porcelain plate bearing a picture of the Great Wall of China. This plate, from the information department, I was told, was customarily presented to all resident foreign journalists when they had successfully completed their assignments in the Chinese capital. In handing it over, an official apologized for its being 'a little late'.

THE 1988 DOCUMENTARY was called *Return to Peking* and I was able to visit and film briefly in the house where I had been held prisoner, although not in the parts that had formed my 'cells'. I also filmed a conversation with my former cook, Siao Kao, who was by then cook to the Irish ambassador. A decent kindly man in normal times, for those two long years he had been forced to prepare food under the watchful eyes of the Public Security Bureau guards and show the prisoner no friendliness or respect. Our meeting at the Irish embassy, in contrast, was memorably warm.

I also intervewed Ying Ruo-cheng, China's best-known actor, who had played a starring role in Bertolucci's celebrated film *The Last Emperor*. Ying, who by now was a vice-minister of culture, had been victimized by Red Guards himself ten years earlier and had been held as a prisoner for a long time, locked up in a theatre props cupboard. We compared notes and when I said I'd been invited to dinner at the Chinese embassy, he exclaimed, 'Ah, then you have been rehabilitated now like the rest of us. I was given just such a dinner too.'

Then – eventually – I met 'Cat-Strangler Chi'. He had scarcely changed at all in appearance, except that now he wore a smart foreign sports jacket with an expensive Western shirt of blue cotton and a coloured tie instead of his austere Mao tunic. To his great credit he agreed to do a filmed interview. He'd now at long last left the ministry and was running an international affairs think-tank, called the Chinese Foreign Relations Institute, and we talked amicably in front of a camera on a carved stone bench in a green and shady garden.

When I asked him what he thought then of the treatment meted out to me two decades earlier, he said what had happened had 'not been meant personally', although it must have 'seemed personal at the time' – and it 'had indeed in some ways been very personal'.

*… he said what had happened had 'not been meant personally' …*

Listening to these somewhat tortured phrases produced in me a strong feeling of compassion for the man beside me, and indeed for all those who had been forced to live through the horrors of ten years of a Cultural Revolution that set neighbour against neighbour, children against parents and grandparents, brother against brother, wives against husbands, and pupils and students against their teachers and professors.

One young taxi-driver, for instance, admitted that he was very ashamed that he had helped beat one of his teachers to death and, even after 10 or 20 years, many other people I met were obviously nursing inner wounds from what they had been forced to do during the Cultural Revolution. Eventually I left Peking feeling a sense of relief that my own nation had never in my lifetime descended into such an abyss. How could any of us know how we would behave when faced with such intolerable pressures?

EQUALLY, I SAW ON THE POSITIVE SIDE that Mao, in his near-lunatic efforts to preserve his extremist legacy of non-stop revolution had inadvertently ensured exactly the reverse. Despite the Tiananmen massacre of students that was to follow the next year, the Cultural Revolution had cured the Chinese once and for all of their previously ingrained tendency to revere and obey dictatorial 'emperor' figures. Although China remains communist in name, it was obvious then from what I saw and heard in Peking that it had turned irreversibly on to a road that was leading at last to higher living standards and a more rational and practical political system. The welcome I received officially everywhere I went was an unspoken act of atonement, and another confirmation of fundamental change.

During the filmed interview with Mr Chi, I deliberately made no mention of Ming Ming. But it had clearly been uppermost in his mind when we first met at a formal dinner given specially for me by the information department in the Number One Peking Duck Restaurant. A place for Mr Chi had been set at my side and he had scarcely seated himself before he leaned confidentially close to my ear and, in a voice that nobody else could hear, he murmured, 'Of course that story about me and your cat is not true, you know. I never ever came to your house.'

> 'Of course that story about me and your cat is not true, you know.
> I never ever came to your house.'

I smiled and assured him quietly that personally I had never believed the story, although I understood why he had mentioned it.

BEFORE I LEFT FOR ENGLAND, I bought a bottle of Chivas Regal, my own favourite whisky, from the duty-free shop for foreigners and took it to Mr Chi's apartment as a farewell gift. I can't say we came to share great personal warmth, yet I am quite sure of one thing: we both benefited inwardly from meeting again in friendly and civilized circumstances to say what we did, even though it was so long after the trauma that had strangely linked our lives.

We had each acted out our role. The political conflict between our countries, in which we had been caught up, had deep historical roots for which neither of us was personally responsible. But as a result of those meetings in Peking in 1988, for me, some indefinable ghosts were gently but firmly laid to rest. I can't be absolutely sure, of course, but I think 'Cat-Strangler Chi' – or more properly Mr Chi Min-tsung – felt the same way too.

# BACK TO BALFOUR

JOHN CHADWICK

FRONTLINES 21

**BACK TO BALFOUR** | JOHN CHADWICK

# 'Back to Balfour again,'

the man from the *Daily Express* said wearily, as I joined him for a beer. 'They blame us for all this, you know'. Didn't I just. He'd recently arrived from Beirut and, sitting on the sun-baked terrace of the Cairo Hilton in his very English brass-buttoned blazer, he presented an easy target. I'd guessed from their gesticulations that the three Palestinian politicians at his table had been giving him a rough time. They vanished as I approached. I'd already had the same treatment.

It was the spring of 1968, half a century since Foreign Secretary Arthur Balfour gave the thumbs up to a Jewish homeland in Palestine, and Britain was still taking the flak. The Suez affair hadn't helped and, more recently, British reporters in Cairo had been effectively quarantined after the Arab débâcle in the Six Day War of 1967. I covered that war with the Israelis, when they wiped out the Arab air forces on the ground and then seized Sinai, Jerusalem and the West Bank as well as the Golan Heights of Syria. Now I was assigned to Cairo, the capital of a chastened Arab nationalist hero, Gamal Abdel Nasser.

**The famous belly dancer, Zoheir Zaki, a nightclub favourite in Cairo**
1968

© author

FUNNY, MY BEING IN EGYPT. A decade or so earlier, working for the *Bolton Evening News*, I'd taken part in my only ever political demonstration – against Britain's Suez adventure, which split public opinion down the middle. It seemed to me then that Nasser had a valid case for grabbing the Suez Canal. So it seemed a pity, now, that the liberator had turned virtual dictator, more and more divorced from everyday life, shielded from reality by a military-political coterie. As a trivial but instructive example, I remember wondering why the very bumpy road to my apartment in the Cairo suburb of Zamalek had acquired overnight a smooth new carpet of glistening black asphalt. It turned out the president was about to call on the Indian ambassador down the road.

Cairo was still sunk in gloom after the Six Day War débâcle. I only realized later that the day I arrived was Nasser's fiftieth birthday. It was not celebrated. There was no doubting who was top dog in the Middle East now. I remembered the contrast between the ebullient Israeli soldiers I'd interviewed during the war and the Egyptian prisoners squatting silently in the Sinai sand, without their boots, clearly expecting something bad to happen. 'Long live General Moshe Dayan,' they chanted. They needn't have worried. They were all sent safely home.

Reuters had been in Egypt a long time. The Royal Palace received the service as early as 1868 and in an office cupboard one day I unearthed an 1883 cable from Sudan, where General Gordon – later speared to death on the steps of his palace in Khartoum – was fighting the Mahdist rebellion.

It described how our correspondent, Mr F. J. Roberts, having been dismounted in the desert, was snatched to safety in the thick of the fighting by an officer of the 9th Bengal Cavalry. Reuters agent in Cairo, Mr Schnitzler, stressed in a letter to London the need for good horses. 'The work of a war correspondent appears to be journalism no longer, but simply horsemanship,' he said. Head office agreed. Another find of mine, a heavy leather-backed cash book embossed with 'Reuters Telegram Company Limited' in gold leaf, contained the entry: 'Paid to Mr Roberts for horse – £40'.

> 'The work of a war correspondent appears to be journalism no longer, but simply horsemanship,' he said.

A century had gone by, but the atmosphere in our stifling offices in Sharif Street, unrelieved by air-conditioning, remained cosily British. Senior staff recalled Kim Philby's frequent visits in the years before the British diplomat, turned KGB spy, defected from Beirut to the Soviet Union. 'A very nice English gentleman,' was office administrator Shafik Bishai's verdict, 'but often very drunk.'

Maybe my northern Anglo-Irish upbringing made me rebel against all this. When I first walked through the doors, eight messengers stood in line to salute. I banned saluting. It worked, except for one dear and friendly man, Saleh, who couldn't bring himself not to salaam as he knocked at my office door each morning with the tiny cup of Turkish coffee on a tray. I had to threaten him with the sack before he obeyed.

Shafik told me it would be my task to 'distribute the sweets'. Sweets? It was the Moslem feast of Bairam, when for years it had been the custom to hand each of the more menial staff a white beribboned cardboard box containing a selection of sticky confections bought at Groppi, Cairo's favoured coffee-shop for foreigners and the Egyptian bourgeoisie. The next time round I asked Shafik how much these cost, and would not the recipients – who I knew had big families to support – rather have the money. He smiled and shook his head. 'They prefer the sweets,' he assured me.

'Well, just ask them, will you?'

He returned after a quick poll in the corridor and said, 'They would prefer the money.'

NEWS WAS HARD TO COME BY and, when something did happen, it was even harder to get it past the censors. You could 'pigeon' it with an airline passenger. The Egyptians knew what went on and when yet another story attributed to a 'traveller' appeared from Rome or London, I'd be summoned to the foreign ministry once again.

One night Israeli commandos took out a power station at Nagh Hamadi on the Upper Nile, but the first we knew of it was on the Reuters wire from Tel Aviv. I rang Egyptian press spokesman Mahmoud Anis, every inch the old-fashioned English gentleman, who asked angrily, 'Do you realize what time this is?'

He did ring back a few minutes later, however, to announce triumphantly, 'Well, I got that official statement for you – the Army says, "No comment."'

'But,' he added, 'don't quote me.'

The Israelis showed their prowess by sending a fighter behind an airliner approaching Cairo airport, which then peeled off and screamed along the Nile, shattering windows with the supersonic boom. We weren't allowed to report it. But there was tragedy as well as farce. We were taken to see a village school near the canal, hit by Israeli bombers that got the wrong target. The bodies of the small victims were laid out in the hall. It looked, and smelt, like a butcher's shop.

In Cairo, however, life went on as usual. The rich remained rich, the poor got poorer. The middle classes went to Groppi for coffee and cakes. Belly dancer Zoheir Zaki danced in the top-floor nightclub of the Hilton Hotel and Egypt's favourite singer, Umm Khalthoum, sang her serpentine melancholy laments of life and love.

More to my taste was the Cairo Jazz Band, created by Colonel Saleh Ragab, musical director of the armed forces, who learned trumpet as a boy after hearing Louis Armstrong records. He raided every regional military band, brought the stars to Cairo and sat them down to read American big-band scores. He told me gloomily one afternoon in the Aladdin Bar that he'd been called before the top brass. 'What is this jazz? Is it some kind of religion?' he was asked. But the band survived and even sneaked in a number called 'Freedom for Iratilim' – read the last word backwards.

TO MEET PALESTINE LIBERATION ORGANIZATION leader Yasser Arafat I was taken by young men in pointed shoes on a ludicrous Hollywood-style ride in a car with closed curtains to a supposedly unknown suburb – I knew almost exactly where I was. From the man in the chequered *kaffiyeh*, I got only rhetoric in response to my questions.

Hoping for some insights into official thinking, I took the lift to the top floor of the offices of newspaper *Al Ahram* to meet the editor-in-chief Mohammed Hassanein Heykal, usually described as 'a close confidant of President Nasser'. The glass-topped table in his office, said this leader of democratic Arab socialism

proudly, was designed by Anthony Armstrong-Jones – then Princess Margaret's husband. But of news he had none. Every Friday, the embassies scoured his flowery piece of rhetoric about Middle East politics. 'Rely usual Heykal daylead,' London would cable. Sometimes it was hard to oblige.

The *Daily Telegraph's* doughty war correspondent Clare Hollingworth, who remembered Cairo from World War II days, flew in from Cyprus and stood with me, gin and tonic in hand, on a balcony at Shepheards Hotel. Bleakly surveying the spreading jumble of rooftops below, replete with lines of washing, rabbits, cats, even the odd goat, she declared, 'God! Haven't they let the place go down?'

But there was fun, too. At the fabled Gezira Sporting Club, Commonwealth expatriates played Sunday cricket and at the Mena House golf course you stood with your driver at the third hole and aimed at the large object behind the distant flag – the Great Pyramid.

> ... at the Mena House golf course you stood with your driver at the third hole and aimed at the large object behind the distant flag – the Great Pyramid.

REVOLUTION WAS IN THE AIR. From next-door Libya, also part of my beat, the news trickled through in September 1969 that a young army officer called 'Gaffadi' had taken power. So unknown was he that we didn't even get Muammar Gaddafi's name right for 24 hours. He soon visited Cairo to pay his respects to Nasser, but frowned at the wine glasses on the banquet table and insisted they were removed. For the Egyptians, not averse to the odd drink, it was the first bad mark against him.

In Sudan a few months later, another mysterious military man took control. We called him 'Mineiri' for a day or two before we got the Arabic consonants in the right order again. Soon, pro-communist groups made an abortive attempt to oust President Nimeiri, and I flew to Khartoum. A trigger-happy soldier stopped my taxi from the airport and marched me off to jail, a disconsolate and still unpaid driver trotting along behind. They hadn't liked the look of my tape-recorder. In the prison courtyard, Marxist textbooks seized from the university, seen as a hotbed of subversion, lay in piles. The soldiers locked me in a cell, deaf to protestations, until a very Sandhurst-style officer turned up. When I said I knew General Nimeiri, he asked, 'Why didn't you say so before, my dear fellow?' and made my erstwhile guard drive me to the hotel.

It was the old Nile-side establishment, with high ceilings and huge fans, to whose elegant front steps those fortunate air travellers of the colonial era were ferried by launch from the Empire flying boats landing on the river.

Right now in Khartoum, things were considerably less romantic. We were shown villas, floors deep in blood, where victims of the attempted coup were slaughtered. Nimeiri himself had escaped through a window. Then the executions began – shooting for the military, hanging for civilian plotters. We were taken to watch the trial of communist leader Abdel-Khalik Mahgoub before a court of army officers whose impressive gold-braided uniforms and flashing eyes betrayed the coming verdict. Guilty. Sentence: death. The defendant looked pleadingly at us reporters, his last link with the outside world. Then we watched him marched off across the sandy courtyard. They hanged him a few hours later.

BACK IN EGYPT, they celebrated the opening of the mighty Aswan Dam. The country that built the pyramids needed Russian engineers for this job and communist leaders were much in evidence at the festivities. Pigeons deputizing for doves of peace were released from baskets, some fluttering uncertainly down again on the fringes of the crowd to be promptly grabbed and enjoyed for supper. The lean and wiry fellahin have a healthy diet.

Not so their overweight leaders, and Nasser himself was to die, not from an assassin's bullet, but a heart attack. After an exhausting Arab summit, I was on a journalists' drinking spree in Cairo when my indefatigable Egyptian colleague Bahgat Badie managed to reach me from the office at the home of a New Zealand correspondent. 'They're playing solemn music. It must be somebody big,' he said. We didn't realize at first just how big. Thank God I'd left phone numbers – no mobiles in those days – or my career might have ended abruptly.

> 'They're playing solemn music. It must be somebody big,' he said.

An hysterical anti-foreigner wave broke over Cairo and rioters thumped the roof of my humble Ford Cortina, but I revved up and got through. Then the masses poured in from the provinces, falling off the packed roofs of trains, for one of the most spectacular state funerals with kings and presidents two a penny. Asked by London for a thinkpiece on likely successors, I named obvious candidates, including Anwar Sadat, and couldn't understand why London didn't issue the story. It had never left Cairo. The censors, when I protested, said they thought such speculation within hours of Nasser's death was in bad taste. Who is to say they were wrong?

FOR WHAT WAS SUPPOSED TO BE A REST after Cairo, I was sent to Munich to organize the Reuters logistics for the 1972 Olympics. But the Middle East haunted me. Palestinian terrorists broke into the athletes' village and took Israeli hostages, and it ended in a bloodbath on the tarmac of Fürsten Feldbrück airfield. Instead of going for a James Bond shootout with too few marksmen, I always thought the Germans might have played for time by letting the Palestinians fly with their captives to Egypt, where I believe the authorities could have defused the situation. It would have been a chance worth taking, anyway.

It looked as if I was stuck with the Middle East. After a couple of years in Scandinavia, Arye Wallenstein in Israel asked for me as chief correspondent under his stewardship. I'd always liked and admired Wally. Fiercely protective of the Jewish state, he was a kindly man. He was a 'Sabra', born in Palestine, and, the ever-present cigarette smouldering between nicotined fingers, he also reckoned he knew what to believe, and what not. His worst experience, he would only tell close friends, had been to stand a few feet away from condemned Nazi war criminal Adolf Eichmann as the Austrian, kidnapped from Latin America to stand trial in Israel, had the noose fastened round his neck and dropped into the void. Only three reporters were invited to attend the execution, for Israel, Germany and the international press. They then had to describe Eichmann's last moments to a news conference, a devastating experience for Wally.

I'd covered war crimes trials myself in Düsseldorf. I remember Bloody Birgitta, as inmates called her, who rode around the Auschwitz death camp on horseback, clad in black leather, witnesses said, and kicked away the bench on which a young girl condemned to the gallows stood and spat at her. Now the same lady stood ramrod stiff in the dock and showed not a trace of regret. Against this sort of background, it's not difficult to understand the mindset of later Jewish generations.

With such knowledge of the Holocaust, however, it was sad on my new assignment in the Jewish state to witness Israeli soldiers batter down doors in a village on the occupied West Bank, drag young Palestinian men out and throw them into the back of a truck. Crossing the so-called Green Line into what were euphemistically labelled the 'administered areas' by the Israelis was like stepping back into another age and culture.

One day I might be flying with the late Prime Minister Yitzhak Rabin, or Defence Minister Shimon Peres, in an Israeli Army helicopter bound for Lebanese border clashes. A few days later I could be interviewing Arab sheikhs squatting in their tented camps in the Sinai desert. On Christmas Eve, I attended Midnight Mass at the Church of the Nativity in Bethlehem, sent the story to London from a phone-box on the Jerusalem road, then drove across the West Bank to Nazareth to get both biblical datelines on the wire in the same day – a first, I think. West Bank leaders were delighted to see I cared about their point of view and one of my treasured memoirs is the 'thank you' letter that Bethlehem's Mayor Elias Freij sent to head office on my eventual return home.

AMID THE NOISY FANATICS on both sides, who always seemed to me to be punching above their real weight, it was refreshing to hear many voices of reason and generosity of spirit. Freij dressed like an old-fashioned English bank manager, in his office above Manger Square, and his views were just as pragmatic. As Israel was here to stay, it made better sense, he argued, for the Palestinians to accept the fact.

> ... it was refreshing to hear many voices of reason and generosity of spirit.

Back on the other side, I found liberal thinkers such as David Landor, for years the government press spokesman, a brilliant and charming ex-Viennese intellectual who had served with the British Army in Palestine. He had no time either for dreams and illusions. The *Jerusalem Post* editor, Ari Rath, who made me welcome in his offices in the days before Reuters had a place of its own in the capital, presented similarly pragmatic views. A few years later, working in Germany, I had the pleasure of bringing him and my old friend Mohamed Abdel Gawad, the head of the Egyptian news agency, together for a chat in Bonn. They got on like a house on fire.

But it seems to me their two cultures are basically different. Not so long ago I met my old Cairo colleague Bahgat again in an Arab capital where I'd been invited to draw up a blueprint for reorganizing the national news agency. In six weeks I'd interviewed just about everyone in the huge building and, amid high praise and lavish hospitality, submitted my report. Bahgat looked at the thick dossier – and me – with incredulity and slapped me affectionately on the back. 'You are wasting your time, my dear,' he chuckled. '*Wasting your time!* In this part of the world, nothing will ever change.' He may be right.

# DATELINE HOLLYWOOD

BRUCE RUSSELL

FRONTLINES 22

**DATELINE HOLLYWOOD** | BRUCE RUSSELL

# For someone who'd grown up

in a small town in Australia, where 'going to the flickers' for a Saturday matinée was a highlight of the week, I had got the plum assignment. Reuters sent me in the late 1960s to Los Angeles. In the Hollywood whose movies fired the dreams of the century, Mae West, Marlon Brando and Elvis Presley were some of the stars I met. Another was Ronald Reagan, whose presidency I would report on later as bureau chief in Washington. There were some ugly stories in California too. I filed how hippie 'flower power' lost its innocence as I covered the Sharon Tate killings and the trial of murder guru Charles Manson.

**Ronald Reagan, Barbara Rush and Frank Sinatra at a dinner in LA after a première of a Sinatra film**
21 May 1959

© Hulton Getty

HER SECRETARY SAID THAT MAE WEST would be delighted for me to come up and see her some time. New in Los Angeles, I had set about with determination to explore Hollywood and meet its stars, beginning with the legends of its history.

Miss West, I noted, had had her apartment decorated almost entirely in white. It was her favourite colour. She was making a cameo appearance in the movie *Myra Breckinridge* and her contract said she was the only actress allowed to wear it – then Raquel Welch turned up on the set in the nearest shade of off-white it was possible to concoct, to set off a blistering row.

I asked her why she favoured the ribald in her humour: 'Goodness, them's beautiful diamonds!' 'Goodness had nothing to do with it, honey.' She said she'd always found it easier to make jokes about sex. As we spoke, she sat beside me inclining her best ear, for her hearing was none too good, and a muscle man walked in with the drinks. I gathered from the looks between them that Miss West was one elderly star who wasn't living entirely in her past.

*... Miss West was one elderly star who wasn't living entirely in her past.*

A request to see Mary Pickford, America's sweetheart of the silent film era, got me, with other selected reporters, as far as a door – just ajar – to a dimly lit upstairs room in her Beverly Hills mansion. Husband Buddy Rogers set his head to the door. 'Mary, some of your friends are here to see you.' From within came a squeak that might have meant anything. That was the end of the visit. The frail old lady was said to enjoy her tipple.

Lillian Gish, a great name of the silent screen, explained how an odd quirk of technology meant that survivors of her era had seemed to weather better than movie queens from the early talkies. 'The lighting was so primitive and the film so grainy that any woman beyond her early teens looked like an old hag on film,' she said. Moviemakers confined themselves to the very young. Actresses had to do their own stunts in those days, she also recalled, describing how she spent hours in brutal weather on an ice floe.

A male legend, Johnny Weissmuller was now a corpulent figure with a small house in one of the duller suburbs. Tarzan had come to earth from swinging on the ropes and vines among the jungle treetops, and the only rope I saw was a piece of cord which attached a motorcar inner-tube to the side of his pokey backyard pool. He slid into that tube and swam in place for half an hour or so for his daily exercise.

CALIFORNIA, WHEN I REPORTED IT, was home to a host of new lifestyles. Most notable, perhaps, belonged to hippie 'flower children', who originated around San Francisco. Their age of innocence soon ended, when a girl walked up to a scruffy bearded little drifter in the Haight Ashbury district and gave him a flower. The drifter was Charles Manson, just out of jail. He was so surprised by this gesture of trust, that he formed the idea of gathering some flower children into a band with himself as their guru, then – when he had brought together 'the Manson family' – he set out to revenge himself on a society that had imprisoned him most of his life by setting his followers against their own class to steal and murder.

In a night of horror for a world not yet inured to cult atrocity, his flower children murdered eight-months-pregnant actress Sharon Tate and her guests at her Hollywood Hills home. I reported Manson's trial through its 171 days. Once, he leaped at the judge to stab him with a pencil, shouting, 'I'll cut your head off, old man.' But perhaps the most dramatic moment was on the day of a major earthquake in Los Angeles. Shaken out of bed, I spent much of the morning reporting a rising death toll, then sped to the courthouse, where Manson-follower Susan Atkins was to take the stand. In the last question before the lunch break, Atkins was asked, 'Who killed Sharon Tate?' to which she replied, 'I did.' Manson drew the death sentence but, as this was not executed in California then, he languished in prison for the killings.

Some writers have tried to cash in, by pretending that Hollywood is sin city, a modern Sodom or Gomorrah. I don't think that was ever true. Real scandals were few. But Hollywood turned a tolerant eye on sexual diversities, and in that way was very different from puritan Middle America. There were always agents to take care of accidents.

Talking to the famous flapper of the 1920s, Anita (*Gentlemen Prefer Blondes*) Loos, I touched on this question of sex. No longer young, but yet a flapper at heart, she giggled so much I feared she might not survive the interview. 'Miss Loos, do gentlemen still prefer blondes?' She thought about that, then replied: 'No. I would say that these days gentlemen prefer gentlemen.' Another gale of giggles.

FROM HOLLYWOOD IN RETIREMENT, I moved to stars of recent vintage, from the black-and-white silents to talkies, Technicolor, 3D and stereoscopic sound. Marilyn Monroe – the tragic beauty who was frightened of going to sleep – had already passed into legend, found dead in her bed in 1962 with a bottle of sleeping tablets beside her. But I met Bing Crosby and Bob Hope, and for good measure their sarong-clad co-star Dorothy Lamour, who confided, 'Boy how I disliked those guys.' Apparently they'd made her life a misery on the set by inventing their own routines and ignoring her.

On a windswept hilltop in the Santa Monica mountains I chatted with Marlon Brando. He had come there to make the gesture of handing his land back to the Indians. I had difficulty in finding this singular event, until I saw Brando being driven by a young US senator of the Kennedy clan, so I decided that the answer was to tail them – although I got the impression they were in trouble too, because they tried several roads and the senator stopped to ask his way. A long line of Indians waited to receive their due of expropriated real estate and Brando was most courteous, but he had put on so much weight it was not easy to recognize him. Certainly nothing of the brooding muscle-bound Stanley Kowalski of *A Streetcar Named Desire* could be seen in that bloated figure. Hollywood's unkind nickname for him then was the 'Great White Whale'.

Paulette Goddard became so nervous when I produced a tape-recorder that I thought she was going to climb up the wall. She ordered me to turn it off at once. Merle Oberon asked me to her

'What do you say to the Queen of England?'

bedroom to see her collection of French Impressionist paintings. A well-known songstress invited me to take her to the movies. Hollywood being what Miss Loos said it was, there were a couple of male actors who came on rather strong. Some stars were as keen to interview me as I was them. Carol Burnett was on her way to Australia to attend the opening of the Sydney Opera House, where another honoured guest would be Queen Elizabeth II. Asked the irrepressible Miss Burnett, 'What do you say to the Queen of England? How did you get your breaks?'

In an interview with Alfred Hitchcock, I chided him that his major American films lacked the humour of his early British classics like *The Lady Vanishes*. I don't imagine my remarks had the slightest influence on one of the leading directors in Hollywood history, but next time I saw him he was with a film crew in London's Soho. The film *Frenzy* laid emphasis on humour, as did another of his last works, *Family Plot*. Sadly neither enjoyed the popularity of tension-laden pieces like *North by Northwest*.

A NEW GENERATION of 1970s celebrities, particularly rock stars, were ill organized in contrast with their Hollywood precursors, who had the studio system to support them. This could make interviews a pain in the neck, like turning up to ask for a group only to be told that no such people were registered in the hotel. They had probably used assumed names. A supposed reception I went to with my wife, to meet a well-known group in a beach house on the road to Malibu, was a glorified pot party.

I was whisked up to Las Vegas to hear Elvis talk about a new television show off-stage during a nightclub intermission. He wore his cream suit with chocolate-coloured inserts at the bottom of the trousers, an outfit supposed to make him look slim, but seen close up he was obviously having problems with his weight and he sweated profusely through his make-up. In 1977, aged 42, he was to die an untimely death, which turned him into one of the cult figures of the century.

Soon after rock king Jimi Hendrix died of a drug overdose in Britain, the loss of Janis Joplin under similar circumstances in Los Angeles was a world sensation. At least one competitor failed to catch up until next day, when his office told him to match it. As a Beatlemaniac, I obviously reacted faster to events in the rock world. I heard him shout down the telephone, 'Who the hell is Janis Joplin?'

Singers I met included country star Merle Haggard, who told me of his astonishment at the reception given his new song 'Okie from Muskogee', which was about the antipathy Middle Americans felt for the 1960s hippies. An audience in Oakland had risen to its feet fluttering American flags. No interview I did got as much play in US newspapers as that one. Haggard had perhaps unknowingly launched the counter-attack against 'flower power' – a political mood that would be exploited by an actor called Ronald Reagan.

**Tears streamed down Reagan's face, organ music surged from the oak-lined walls, white doves flew from white cages.**

In my time in Hollywood, I watched Reagan read the eulogy to his old friend, Robert Taylor, at a funeral in the lushly sentimental Forest Lawns cemetery, lampooned by English author Evelyn Waugh in his novel *The Loved One*. Tears streamed down Reagan's face, organ music surged from the oak-lined walls, white doves flew from white cages. Later I interviewed him as governor of California and met him again when he was among the most popular presidents of US history.

He seemed to me by then to be largely out of it, ageing and deaf, making mistakes in news conferences and unwilling to meet most visitors at anything more committing than a photo session. Interviews weren't exciting. He had scripted answers. He made the same speech time and again, as his wife Nancy sat gazing raptly, as if she'd never heard a word of it. Gore Vidal waspishly dubbed him 'our acting president', yet he was more effective than many gave him credit for – as the Russians found as he engaged them with Star Wars in a last ruinous bout of the Cold War arms race.

# THE DEATH OF CHE GUEVARA

CHRISTOPHER ROPER

FRONTLINES 23

## THE DEATH OF CHE GUEVARA | CHRISTOPHER ROPER

# Summarily executed, in October 1967

at the age of 39, Ernesto 'Che' Guevara became a cult hero around the world, a revolutionary icon untainted by the corruption of power. I was the Reuters reporter who broke the news of his death in the dry scrubby forests of Eastern Bolivia.

In retrospect, it is hard not to be influenced by subsequent events – by the profound cultural and political changes that have swept the world. Guevara died a year before student-led upheavals sent tremors through Western capitals and destroyed the presidencies of Lyndon Johnson and Charles de Gaulle.

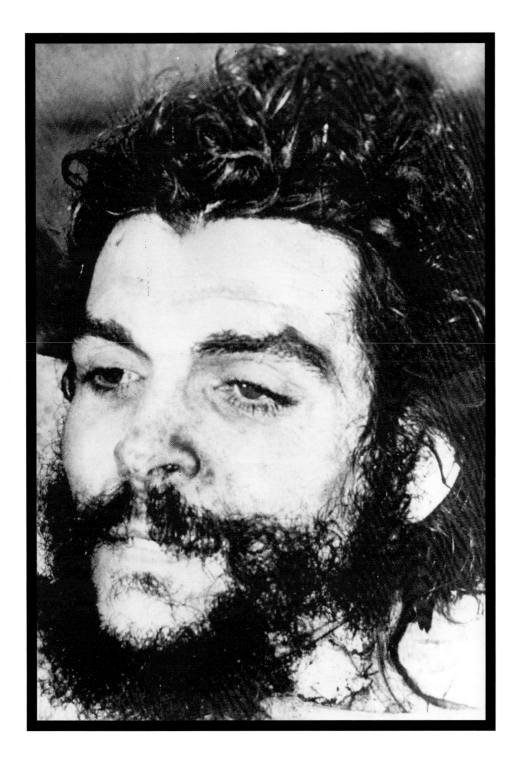

**Che Guevara, shortly after his death**
09 October 1967

© Hulton Getty

LATIN AMERICA BARELY FIGURED in the news pages of the British press and it hadn't yet become a popular destination for back-packers or students in their gap year. Cocaine was still an exotic substance that barely registered in my consciousness when I was sent to take over the Reuters office in Lima in September 1966. As for Guevara – the Argentine-born revolutionary had made the front pages when he resigned from Castro's government in 1965, but his subsequent movements interested only a minority. President Kennedy's 'Alliance for Progress' seemed to have contained the threat of rural insurrections of the kind that had led to the overthrow of Fulgencio Batista in Cuba a decade earlier.

All that changed in early 1967, when ex-Reuters journalist Murray Sayle, a larger-than-life Australian, took time off from covering a round-the-world yacht race for the *Sunday Times* to visit land-locked Bolivia. He broke the news that a guerrilla encampment had been discovered near Camiri, a tiny oil town so remote that, by scheduled flights, it would take three days' travelling from Lima, via La Paz and Santa Cruz. The Bolivian government claimed that it had uncovered the headquarters of an ambitious plan by Che Guevara to raise a continental guerrilla army.

**The Bolivian government claimed that it had uncovered the headquarters of an ambitious plan by Che Guevara to raise a continental guerrilla army.**

It seemed utterly far-fetched. The consensus of Lima-based foreign correspondents was that General René Barrientos, Bolivia's military ruler, was using the story to squeeze more aid out of Washington. No one took very much notice until the Bolivians produced the prize exhibit – Regis Debray, a young French intellectual who had been recruited by the Cubans to publicize the Latin American revolutionary struggle. A year earlier, he had published a pamphlet in Havana called 'The Revolution within the Revolution', which laid out Guevara's belief that, contrary to Soviet orthodoxy, the foundations of the Latin American revolution had to be laid in the countryside, supported by the peasantry and far from the corruption of the city.

It soon became clear that the trial of Regis Debray, before four military judges in Camiri, would be a major media event, with a revolving cast of around 200 journalists from Europe and North America crowding into a town that was totally unprepared to receive them. The wheels of Bolivian justice ground slowly, but once the trial got under way in July, we had to be there.

I NEEDED A CRASH COURSE in the complexities of international revolutionary theory to understand exactly why the Cubans and the Soviets could be both close allies yet in total disagreement about Latin America. I had an excellent tutor in Richard Gott, the *Guardian's* correspondent in the region, who was writing a book on rural guerrilla movements.

Gott already knew the very exotic delegation of international Marxists, who arrived in La Paz under the banner of the Bertrand Russell Peace Foundation: Robin Blackburn and Perry Anderson of the *New Left Review*, Tariq Ali, former president of the Oxford Union, and Ralph Schoenman, Bertrand Russell's American secretary. Schoenman was the only member of the delegation who reached Camiri with press credentials – from a small left-wing weekly. He was not alone in mixing his roles. Among the journalists, there were at least one member of Israeli intelligence, one CIA agent and one Cuban agent. Others, whom we suspected of such affiliations, were probably innocent.

Keeping the story alive for weeks on end was a real challenge, as the outcome of the trial was never in doubt. The Bolivian military and their allies in Washington wanted to expose an international communist conspiracy, with Regis Debray and Ciro Roberto Bustos, an Argentinian who had been arrested with him, as living evidence of the terrorist threat. Debray's defence was that he was simply a journalist plying his trade. The facts were not in dispute: Debray had spent some weeks with Guevara and his small band of Cuban and Bolivian volunteers, and had then been arrested as he tried to leave their theatre of operations.

My abiding memory of eight or nine weeks in Camiri is the rare pleasure of idleness without guilt. The court sat each morning for two or three hours; we filed our copy through a special facility set up by Cable & Wireless for the duration of the trial – then we were free to swim in the river, flirt with the local girls, play chess and drink and talk with other journalists.

ANOTHER MONTH AND I MIGHT HAVE GOT BORED, but I actually remember it with unmixed pleasure. Camiri was, and probably remains, a grid of unpaved streets around a central plaza, with low wood and concrete buildings roofed with corrugated iron. An Italian who had arrived in 1945 and enjoyed excellent relations with the local military ran the only restaurant. We could only guess at his past; it wouldn't have been polite to ask. The trial of Regis Debray must have been a once-in-a-lifetime bonanza.

One weekend in early October, Richard Gott suggested that I should accompany him to Santa Cruz, where American Green Berets were training Bolivian troops in counter-insurgency warfare techniques. Richard thought rightly that we were more likely to find a fresh angle at La Esperanza, the sugar mill where the Americans were based. In any case, Richard was by then working as a researcher for Brian Moser, a television producer, who had come to Bolivia to make a film for Granada's *World in Action*.

Santa Cruz is the capital of Eastern Bolivia and at that time it was enjoying an economic boom, based on oil, agriculture and dramatic increases in land values. It was hard to imagine that the poverty-stricken highlands around La Paz and the rich lowlands around Santa Cruz were both part of the same country. Until air travel altered the social geography of Latin America forever in the middle decades of the twentieth century, it had taken less time for a plantation owner in the Beni region of Bolivia to travel to London by boat than it did for him to reach La Paz.

Sparsely inhabited, and tightly controlled by the military ever since the Chaco War, which had pitted two of the continent's poorest countries, Bolivia and Paraguay, against one another in the 1930s, south-eastern Bolivia was an unpromising seed-bed for a continental revolution. We now know that Guevara had chosen it for two reasons. The first was its proximity to Argentina, the real focus of his revolutionary strategy, and the second was a climate that wouldn't adversely affect his asthma. He was accompanied by tried and trusted Cuban companions, who had fought with him in the Cuban sierras more than a decade earlier, but neither they nor their Bolivian recruits knew much about the area in which they had chosen to establish their headquarters.

Sitting over cold beers on Sunday 8 October, talking over the evident seriousness with which the American special forces viewed the threat posed by Guevara, we were hailed by a sergeant, whom we had met earlier in the day at La Esperanza. 'You guys should get down to Vallegrande. They've captured Che!'

Easier said than done. It was 8 in the evening and Vallegrande was around 125 miles away over dirt roads. It was hard to find a driver who would take us there that night; they weren't worried about the guerrillas, but they weren't keen on carrying foreign journalists through the military roadblocks that we would certainly encounter.

THEY NEEDN'T HAVE WORRIED. We rolled into Vallegrande in the early hours of Monday. Here was a little town in the rolling foothills of the Andes, even less touched by the outside world than Camiri, which was on a main road from Santa Cruz to Argentina. That morning, however, Vallegrande was buzzing with the news that a battle had been fought between a Bolivian Army patrol and the guerrillas. We also learned that operations were effectively directed by two Americans of Cuban origin. We discovered their names by the simple expedient of going to the town's only hotel and checking the register: Felix Ramos and Eduardo Gonzalez.

We waited most of the day on a small grass airstrip, rumours swirling through a small but excited crowd. Brian Moser discovered that he had only two or three shots left in his camera and no more film. My main worry was how my story could be filed. Unless I could get the news to La Paz, my rivals would arrive in hired planes and possibly file before I could get back to Camiri. However, there had been several false reports of Guevara's capture or demise, one just ten days earlier. I had actually to see Guevara, dead or alive, before writing a word.

In the late afternoon, a small helicopter swirled into view out of the setting sun. As it circled the field, we could see a bundle strapped to one of its runners. Once the helicopter had landed, soldiers prevented our approach, but we saw the bundle loaded into the back of a battered blue van. Our driver, by now as excited as we were, gave chase. We crowded around the van as it

'You guys should get down to Vallegrande. They've captured Che!'

stopped in front of iron gates. 'Let's get the hell out of here!' shouted a burly figure in combat fatigues. He later pretended not to understand English, but he was clearly one of the Cuban Americans who were directing affairs.

Despite the best efforts of the soldiers, the crowd pushed into the compound, where Guevara's body was laid out on a slab in the improvised morgue. Richard, who had interviewed Guevara in Havana, was in no doubt that the Bolivians had indeed killed the Argentine guerrilla leader. A black and white photograph of Guevara, lying with his eyes wide open, has been reproduced many thousands of times over the years. It was almost my first encounter with violent death, and his clear gaze remains fresh in my memory. There was no fear in those eyes. What, I wondered, had he seen in the situation that I couldn't see? How had he managed to die without being overcome by desperation and despair. The bullet hole through his torso told us that if he had indeed been captured, he had subsequently been summarily executed.

*... Guevara's body was laid out on a slab in the improvised morgue.*

We didn't remain long. For one thing, we were afraid that we might be prevented from leaving the town. We did, however, find a telegraph office, where an operator tapped out messages in Morse code to the telegraph office in La Paz. More hopeful than confident, I sent a one-paragraph story to Hector Villegas, the excellent Reuters stringer in La Paz, care of Cable & Wireless.

After leaving Richard and Brian in Santa Cruz, I persuaded the driver to take me back Camiri, where I knew I could find a telex and file the full story. We had by then been awake for around 36 hours, but our driver understood exactly what was required. At some point during that long night, we stopped at a roadside bar and persuaded its owner to tune into the BBC World Service: 'Reuters correspondent in La Paz has reported that Bolivian troops have killed Ernesto Che Guevara, the former associate of Fidel Castro ...' So my cable had got through and the first hurdle was cleared. The next day in Camiri, I filed a long piece, which, in a unique double, appeared under my byline on the front pages of both the *New York Times* and *Izvestia*.

So what had Guevara seen? My story compared his appearance to a medieval painting of St John the Baptist and he became an iconic figure in death for millions who had paid little or no attention to him while he was alive. The years since his death have seen armed revolutionary movements successful in Nicaragua and close to bringing governments to their knees in Argentina, Guatemala, El Salvador, Peru and Colombia.

As I write, the United States is pouring military aid and combat troops into Colombia, in an effort to prevent the country slipping out of central government control. Rural guerrillas under the leadership of one of Guevara's contemporaries, Manuel Marulanda, have been quietly enlarging their spheres of influence in rural Colombia over the past three decades. It's just possible that Guevara was more clear-sighted than many of the journalists, who mostly reported his death as the final chapter of a revolutionary odyssey.

# THE WAR AMERICA LOST

RONALD CLARKE

FRONTLINES 24

## THE WAR AMERICA LOST | RONALD CLARKE

# 'As Vietnam goes,' said the Pentagon,

'so will the free world.' It didn't happen that way in the end, but that was America's domino theory. If Vietnam fell, Communism would sweep the globe. The country had been partitioned. That happened at the end of French colonial rule in the 1950s, but before long South Vietnam, backed by the West, was facing an insurgency supported by Ho Chi Minh's Communist North. The US entered the war in 1964, when North Vietnamese torpedo boats attacked the American destroyer *Maddox* in the Gulf of Tonking – and by the time I was in Saigon as Reuters bureau chief, four years later, nearly half a million American servicemen were involved in trying to defend the South against the communist Viet Cong guerrillas and troops from North Vietnam.

**South Vietnamese children flee the scene
of a misdirected napalm attack by their own
troops. Kim Phuc (centre) has ripped off her
burning clothes**
08 June 1972

© AP photo

I SUPPOSE THAT IF I HAD TO THINK of a dateline in Vietnam, it would be Bien Hoa. Not the big American air base of that name, although that was part of the story. The place that I remember, though, was a village. I sat one evening, on what had seemed to me a quiet hillside, and sipped a glass of wine, when I saw it bombed and burned to rubble.

I had spent most of that day trying to find the fighting, amid the usual conflicting reports, when the commander of some American tanks invited me to add my car to his column. Twenty minutes of random sniper-fire later,
I decided that the only person who hadn't got some armour around him was me, so I waved goodbye and drove off the road to the edge of what, as I say, seemed to be a quiet hillside, where I stopped and got out the bottle of white wine and a cake that had been intended for my picnic lunch.

My haven was shattered by South Vietnamese Sky Raiders and US Super Sabre fighter-bombers screaming through a ravine beneath my dangling feet to rain high explosive and napalm on that village. I remember how I felt strangely safe and curiously detached – an observer who could do nothing – as flames 20 feet high scorched the side of the hill.

Within minutes the planes had gone and, in the eerie silence, I drove down there. The place belonged now to a half-dozen stray dogs and a family of ducks on the pond. Not a building was intact. Villagers, who had fled their homes, streamed back to see a few brick walls pockmarked by bomb splinters in a big patch of fire-blackened earth. This was strewn with the corpses of North Vietnamese soldiers, buffalos, cows and pigs. Some of the people sawed off the legs of the cows to eat, while aid workers, handkerchiefs over their mouths, threw lime on the bodies in front of the church. Its façade of yellow brick had been blown in and the roof ripped off. A statue on the altar had lost its head.

'We wanted to avoid blowing up the village, but finally we had no choice,' a US military adviser told me – and then I asked why, and began to put together the jigsaw pieces of the battle that I'd stumbled across.

**'We wanted to avoid blowing up the village, but finally we had no choice,' a US military adviser told me ...**

This had to do with the other Bien Hoa. The sprawling American base just 20 miles north of Saigon, or Ho Chi Minh City, as it is called now. Some 1500 North Vietnamese troops had been ordered to attack it, and 500 of them had deployed, as part of the advance, in the village that was also called Bien Hoa.

That was where the South Vietnamese, with their US advisers, caught up with them. The village had been a cluster of neat tin-roofed houses; home to about a thousand people, many of whom were Roman Catholic refugees who had fled from the communist North in the 1950s after the French went away. The government had expanded it as a model settlement that was intended as a showcase for how good life could be in the South for people like that. Vietnam was, after all, as Americans were always told, a war for hearts and minds.

Three times the South Vietnamese attacked the village. Firing from inside the church and from positions in homes and ditches, the North Vietnamese drove them back. Then the South Vietnamese commander called a ceasefire when, for 15 minutes, helicopters used loudspeakers and dropped leaflets to tell the villagers to move out. Most had already fled anyhow. It was during that interlude, I suppose, that I sat down on the nearby hillside. Then the air strike went in. No North Vietnamese reached the other Bien Hoa. The village paid the price.

It wasn't a big battle, but it was the kind of engagement that had begun to happen almost anywhere, at any time, across South Vietnam as the character of the conflict changed. The North and the Viet Cong were turning it into a war of attrition, with a new campaign of 'postage stamp' attacks – brief assaults at roughly the same moment in various parts of the country.

THAT SWITCH OF STRATEGY followed their heavy losses in the famous Tet Offensive at the end of January 1968, when they launched a full-scale drive against Saigon and 30 provincial towns and took the South, which was enjoying the Tet lunar new year festival, by surprise. One of my predecessors, James Pringle, sent his story by teleprinter in a darkened Reuters bureau as North Vietnamese troops crept by his window, and the fighting in Saigon reached the lawn of the presidential palace.

The Americans finally claimed Tet as a victory, citing 60 000 communists dead, and it was this mauling that led the North

Vietnamese and the Viet Cong commanders to change their strategy – although elsewhere in this volume another colleague, Stephen Somerville, tells how he learned long afterwards that some of their agents told them that a further big push like Tet would be worth the risk. Those counsellors reckoned that a new all-out offensive could prove too much for American public opinion back home, and might thereby hasten the end of the war.

Perhaps they remembered how a demoralized France had packed up to go when its fortress of Dien Bien Phu fell to the communists in 1954 after an epic 55-day siege. The French lost more than 15 000 killed or taken prisoner at Dien Bien Phu. In mourning, a stunned France heard how General de Castries, the commander, ordered his guns to shell his headquarters rather than surrender – and it was around then that Secretary of State John Foster Dulles etched the phrase 'row of dominoes' on American foreign policy.

In the event, however, fighting against the United States in the late 1960s and after the Tet campaign, the Vietnamese communist commanders decided on their new 'postage stamp' strategy of attrition – to hit and to hurt and then melt away. American bombers pounded the North's capital of Hanoi and its port at Haiphong. In the South, besides night-time rocket attacks on Saigon or a brief sally inside the city, small-scale but savage clashes might suddenly flare up anywhere.

Reporters would wake up in their Saigon hotel rooms and make firemen trips to the flashpoints, rather than stay in the field for days. No war could ever have been covered so fully for the media. Military helicopters were available to rush correspondents to 'hot spots'. Briefing officers were on call day and night. A New York reporter in Saigon once was instructed to interview six New York servicemen who had been in combat. Next morning six men, pulled from their battle areas, were lined up in Saigon to be interviewed. There was no censorship and the only restriction on foreign correspondents was not to report future troop movements – a necessary rule to save lives.

Each afternoon when we were in Saigon, we would go to the 'Four O'clock Follies', the name given by correspondents to the daily military briefings. A South Vietnamese officer would report on the day's events with a young private acting as interpreter. If the interpreter made a mistake, the briefing officer – they all knew English – would smack him across his head.

American briefing officers at first gave precise details of ground won or lost and of casualties. But as the war went on and the tolls lengthened, they often preferred phrases such as 'damage was moderate' and 'friendly casualties were light'.

In the week leading up to that Bien Hoa attack, for instance, the cost was high. US military sources said more than 5000 North Vietnamese and Viet Cong, 350 South Vietnamese and 250 Americans were killed.

Many of the US conscripts I talked to had little idea why they were in Vietnam and were looking forward only to the 'Freedom Birds' that might one day fly them home. Drugs, easily obtainable, were a way of escape, but I did not find them as widespread as many reports suggested. I do remember being taken on a helicopter flight by a pilot who, once away from base, removed his helmet and earphones and spent the next 40 minutes holding a portable radio to his ear and singing to pop music. When North Vietnamese in the jungle below fired rockets at us, he shouted back, 'This is great. We're being attacked. Put your feet over the side and wave your press badge at them.'

THE WAR TURNED SAIGON, which had been the 'Paris of Asia' under the French, to a dirty noisy city of litter-strewn streets and thousands of smoke-belching mopeds and rickshaws – and the bar girls.

Many older Vietnamese talked nostalgically of the elegant days of French rule, when Graham Greene drank with planters on the balcony of the Colonial Hotel, overlooking the Tu Do boulevard and its fashionable shops. Beautiful Vietnamese women in their tight-fitting *ao dais*, the neck-to-ankle national dresses, still tottered along the Tu Do on their high heels, but now many were on their way to work in bars.

> Reporters would wake up in their Saigon hotel rooms and make firemen trips to the flashpoints …

> … as the war went on and the tolls lengthened, they often preferred phrases such as 'damage was moderate' and 'friendly casualties were light'.

Saigon had become a city of contrasts, packed during the day and silent at night under a curfew. Vietnamese who had come to the city to cash in on the presence of US servicemen often spent their nights sleeping under pieces of cardboard in fields. Americans, who packed Saigon on leave, were greeted by choruses of bar girls. Their routine never changed. They greeted an American with, 'Hey Johnny, you want good time?' If he did not, he was dismissed with a gruff, 'You number one Cheap Charlie.'

ON A MORNING IN MAY 1968, I had snatched a few hours' sleep after working through the night, when I walked into the bureau to be told North Vietnamese and Viet Cong forces had again attacked the city. Two Reuters correspondents, Bruce Piggott and Ronald Laramy, had left to cover the fighting. 'See you later then,' Laramy shouted as they drove off with two other correspondents, Michael Birch, of the Australian Associated Press, and John Cantwell, of *Time* magazine.

I filed reports on US and South Vietnamese briefings on what became known as the 'Mini-Tet' Offensive in a strangely silent bureau. Suddenly, the door was flung open. Frank Palmos, a freelance reporter who had been given a lift in the office car, burst in shouting, 'They are all dead, they are all dead.'

'What are you talking about?' I demanded.

He said he had left the car just before it ran into a Viet Cong position and he had seen the four correspondents shot. One of them had shouted, '*Bao Chi, Bao Chi!*' 'Press, Press!' to the Viet Cong. They mimicked him, '*Bao Chi, Bao Chi!*' Then they opened fire.

Our Vietnamese office manager Pham Ngoc Dinh immediately drove to the scene, to return with tears streaming down his face. 'They are all dead,' he said simply.

'They are all dead,' he said simply.

Later that day I knelt on the floor at a US Army ambulance post and identified the four to a sergeant who stood over me, chewing gum.

The Mini-Tet ended in another defeat for North Vietnam and the Viet Cong, but the war dragged on. A US Army officer, Lieutenant William Calley, would be found guilty at court martial of a massacre of 20 Vietnamese civilians at Mylai. A news picture of Vietnamese children as they ran screaming from a napalm attack haunted the world. Unrest flared in campus riots at home. The United States would lose more than 45 000 dead before, in 1972, President Richard Nixon withdrew US combat troops. A peace pact was signed in Paris. America had lost. The North Vietnamese flag soon flew over what was again a unified country.

**GET IT RIGHT!**

JOHN SUCHET

FRONTLINES 25

## GET IT RIGHT! | JOHN SUCHET

# I joined Reuters as a graduate trainee

in London in September 1967. Nine months later I was posted to the Paris bureau and found myself out in the streets covering the student revolution of 1968 that so weakened the presidency of Charles de Gaulle that he resigned within a year. From one historic event to another: America, desperate to extricate itself from Vietnam, joined the North Vietnamese round the table for peace talks – in Paris.

**Press photographers scramble to get images
of the Paris riots of 1968**
14 May 1968

© Hulton Getty

I HAD BEEN THE WORST HISTORY STUDENT my school had known. I remember gazing out of the window as we were taught about the revolutions that swept across Europe in 1848. Now, a swift century and a quarter later, I was on the streets of Paris witnessing events of similar proportions.

Someone once said that journalism is the first draft of history. From learning – or failing to learn – about history in the classroom, I was witnessing it.

In 1968, President Johnson, his health and spirit broken by the Vietnam War, had decided not to run for re-election. Demonstrations against American involvement in Vietnam, which had been growing in intensity since 1965, exploded, not just across America, but in Europe too. They were to culminate, in 1970, with the killing of four students at Kent State University by the Ohio National Guard.

The student revolution that took place in Paris in May–June 1968 was ostensibly to do with a change in the education curriculum. The students, who raised the Red Flag, used wrecked cars to barricade the streets and fought the CRS riot police with cobblestones and Molotov cocktails, were really protesting about the Vietnam War, disillusionment with government and the empowering of youth.

Ironic, then, that Paris was chosen as the site of the Vietnam peace talks – the ultimately fruitless negotiations between the Americans and North Vietnamese. And I – fresh out of university, a journalist for less than a year – was assigned by Reuters to cover them.

The talks took place every Wednesday morning at the International Conference Centre in the Avenue Kléber. They began at 9 and finished any time between noon and 2 pm. If things went particularly badly, there would be a walkout early on.

MY COMPETITORS' CORRESPONDENTS – from Associated Press and United Press International – and I would stay behind the barrier outside the entrance for an hour or so (less, as the weeks went by), then cross the broad avenue to the Café Venice, to consume numerous coffees and croissants, read the papers and gossip about each other's newsrooms.

Around noon we would resume our places behind the barrier,

to wait for the spokesmen for the two sides to come out and make a statement: the American first, on behalf of Averell Harriman, in English; then the North Vietnamese, on behalf of their chief negotiator, Xuan Thuy, in French.

That would be followed by an unseemly dash back to the Café Venice and its single telephone to send the details through to our offices. Seconds counted. Reuters would compare the time of its 'snap', sent around the world, to that of AP and UPI. If I was beaten to that phone ... It didn't bear thinking about.

ON ONE FATEFUL DAY the familiar routine took place. But there was a new North Vietnamese spokesman, and he spoke French with a heavy accent. A very heavy accent.

I hastily scribbled down his words and dashed across the road, breathing a sigh of relief to be first to the phone. I filed my report and thought no more about it.

> I filed my report and thought no more about it.

That evening I got a call in my flat from the World Desk in London, 'We've had a telex from our desk in Asia. Ho Chi Minh's people are recalling their team from Paris, after what they said to reporters today about the latest American position. It's a major story, and you were first with it. Well done. By the way, just check your notes to make sure you got it right ...'

The smooth *pâté de foie* and the Beaujolais I had just consumed rose in my throat. With trembling hands I opened my notebook – and realized the scrawl I had been unable to read when I phoned through my report was still indecipherable. In my haste to get the story across, I had reported the interpreter's words that I could read and ignored those I couldn't, filling the gaps with what I imagined he had said.

In so doing, I had put into Xuan Thuy's mouth a far stronger reaction to the latest American proposal than he had in fact given, followed by a threat to withdraw which – couched in the subtle language of diplomacy – had in reality been far less than that. The summons from Hanoi had no doubt been to seek an explanation for their team's making such a threat without first referring it back to Ho Chi Minh.

Hands trembling even more, I telephoned the World Desk and suggested it was just possible that I might slightly have misread my own notes. Perhaps, I said, we ought to

… the three
qualities that
matter most
are accuracy,
accuracy and
accuracy.
In that order.

make a correction. 'Yes,' said the voice drily, 'we ought.'

It's said you have to make a mistake to learn. Through that incident – still indelibly etched on my mind – I learned the single most important lesson in journalism: the three qualities that matter most are accuracy, accuracy and accuracy. In that order. And accuracy is the hallmark of Reuters.

As for the peace talks, they continued fruitlessly for some months before finally fizzling out. The war on the ground intensified, as American troops became more and more embroiled in a conflict that, it slowly became clear, they could not ultimately win.

I WAS A CHIEF SUB-EDITOR at Independent Television News – and about to become a reporter for it – when I watched the pictures of the victorious North Vietnamese tanks rolling into Saigon. It was one of my regrets that I never went to Vietnam to cover the war in which I so nearly played an unwitting part.

# MIDEAST: DAVID AND GOLIATH

PATRICK MASSEY

FRONTLINES 26

## MIDEAST: DAVID AND GOLIATH | PATRICK MASSEY

# At about 9.30 one bright London

spring morning in 1967, I strolled into head office to find that the editor, Stuart Underhill, wanted to see me. 'You're booked on a plane to Tel Aviv. It takes off at 12.15,' he said. No time to go home and pack. My wife took a suitcase to Heathrow and I piled into a cab, where I studied my brief. War was brewing in the Middle East. Egypt had that day sent a mighty army to Israel's frontier. Syria and Jordan had massed troops on its eastern flank. It was the start, for me, of almost a decade of reporting the region for Reuters. I would cover the way that Israel's astonishing triumph in the Six Day War set history there on a new course, changing the conflict of Arab and Jew in Palestine from a sideshow to a Cold War nuclear flashpoint, as oil was held to ransom and Islamic militants proclaimed a holy struggle to recover Jerusalem.

**The Six Day War: a blindfolded Syrian
prisoner in the hands of Israeli troops on the
Golan Heights**
12 June 1967

© Hulton Getty

I AWOKE IN TEL AVIV on 5 June 1967 to a deceptive calm. Traffic was light. Pedestrians moved at an unhurried gait. Only a handful of Israeli insiders knew how the date would be branded deep on history.

In May, the Arabs, led by Egyptian President Gamal Abdel Nasser, had torn up past agreements and uttered threats to annihilate Israel, but most Israelis, and a wider world, had been lulled by Israeli assurances that diplomacy would prevail.

Many Western journalists, who had rushed to Israel to cover a war, decided it was safe to fly home. One was Winston Churchill, grandson of the wartime leader. 'There will be no war,' he announced confidently on returning to London. He and others later had trouble finding flights back to Israel when fighting did start.

I drove to Galilee that morning to write feature stories. As I left Tel Aviv, I did not know that Reuters permanent man in Israel, Ayre Wallenstein, a fifth-generation Israeli who was privy to the highest secrets, had prepared a bomb shelter under his kitchen table. He had been told, in strictest secrecy, that Israel was set to launch a dawn aerial assault to destroy the air forces of Egypt, Syria and Jordan – the most daring pre-emptive strike in modern history. Had it failed, Tel Aviv could have faced ferocious retaliation.

At mid-morning, Israel radio announced that hostilities had started. It was vague on detail, but Wallenstein knew by then that his kitchen table would not be needed.

I raced back from Galilee to catch up with Israeli forces in the Egyptian Sinai desert. Not until after midnight did Israel disclose that virtually all of the enemies' air forces had been destroyed on the ground and that its armour was pushing deep inside Arab territory under an Israeli-controlled sky. Failure of the air strike could have left Arab troops clear to push into Israel in overwhelming numbers and perhaps wipe the Jewish state off the map. But the pre-emptive attack succeeded beyond the wildest dreams of Israel's high command and history would now point in an entirely different direction.

*... the pre-emptive attack succeeded beyond the wildest dreams of Israel's high command ...*

I rode an Israeli Army truck across Sinai, gaping at a sandscape filled with shattered tanks and guns, testimony to the crushing defeat that smote the hosts of Egypt. Alongside many tanks, I saw heaps of boots, discarded by Egyptian soldiers as they fled west towards the Suez Canal. The advance was so swift that traffic jams built up, as vehicles jostled on paths through the desert minefields.

Six days later it was all over. Mastery of the sky enabled Israel to capture the Sinai peninsula from Egypt, as well as the Golan Heights from Syria and the West Bank of the Jordan from the Arab Legion of King Hussein. Israeli soldiers stood in control everywhere from the Suez Canal to the River Jordan. The victory was an object lesson in the importance of air power and set a pattern for Middle East history for the rest of the century.

IN THE DECADES LEADING UP TO 1967 the conflict there had registered a scant impact on the consciousness of the outside world. Arab–Jewish enmity sputtered from the turn of the century, when Jewish refugees from Eastern Europe streamed into Palestine, which then belonged to the Turkish Empire. In the days of a British mandate, from 1917 to 1948, hostilities grew fiercer, until open warfare marked the birth of the Jewish state in 1948.

Until the Six Day War, too, Israel looked like a plucky little David up against a Soviet-backed Arab Goliath and it was in this atmosphere, shortly before the conflict, that I had heard Foreign Minister Abba Eban assure reporters, 'We do not seek a single extra foot of Arab territory.'

His view was not universally shared in Israel. A strong current of Israeli opinion favoured using Arab belligerence as an excuse to burst out of the strategically awkward confines in which Israel had been left by previous indecisive conflicts.

'It'll be years before we get another chance like this to give ourselves defensible borders,' an Israeli major told me.

After the war, many Israelis hoped their victory would make the Arabs sue for permanent peace. When this hope was dashed, there began a slow but profound shift in Israeli psychology. With their backs no longer against the wall, Israelis began relishing the role of top dog. From plucky little David, Israel had metamorphosed into a regional superpower.

I found the changed atmosphere most noticeable on returning to Israel in 1969, two years after the war. A conviction had gained ground that Israel should be in no hurry to hand back the captured territories. Certainly in the case of Jerusalem, which before the war had been divided between Israel and Jordan, Israelis were virtually united in believing that the Arab half should never be returned. Much of this reflected the Jewish people's deep historical and religious roots in Jerusalem. The 1967 victory had restored access to Judaism's holiest shrine, the Western Wall of the Temple.

By that time, the concept of Jewish roots was being extended to the West Bank, an area predominantly populated by Palestinian Arabs. Hebron was the first focus of attention. The town had contained an important Jewish community up to the 1920s, when massacre and expulsion drove the Jews out.

Israeli Defence Minister Moshe Dayan, a fervent believer in permanent occupation of the West Bank, told us enigmatically, 'We must create facts on the ground.' The Old Testament was scoured for West Bank place names, the existence of which in the scriptures was taken as proof of Israel's divine right to rule them. Archaeological excavations sought out ancient Jewish artefacts to bolster the argument. And there began the most important fact-creation of all – the establishment of Jewish settlements on land where Palestinian Arabs had lived for generations.

IN CONTRAST TO THE GRIM DEFIANCE of the pre-1967 years, an Israeli mood of self-congratulation blossomed. Once when I asked a military spokesman about a report of Israeli arms sales to Singapore, he replied jovially, 'Well, you know, I wouldn't put anything past these Israelis.'

In the 1950s, Israel's closest ally in the West had been France. So close was this friendship that Israelis at one time contemplated removing the English language from their street signs and replacing it with French. Much of the Israeli air force came from French factories and the Mirage 3 fighter-bomber was credited with being the decisive weapon system in winning the Six Day War.

President Charles de Gaulle changed all that. He even refused to allow delivery of navy patrol vessels that Israel had already paid for. Israelis responded by sneaking the craft out of Cherbourg and sailing them home to a heroes' welcome: more fodder for Israeli pride.

Where the French backed out, the United States stepped in with a massive supply of arms, including some of the most formidable aircraft, notably the F-15 fighter and the F-16 ground attack airplane. Sporadic clashes between Israeli and Arab aircraft provided useful data for the Great Power arms makers. American equipment invariably bested the Soviets'.

By 1970, Israel felt powerful enough to start imposing its will on Arab governments. I was then in Amman, covering the Black September civil war. The Palestinian guerrillas of Yasser Arafat, also just then making spectacular hijacks of Western airliners, sought to overthrow the pro-West King Hussein in the quest for a base from which to wage a war on Israel.

WITH OTHER CORRESPONDENTS, I was penned up in the Hotel Intercontinental and told that anyone moving outside would be shot. Electric power and telephones had been cut. How to file copy? I had established a contact with a communications officer at the British embassy just up the road. He would visit the hotel in an armoured car to collect my copy and transmit it to London on embassy links. Others clamoured for the same facility, but the embassy man insisted – one person's copy only. So we ended up writing a pool story that the Foreign Office could distribute to other media.

From what we saw from the roof and reports trickling into the hotel, it seemed that Palestinian forces, backed by Syrian tanks, might defeat Hussein. Then Israel pushed troops and heavy artillery up to the Jordan border and said any Syrian aircraft venturing into Jordanian skies would be shot down by the immensely superior Israeli air force. Syria heeded the warning. Hussein's rag-tag air force, with no worry about opposition in the sky, chased the Syrian tanks back across the border. The Palestinian bid to use Jordan failed and thousands of defeated commandos fled to neighbouring Lebanon. Their presence and retaliatory strikes by Israel soon ignited the vicious civil war that lasted into the late 1980s.

But in 1973 came a devastating blow to Israeli self-confidence. Just as nobody expected the Israeli attack in 1967,

Sporadic clashes between Israeli and Arab aircraft provided useful data for the Great Power arms makers.

so hardly anyone foresaw a lightning onslaught in October by the forces of Egypt and Syria. Egyptian President Anwar Sadat, who had succeeded Nasser three years before, sent his armour to storm across the Suez Canal. Syria smashed at Israeli positions on the Golan Heights. The Arabs used Soviet weapons that had never been seen before. Particularly deadly was the hand-held SAM-7 missile that wrought havoc with Israel's proud air force. I covered that war from Jordan, where King Hussein opted to stay out of the main conflict and contented himself with sending tanks to join the Syrians on the Golan Heights.

Fed by tales of Israeli reverses, a tide of jubilation rolled over the streets of Amman. Joyful officials explained to me that the Syrians would march through Israel by the weekend and that Jerusalem would soon return to Arab hands.

In the event, as Syria hesitated on the Golan and Israel made a daring counter-thrust across the Suez Canal, the Arabs were checked. Israeli troops advanced to some 60 miles from Cairo and almost within hail of Damascus. Then we were stunned to learn that US nuclear forces were on high alert. Soviet President Leonid Brezhnev had issued a warning of grave consequences if the Israelis moved in to wipe out the trapped Egyptian Third Army near Suez.

IT REMINDED THE WORLD that the Middle East now belonged to the Cold War. As petrol prices around the globe soared, so the October War also provoked Saudi Arabia and some others in the Organization of the Petroleum Exporting Countries (OPEC) to unleash the oil weapon and embargo supply to the West for its support of Israel. The war was the trigger for OPEC to seize control of oil pricing from the Western multinationals. The price of a barrel of oil quadrupled in a year.

The immediate nuclear crisis was resolved, with the Third Army allowed to go home and Israel staying in control of territory it had held before the 1973 Arab attack. Jordanians wept bitterly at the failure to regain Jerusalem. The Egyptians salvaged pride by recalling their successful initial thrust across Suez and, with a little adjustment of hindsight, came to see the October War as a stirring victory. For Israel, knowledge of how near it came to defeat dented a pervasive self-confidence. A conviction grew in higher circles that some accommodation

was needed with the Arabs – a sense shared in a wider world afraid that the quarrel with the Palestinians might risk a nuclear war or shut off its oil again.

IN JULY, I ARRIVED IN TEL AVIV for a four-year stint as Reuters chief correspondent. The Israeli Labour Party, which had governed Israel since its birth in 1948, had been thrown out of government and replaced by the right-wing Likud bloc under its hawkish Prime Minister Menachem Begin.

The decisive factor behind Begin's victory was the swelling population of Sephardic Israelis – Jews of North African and Middle Eastern stock – who took a more hawkish view than did the Azhkenazi Israelis, those immigrants from Eastern Europe who had founded the country. Begin, though himself an Azhkenazi, shared the view that the West Bank should be forever part of *Eretz* Israel, the biblical Land of Israel. He harnessed Sephardic support in this cause.

But the lesson of 1973 had not been lost on Begin. He knew that, to secure Israel's borders in the long term, he must make peace with Egypt. It had become clear to Western diplomats that President Sadat did not espouse the firebrand Arab Nationalism embraced so passionately by Nasser. Moreover Sadat had expelled the thousands of Soviet advisers imported by Nasser and started turning to the West, in hopes of aid to restore a sorely depressed economy. Highly secret negotiations began.

Three months after my Israeli assignment commenced, Sadat stunned the world by announcing he would travel to Jerusalem to talk peace. The move scandalized hard-line Arab states, among which Egypt soon became a pariah, but the Israelis welcomed him with glee. We stared in disbelief at a succession of spectacles – Sadat and Begin side by side at a press conference, Sadat sitting on a sofa chuckling alongside former Israeli Prime Minister Golda Meir, Sadat addressing the Israeli Knesset (parliament).

> … Sadat stunned the world by announcing he would travel to Jerusalem to talk peace.

But negotiations were long and difficult. Sadat did not wish to cut himself off completely from fellow Arabs by totally abandoning the Palestinians in exchange for the return to Egypt of the Sinai desert. He struggled to persuade Israel to allow the

West Bank a strong degree of independence. Begin refused anything more than a very limited Palestinian autonomy with essential power in Israeli hands.

Eventually a compromise left the Palestinians and other Arab states highly dissatisfied, but was presented by Egypt as a big step forward for the Palestinian cause. In 1978 Sadat and Begin signed a peace treaty on the White House lawn under the benign eye of President Jimmy Carter.

Sadat would hold four summits with Begin to seek Palestinian advancement. Begin stubbornly blocked all efforts to prise Israel's grip from the West Bank. Instead he promoted a huge influx of Jewish settlers to make homes on confiscated Arab land. The Palestine Liberation Organization waged continuous guerrilla warfare, directed by Yasser Arafat from his headquarters in Beirut. From south Lebanon, guerrillas lobbed rockets into Israeli towns in north Galilee.

Then in 1981 Sadat was assassinated at a Cairo army parade by Moslem fundamentalist soldiers who opposed peace with Israel. That reminded the West of how the conflict in Palestine now also had the dimension of a holy war for many – especially young – people across the Islamic lands over the status of the sacred city of Jerusalem. The Sadat killing rang alarm bells in Israel, but then successor Hosni Mubarak, a former air force general, opted to continue a policy of peace and aid from America in Egypt.

NEXT YEAR I TRANSFERRED TO CAIRO as bureau chief there. That spring Begin, persuaded by his super-hawk of a defence minister, Ariel Sharon, that a military solution to Palestinian terrorism was possible, sent the Israeli Army into Lebanon to the gates of Beirut. Cairo was quiet, so I was dispatched to help cover the conflict. There I tasted the experience of being bombed by the Israeli pilots I had been used to meeting at cocktail parties in the plush suburbs of Tel Aviv.

Despite a stranglehold on Beirut, Israeli soldiers rarely ventured into the Moslem sector. The wisdom of that was demonstrated by an incident near our hotel, when two Israeli soldiers at a sidewalk café were shot dead by gunmen who disappeared in the back streets. I remember an Israeli armoured patrol touring the streets bellowing in Arabic for the killers to be surrendered. An ominous silence persuaded them to withdraw.

Begin did not directly assault PLO guerrilla strongholds, but he secured their withdrawal. Arafat and his troops were taken off by sea and distributed to a half dozen or so other Arab countries. Then followed a massacre of Palestinian civilians in refugee camps outside Beirut by Lebanese Christian militias, guided to the sites by Israeli troops who were in Lebanon under the orders of Sharon. Those killings dismayed a large body of Israeli opinion, including Begin himself. He resigned, withdrew from politics, and spent his last days in sorrowful isolation. Removal of the Palestinian guerrillas was a hollow victory for Israel. Casualties in Lebanon had been, by their standards, unacceptably high. In a short time the guerrillas drifted back and resumed their war. Islamic militants had a bigger role.

In 1983 I left the Middle East for a posting in Tokyo. I watched from afar such sensations as the surprise peace accord in Oslo between Arafat and an Israeli government led by doveish Yitzhak Rabin – then how an Israeli fanatic assassinated Rabin and the peace process began to unravel. Even as I write, there is fighting again for Jerusalem. Veterans of the Middle East may have imagined in the early 1990s that the conflict would not outlast the twentieth century. Now we know better.

> Removal of the Palestinian guerrillas was a hollow victory for Israel.

# JUST WHAT DID HE SAY ON THE MOON?

PETER MOSLEY

FRONTLINES 27

## JUST WHAT DID HE SAY ON THE MOON? | PETER MOSLEY

# Neil Armstrong and Edwin 'Buzz' Aldrin

stepped on the moon and planted the Stars and Stripes on the lunar surface on 20 July, by America's clocks, in 1969, watched on television by the rest of the world. At Mission Control, reporters were as spellbound as everyone else. Hard to believe, on that day, that when the superpowers began their Cold War race in space back in the 1950s, it had taken almost everyone by surprise. Reuters, I remember, was no exception. I'd just joined as a junior sub-editor, when Moscow Radio's announcement on 4 October 1957 of the launch into orbit of the first man-made Earth satellite, called 'Sputnik 1', woke up a sleepy overnight shift on the desk. What the hell is an Earth satellite? It went, 'Bleep, bleep, bleep'. Enthralled and baffled, we listened to the radio signals from space.

**The Apollo II Moon Landing:
Neil Armstrong snapped Buzz Aldrin
alongside the US flag**
20 July 1969

© Hulton Getty

THE AMERICANS, who had long assumed a technological ascendancy over the Soviet Union, were caught on the wrong foot by Sputnik 1. Their space programmes were under-funded and, even on the drawing board, they had nothing to match the Soviet triumph. Their rockets were relatively puny and prone to fail. Some suspected that in a post-World War II division of spoils, Russia had acquired the best German rocket scientists. Wernher von Braun, who gave the Germans their wartime V 2 missiles, had yet to design the Saturn V Moon-blasters for America.

The Russians soon rubbed salt in the wound to US pride. A month later Sputnik 2 carried a dog called Laika to orbit the earth – then perish in space with no hope of rescue – in what was soon portrayed in the West as a sacrifice on the altar of Cold War rivalry that merely confirmed the callous brutality of the communist regime. As with Sputnik 1, Reuters was ahead with news of the launch, thanks to its 24-hour radio monitoring station at Green End, north of London.

Still greater humiliation for the Americans lay ahead. On 11 April 1961, Russia put a man in orbit and brought him down to Earth again. Moscow celebrated, although, as Robert Elphick, who was the Reuters man there, recalls, the historic event of Yuri Gagarin's flight was almost upstaged by another amazing phenomenon: in an easing just then of Soviet austerity, there were suddenly oranges for sale.

President John F. Kennedy had finally had enough. It did no good to keep denying that the superpowers were engaged in a space race. The only option for America was to win it. Six weeks after Gagarin's flight, Kennedy committed the United States to landing men on the moon by the end of the decade. In the years that led up to Neil Armstrong's walk on the lunar surface, the focus of space reporting switched from Soviet technical triumphalism to the 'human interest' story of America's élite corps of astronauts and would-be moon-walkers.

Reuters, I remember, had the great good fortune to have as a 'string' or part-time correspondent down at the Cape Canaveral

> Six weeks after Gagarin's flight, Kennedy committed the United States to landing men on the moon by the end of the decade.

– later the Kennedy – space centre, a true astronaut groupie. The redoubtable Mary Bubb was a whisky-drinking, chain-smoking, raunchy and raucous woman with an intimate tale to tell about most of America's new heroes. Reuters saw itself then as a family news agency. The staff writer's job when editing Mary's file was to take care – in excising some of the wilder kiss-and-tell titbits – not to lose any of the immaculate technical reportage. Mary knew her spacecraft just as well as her spacemen.

Later, she added to her 'strings' the job of being an agent for the brand of soap that had been chosen to travel to the moon with the astronauts. The task then was to spot the plug for that soap that seemed to slip into most of her stories. Mary also wrote for *Women's Wear Daily*, which may be why she wore new and ever more outrageous hats for every space launch.

An unforgettable story she told me when I was Reuters correspondent in Houston never appeared on Reuters, nor as far as I know in *Women's Wear Daily* or anywhere else. It concerned the flight test of the first 'space loo', which made its debut aboard the Skylab spacecraft. It seemed that the US air force had a sergeant whose bodily control was so well honed that he could relieve himself any place, any time on the word of command. A prototype space lavatory was loaded aboard an aircraft, which was flown through a high altitude parabolic arc to simulate a few moments of weightlessness at the top. While NASA and the military top brass leaned forward for a better look, the sergeant duly did his thing. Unfortunately, an internal fan designed to propel the waste into a container had been wired the wrong way round. The aircraft made an emergency landing.

If only all NASA failures had been as harmless. There was the tragic loss during testing of an Apollo command capsule of Virgil 'Gus' Grissom, a veteran of the trailblazing Project Mercury sub-orbital flights, Ed White, the first American to walk in space, and novice astronaut Roger Chaffee. They were incinerated in a launch-pad fire on 27 January 1967. The American public was spared none of the horror. In 1986, a schoolteacher called Christa McAuliffe, who had been chosen as the first ordinary US citizen to fly in space, would perish with all six others aboard in the explosion of the Challenger space shuttle. Her children would be among millions who watched on television.

IN CONTRAST, MOSCOW preferred to stay tight-lipped about the cost in lives as men challenged the new frontier of space, although there were plenty of unconfirmed reports of catastrophes. The world did, however, discover the fate, just three months after the Apollo disaster, of cosmonaut Vladimir Komarov. He was already a hero for flying the Voskhod I capsule into orbit, when he took up the much bigger Soyuz spacecraft on its maiden flight. It went out of control during his return to Earth and Komarov plummeted four and a half miles to his death. In June 1971, as America pressed home its advantage in space, Russia lost three cosmonauts aboard another Soyuz returning to earth after docking with a space station.

I remember that episode well, because only hours before, I had returned home to Houston from a long reporting trip across the south and south-west United States. Feeling tense, I took a tranquillizer and plunged into a deep sleep. Sometime in the early hours, my wife woke me to say that Reuters in New York was on the phone, demanding quick NASA reaction to the Soviet disaster. I woke up some officials, put together a brief story and telephoned it to New York before going back to bed. I thought it had all gone smoothly, but my wife told me next morning it had taken me more than an hour to dictate my story, speaking at about two words every ten seconds, like a tape-recorder with a failing battery. That knockout pill was more potent than I had realized. The telephone bill was horrific.

A WIDER WORLD SAW NEIL ARMSTRONG'S Apollo 11 moon landing on 20 July 1969 as the epic clincher of America's space race victory, although critics can argue that, in scientific terms, the Apollo programme was a gaudy sideshow and that, by concentrating on orbital space stations, Russia was the real winner.

Alan Paterson, who led the Reuters team, remembers that Houston was in party mood. Unbeatable Texas-sized offers to the press corps included 1000 burgers 'for only 350 dollars'. Texan pride was unbridled when Armstrong and co-pilot Buzz Aldrin landed their Lunar Excursion Module after a tricky final descent and reported, 'Houston,

The *Houston Chronicle* seized on that for a splash headline: 'Man's First Word on Moon: HOUSTON!'

Tranquillity Base. The Eagle has landed.' The *Houston Chronicle* seized on that for a splash headline: 'Man's First Word on Moon: HOUSTON!'

More fun with 'first words on the Moon' was to follow, raising a question that may never be answered. Did Armstrong fluff the most memorable sound-bite in history? The Reuters staffers were sure that they heard him say, 'That's one small step for man, one giant leap for mankind.'

The official NASA version inserted an indefinite article, so that it had him declare, 'That's one small step for a man …' It made better sense. NASA denied the Reuters version and we had to go along with them, and Armstrong later also insisted that the 'a' was in there. Maybe it got lost in the crackly transmission. Next time they play the quote, listen hard and see what you make of it.

SOME ASTRONAUT UTTERANCES were not meant to be overheard. When John Young, commander of Apollo 16 in April 1972, was cooped up in the lunar module with Charles Duke and preparing to get a night's sleep, he thought his Earth link was switched off. 'I got the farts again, Charlie,' he said.

He went on to blame the oranges and potassium he had been ordered to eat to head off potential heart problems during weightlessness. Mission Control sent a signal to warn him that the world could hear what he was saying, but Young must have missed it. 'I mean,' he said, 'I haven't eaten this much citrus fruit in twenty years. And I'll tell you one thing, in another twelve f***ing days, I ain't eating any more.'

The Houston press corps was so delighted with this break from the usual puritan NASA-speak that Young got a gift on his return – a bag of oranges.

Reuters appointed me as permanent staff correspondent in Houston late in 1969, just in time for Apollo 13, the third lunar landing. By then, moon missions had become somewhat routine and news cover was scaled down – until a tank containing oxygen blew up to cripple that spacecraft and threaten to maroon its three crew in space. In terms of column inches and prime-time headlines around the globe, this nail-biting drama was probably an even bigger story than the first lunar landing.

News of the explosion, which happened halfway to the

moon, brought all the New York and Washington correspondents who had decided to 'leave this one to the wire agencies' hurtling back down to Houston. Some reporters missed their deadlines, victims of a notorious 20 mph speed trap at nearby Webster, a township that derived much of its income from traffic fines. Those who argued spent the night in a cell.

> ... as the astronauts' parachute broke through the clouds, cheers and prayers were heard from hardened journalists in the pressroom.

Ace rewrite men from New York took over the story from some of the seasoned American space writers, whose protests were overruled, and some of the copy turned lurid indeed. Newspapers liked that. Reuters London told us in a dispiriting cable: 'Know you telling it like it is, but 'tis cold comfort to be right when opposition getting all the play.'

In the end, as the astronauts' parachute broke through the clouds, cheers and prayers were heard from hardened journalists in the pressroom. One woman reporter fell to her knees in front of the display screen.

More Apollo missions followed, until Apollo 17, the only night launch of the mighty Saturn V rocket that propelled mankind to the moon. A spectacular *son-et-lumière*, its shockwaves pummelled the chests of onlookers and roused the bird life of Cape Canaveral to a false dawn.

But American taxpayers had tired of the Apollo spectacle, with its stratospheric costs, and the programme was cut short. Left with redundant hardware, NASA, satisfied it was no longer trailing in the great space race, felt able to join Russia in a joint Apollo–Soyuz mission. Some true believers saw that as a triumph rather for public relations, as Cold War tensions abated, than for science.

# THRILLA IN MANILA

RICK NORSWORTHY

FRONTLINES 28

**THRILLA IN MANILA** | RICK NORSWORTHY

# Muhammad Ali and Joe Frazier

fought the third and final of their brutal encounters on 30 September 1975. Each had won once. The rubber match was the 'Thrilla in Manila', where Ali, now 33, cockily planned to demolish Frazier. Those 14 rounds in Manila went by in a blur but, looking back, I seem to remember every punch. I'd begun in the news business as a copy boy in Savannah, Georgia, and now as Reuters editor for Asian services, I was in the agency's team in Manila for the greatest fight of the century. I can't remember a more exciting moment in my time as a journalist – but as Ali, stricken by Parkinson's disease, lit the Olympic flame in Atlanta 21 years later, I realized it should have been one of the saddest, too.

**Muhammad Ali connects with a right to the head of Joe Frazier during the ninth round of their famous fight**
01 October 1975

© AP photo

AT THE AGE OF 12, CASSIUS CLAY told a policeman his bicycle had been stolen and, 'I'm gonna whup whoever done it.' The policeman, Tom Buttkins, said that he had better come to his boxing gym in his hometown of Louisville, Kentucky and learn how to fight. Just 11 years later in 1964, when he was 23, he stunned the boxing world by stopping the giant Sonny Liston in the seventh round, depriving him of his heavyweight title. He clinched it the next year, knocking Liston out in round one with a 'phantom' punch that many at the ringside said they didn't see.

As I took a quick breather before the Frazier fight, I watched the crowd of 28 000 pouring into the sweaty Manila Coliseum and wondered how many of them were aware that Ali had fought some of his most crucial and toughest battles outside the ring. In the crowd were President Ferdinand Marcos of the Philippines, his wife Imelda and their entourage. Imelda appeared almost as laid back as Ali and, some said, almost as beautiful.

Clay had joined a black nationalist religious movement called the Black Muslims, changing his name to Muhammad Ali because Clay was his 'slave name' and refusing the draft during the Vietnam War for reasons of faith. Stripped of his title and sentenced to five years in prison, he was a hero to the anti-war protesters, but he had to wait a long time for the acclaim of Middle America. His refusal to serve had nothing to do with cowardice. An earlier champion, Joe Louis, for example, served in the army in World War II and was kept out of harm's way doing exhibition matches for the troops.

After an appeal, the US Supreme Court stepped into Ali's corner and, at the age of 28, he was allowed to seek the heavyweight title again. Boxing journalists said the fastest feet in the business had lost their bounce in his years of enforced idleness in the prime of his manhood, but he regained his title by knocking out George Foreman in Kinshasa in eight rounds in 1974. Now he had to see off Frazier, the man he'd outpointed in that year, but who, in 1971, had whipped him over 15 rounds.

RONNIE BACHELOR AND ALAN THOMAS were at ringside for Reuters. Ronnie was the fastest hand on a story anybody ever met, and he was going to telephone a round-by-round commentary to New York, where they had a new-fangled thing called a video display unit. Computers were beginning to revolutionize the delivery of news, and this new technology enabled sub-editor David Nicholson to transmit his report direct to the world instead of relying on a teletype operator. Alan, who had an eye for detail and quote, crafted colourful 'sidebars' and I sat behind them to edit the copy. Budgets were tight and sports editor Clare McDermott in London fretted when I opened that direct telephone line three minutes early, rather than stay on telex, to dictate the pre-fight 'scene setter', but what a scene we had to set!

During the pre-fight ceremonies in the ring, Ali looked down at Ronnie and Alan, smiling, and said, 'This is gonna be just a workout.'

'This is gonna be just a workout.'

For the last few days we had watched Ali work out. And we had watched Frazier work out. Although nobody sneered at Ali's claim to be 'The Greatest', few thought the Thrilla would be just another workout for either man. After working out, Ali would stroll around naked and talk to reporters while weighing, showering, towelling, being massaged. He certainly was not ashamed of his light brown hairless body. It seemed to many of us that the only time Ali wore clothes was in the ring. But mostly he talked about himself. When he was not talking about himself, he was talking about Frazier, mostly with contempt and derision. 'That nigger has taken too many to the head,' was one of many unworthy and uncharacteristic remarks made by both Ali the champion and Frazier the challenger before and during the fight.

ALI MAY NOT HAVE WANTED TO FIGHT in Vietnam – 'I ain't got nothing against them Viet Congs' – but he certainly seemed to have something against Frazier. Both fighters had reputations as gentlemen of the ring, but there was no doubt that this was a grudge match. One veteran boxing writer close to Ali said that Ali despised Frazier because Frazier was not beautiful.

Ali's pre-fight vitriol had got to Frazier and he responded in kind. He told Ali at a pre-fight meeting in Manila that he was going to beat his 'half-breed ass'. He had got under Ali's skin by calling him 'Clay'.

Others thought the real reason for Ali's apparent hostility was because Frazier was one of the only two people who had beaten him. The other was Ken Norton. But Ali seemed to have dismissed any lessons from the 15 rounds in 1971 when he lost to Frazier, as he smiled and joked in his corner before the fight. As the master of ceremonies went through the introductions of other boxers in the crowd, Ali acted as his own cheerleader, waving his gloves, a signal for his fans to start the familiar chant of 'Ali, Ali'. There were also signs of the real Ali, who usually attacked his opponent verbally, but without bitterness, before a fight. Always the poet, he had come up with:

*This may shock and amaze ya,*
*But I'll retire Joe Frazier.*

RINGSIDERS HEARD THE CHAMPION say to his manager, Herbert Muhammad, 'Don't worry, I'm gonna whup this nigger.'

Ali answered the first-round bell with an arrogant stance as Frazier charged. Many fighters would have quit on the spot, on seeing the menacing expression on Frazier's face as his 200-odd pounds thundered towards the champion, but Ali stood his ground and fired punches at the challenger. The champ seemed indestructible. His old battle-cry and strategy of 'Float like a butterfly, sting like a bee' seemed to have been forgotten, as Frazier stayed in close in an attempt to deprive the champ of the advantage of his longer reach. It did him no good and his legs wobbled two or three times in the first round. In the second, Ali poured on more punishment. Someone from the champion's corner shouted, 'He won't call you "Clay" any more, Muhammad.'

By the third, the crowd began to smell blood. When Ali tired of punching Frazier, he held him at bay with his left arm. The sweat pouring off Frazier flew into the air with every punch Ali landed. At least twice, it looked like the third round could be the last.

But in the fourth, Frazier was punching back, although Ali's shots to the head were still finding their mark. Angelo Dundee, Ali's trainer, felt it necessary to shout from the corner, 'Stay mean, Champ.' When the round ended, Ali glowered at Frazier and called him an ugly dumb chump.

The fighters spent the fifth round in Ali's corner, with Frazier landing punches to Ali's kidneys that could be heard several rows away. Dundee and manager Herbert Muhammad looked worried and seemed to be sweating as much as the fighters. 'Get out of that goddam corner,' Dundee shouted. Frazier was beginning to prove to Ali that despite all those past punches to the head, he was still championship material.

The sixth round looked as though it might be the turning point. As in the first round, Frazier came in close, but this time he landed left-hook after hook on Ali's head. Two hooks with all Frazier's weight behind them caught Ali's jaw and seemed to work their way down to his legs. *Sports Illustrated* magazine reported that Imelda Marcos looked down at her feet and her husband winced. After the fight, Frazier told reporters, 'I've seen walls tumble down behind blows like that.'

Arguments over whether or not Ali could take a punch were resolved when he came out to fight the seventh. Somebody at ringside heard him say, 'Old Joe Frazier, I thought you were washed up.'

'Somebody told you wrong, pretty boy.'

Frazier continued his barrage through the tenth round, when most ringsiders were saying it had become an even match and Ali sat down, head drooping, and looked like he might never get up from his stool. He would tell reporters, 'I felt like I was dying.'

Sports writers love and sometimes abuse the word 'courageous', but that was the word that came to mind when Ali answered the bell for round 11. We realized then that the youthful fighter who wrote poems, floated like a butterfly and stung like a bee had reached maturity, no matter who won.

Ali was trapped in Frazier's corner in that round and blow after blow mauled his face, then he used his reach to bloody the challenger's mouth and batter his eyes. Ali summoned what must have been the last ounces of his reserves in rounds 13 and 14. 'Ya gotta knock him out, Champ,' shouted Dundee as 14 began. 'He's all yours.'

Ali poured on the last punches of the fight. At the bell, the referee guided the nearly blinded Frazier towards his corner,

> Two hooks with all Frazier's weight behind them caught Ali's jaw and seemed to work their way down to his legs.

where his manager, Eddie Futch, told his man he was going to throw in the towel. 'But I want him, boss.'

'You're blind, Joe, you can't see.'

The bell for round 15 never rang and Muhammad Ali was still champion, although he dropped apparently lifeless in his corner. One report of the fight said Ali took 440 of Frazier's wall-breaking punches.

'... the best heavyweight fight of all time.'

ALAN THOMAS WROTE THAT NIGHT, 'Veteran newsmen, witness to the blood (all Frazier's), class (all Ali's), and courage (honours shared) ... rated the searing clash as the best heavyweight fight of all time.' Ali's purse was a guaranteed minimum of $4.5 million and Alan wrote, 'There were those who felt he earned every cent.'

The fighter told journalists again, 'I am the greatest.'

His later fights never made such drama. After ten defences, he lost his title to Leon Spinks in February 1978, but regained it for an unprecedented third time later that year when he defeated Spinks over 15 rounds. He then announced his retirement, only to return to the ring again to meet Larry Holmes in a title fight on 2 October 1980. Holmes knocked him out in the eleventh and Ali retired for good after losing a decision to Trevor Berbick in 1981.

The beatings that morning in Manila when he fought Frazier should have proved ammunition for anti-boxing campaigners. In 1996 in Atlanta, there was more ammunition for them when Ali, the fighter who America's establishment had once reviled, was chosen to light the Olympic flame.

Reuters correspondent John Mehaffe called it 'one of the most poignant moments in Olympic history'. The stadium applauded as the familiar figure was bathed in light, then the applause died to a shocked silence as the ravages of Parkinson's disease on the most dazzling sporting personality of the century became apparent. His left hand shook uncontrollably. By sheer force of will, Ali lifted the torch with both hands, narrowly missed scorching his right arm, and lit the flame. He was the greatest, but he paid a terrible price.

# 'AMERICA CANNOT DO ANYTHING'

PAUL TAYLOR

FRONTLINES 29

**'AMERICA CANNOT DO ANYTHING'** | PAUL TAYLOR

# When Ayatollah Ruhollah Khomeini

arrived unannounced at Orly airport in October 1978 and our airport stringer (part-time correspondent) called to report the news, I got my lucky break in journalism. As a 24-year-old graduate trainee journalist in the Paris bureau, one of my tasks – between weekend duty and night shifts tabulating sports results – was to keep an eye on political exiles who congregated in Paris, plotting revenge or revolution. My contacts included a group of Iranians who drove my colleagues to distraction by calling every day with unverifiable reports of a swelling revolt against the Shah's rule. Among them was Abolhassan Bani-Sadr, an economist who went on to be Iran's first president after 2500 years of monarchy. The day after Khomeini landed, I asked Bani-Sadr if he could put me in touch. We arranged for me to interview the Ayatollah a few days later and thus was born my nickname, 'Ayataylor'.

**Mourners at his funeral struggle to touch the body of Ayatollah Khomeini. The event was so frenzied that eight people died and hundreds were injured**
06 June 1989

© AP photo

THE DOOR OPENED in a nondescript suburban bungalow near Paris and I was ushered into a bare room, lit by a naked light bulb, with a few cushions on the floor. A frail white-bearded old man in dark robes and a black turban sat cross-legged on a Persian rug. There was no handshake, no eye contact. My interpreter motioned me to sit on the floor and the interview began.

Ayatollah Khomeini spoke into a cassette recorder in a faint monotone. His answers fuelled one of the great upheavals of the twentieth century – the Islamic Revolution in Iran.

'We will end foreign domination in Iran. America cannot do anything,' the ascetic Shi'ite Moslem cleric vowed in our interview in the village of Neauphle-le-Château near Versailles.

'Do not be afraid to give up your lives and your belongings in the service of God, Islam and the Moslem nation,' Khomeini

**'We will end foreign domination in Iran. America cannot do anything,'**

told his followers in one of the taped messages that sent millions of unarmed demonstrators into the streets to brave the Shah's army and the hated Savak secret police.

Exploiting a national network of mosques, the Shi'ite cult of martyrdom, and the indecisiveness of Shah Mohammad Reza Pahlavi, Khomeini replaced one of the Middle East's richest US-backed oil monarchies with an austere theocratic state.

THE CONTRAST BETWEEN THE SHAH, whose imperial family flaunted its fabulous petrodollar wealth in gaudy ceremonies, and the Ayatollah, who lived frugally on a diet of bread, fruit, nuts and yoghurt, could hardly have been more stark. Twice a day, the stern old man, his black turban indicating descent from the Prophet Mohammed, crossed the Route de Chevreuse under French police guard to lead prayers and deliver sermons in a blue-and-white tent pitched in the garden of the two-storey house that served as his headquarters.

Students, businessmen, clergymen and politicians flocked to Paris from Iran, Europe and the United States to talk and pray with Khomeini after President Valery Giscard d'Estaing gave him temporary refuge. The Ayatollah listened to moderate advice but held firm to his course, dismissing calls for compromise to avert

bloodshed. 'There will be no compromise with the Shah. Until the day an Islamic republic is established in Iran, the struggle of our people will continue,' Khomeini said in the interview.

He had launched his battle to drive the Shah from his 'Peacock Throne' in 1962–3, condemning the monarch's land reforms as un-Islamic and denouncing the privileges of US advisers and oil companies in Iran. He was exiled first to Turkey, then to the holy city of Najaf in Iraq, before coming to France.

In Neauphle-le-Château, Khomeini was surrounded by a circle of Western-educated aides who went on to play key roles in the early revolutionary governments before being sidelined by Islamic hardliners. A large sign in English and Persian outside Khomeini's headquarters proclaimed 'The Ayatollah has no spokesman'. But the men who assured journalists that Iran would be a liberal Islamic democracy would qualify nowadays as spin doctors.

Bani-Sadr acted as his interpreter and secretary. He was elected the first president of the Islamic republic in 1980, before being hounded from office by hardline mobs a year later, fleeing for his life to the French capital.

Sadeq Qotbzadeh, a former anti-Shah student activist expelled from the United States in 1969, became head of radio and television, then foreign minister. He resigned in 1980 after trying unsuccessfully to end the hostage crisis, and was executed in 1982 for allegedly plotting to overthrow Khomeini. The hostage crisis, when students occupied the US embassy in Tehran, followed a decision by the United States to admit the deposed Shah for treatment for the cancer from which he died.

Khomeini's second son Ahmad, a mullah (clergyman) was his closest aide during his decade at the helm of the Islamic republic and the key link with the students occupying the US embassy. He died in 1995. The Ayatollah's wife, Batul, accompanied him in France but played no public role.

INTERVIEWING KHOMEINI was a strangely impersonal experience. I had to submit questions in writing, and Bani-Sadr translated the written replies before I was admitted for our brief meeting. Khomeini stared at the

**Interviewing Khomeini was a strangely impersonal experience.**

carpet while speaking rather than seeking eye contact with the interviewer.

Some of his statements required interpretation. When he said 'We will cut off the hands of foreign agents', his aides hastened to explain he meant rooting out foreign domination in Iran, not severing limbs. Nevertheless, I felt my hand instinctively feel for my shirt cuff.

As the revolution moved towards a climax, sending world oil prices soaring to record levels, the French authorities who had initially treated Khomeini with caution, warning him three times to refrain from political statements, gave him VIP treatment.

Two weeks after the Shah left Iran on 'holiday' on 16 January 1979, never to return, the Ayatollah, his entourage and dozens of journalists boarded an Air France jumbo jet for Tehran, despite threats by the Iranian government to shoot the plane down.

The volunteer crew had taken on twice the normal load of fuel in case they were forced to turn back. The plane had to circle for more than half an hour over Tehran while final negotiations for permission to land were conducted. A crowd estimated at more than one million people was waiting to greet the revolution's spiritual leader as the Air France stewards helped him down the gangway at Mehrabad Airport.

Ten days later, the remnants of the Shah's last government under the hapless prime minister, Shahpour Bakhtiar, later assassinated in Paris, were swept away in street battles and Khomeini's supporters seized power.

I had my suitcase packed and my ticket for the flight with Khomeini to Tehran when my bureau chief telephoned to say I must yield my place to a more senior Reuters journalist. The editor had decided they could not send a trainee to a civil war. I was mortified but obeyed. I covered Khomeini's departure and went back to night shifts and sports results, watching the triumph of the revolution on television.

Nine months later, when militant Iranian students occupied the US embassy and took the staff hostage, my chance came and I spent eight fascinating months in Tehran covering presidential and parliamentary elections, the aborted US raid to rescue the hostages and power struggles between Islamic hardliners and Western-educated liberals in Khomeini's entourage.

## THE IRON LADY

PETER GREGSON

**THE IRON LADY** | PETER GREGSON

# Shopkeeper's daughter, Margaret

Thatcher, swept to power in a 1979 election to be the prime minister of Britain for more than a decade, was driven by a sense of destiny and a resolve to forge her mark on history. She broke a coal miners' strike to smash trade union power and defied the rules of war to send troops aboard ship against superior land-based air power to recapture the Falkland Islands from Argentina. She enraged the European Union, rebuked Ronald Reagan and chastised Mikhail Gorbachev. As Reuters lobby correspondent, I reported about an 'Iron Lady' – as she was famously nicknamed by a Soviet newspaper – who seemed to think that she didn't just run Britain. She ruled the planet. But the virago image wasn't the sum of this extraordinary person.

**Margaret Thatcher stands out at a
conference of the UK Conservative Party**
12 October 1994

© Reuters. Photo by Ian Waldie

DESPITE HER STATURE ON THE WORLD STAGE, she isn't a big woman. People always talked about her trademark black handbag, but I remember her shoes. She always wore rather tall heels. Once she staged a reprise of the famous episode where Nikita Khrushchev banged his shoe in the United Nations. Demanding a rebate for Britain at a European summit budget meeting, Thatcher suddenly rapped the table with one of her high heels and stridently declared, 'I want my money back.'

She had other sobriquets besides the Iron Lady. She was 'Mrs T' or just 'Maggie'. One wag dubbed her the 'Great She Elephant' after the official title of the senior wife of the King of Swaziland. In a Fleet Street headline she was 'Attila the Hen'. It made a point. The formidable right-wing free marketeer, who vowed to scrub socialism out of the fabric of society, used to portray her policies in the everyday language of a housewife.

Before one meeting in Parliament, an aide arrived to set up the room and found Thatcher there ahead of him – standing on a chair in her stockinged feet, reaching at full stretch to dust the top of an oil painting. 'Women clean properly,' she told him over her shoulder.

And, of course, she *was* a housewife. In their tiny flat at the top of 10 Downing Street, the grocer's daughter from Grantham, Lincolnshire, made the breakfast tea and toast for husband Denis, listening to the *Today* programme on the BBC Radio 4 channel before heading downstairs to her phenomenal workload.

Always well groomed, she made subtle style changes to her wardrobe and her hair on taking office to soften the rigid façade of a warrior queen. Aged 53, she took elocution lessons, to lower her rather squeaky – some said shrill – voice by a good half octave.

THATCHER ALWAYS FLEW ABOUT THE GLOBE in a Royal Air Force VC10, an elderly aircraft by then, although a triumph of early jet-age plane-building. It never rivalled the Boeing 707 as a commercial airliner, because it cost too much to run – but it was robust, over-powered and very British. She adored it. The snag was, that it was rather noisy and, at 35 000 feet, you could not always catch the nuances when she held news conferences on

issues ranging from the Middle East to the Poll Tax. She'd also mingle socially on board, as best as she could in the narrow confines of the cabin, inviting the travelling staff and press corps up front to the VIP section, where they were offered champagne that she insisted on paying for personally, so that it would not be at the taxpayers' expense.

It was always more fun on foreign trips when husband Denis came along. He was a successful wealthy businessman and not at all the buffoon, obsessed by gin and golf, of the satirists. A divorcee and a decade older than she was, he had backed his wife's early political career and he was very protective – he'd tell her when it was time to call it a day and go to bed, and she'd tell him off for drinking too much.

With a twinkle in his eye, Denis did play up to his public persona. On one trip, he came down the airplane aisle to push his head through the curtains to the rear galley – rather than risk the VIP one up front – to ask for a large gin and tonic. 'Make it snappy,' he whispered.

Too late. Moments later came the tap-tap-tap of those high heels. 'Denis – I thought there was going to be *no* gin on this trip.'

'Just tonic, dear, just tonic,' Denis spluttered, downing his drink.

A barrister and chemist by training, Thatcher was always well briefed, whether for summit meetings with other world leaders or the twice-weekly question time in Parliament that the combative Mrs T called the highlight of her week. She had a razor-sharp brain that reminded me of a card index, dealing with questions at opposite ends of the political spectrum with just a slight pause between them, as the right briefing notes slotted into place in her mind, before delivering a comprehensive answer. A workaholic with no outside interests, she normally had only about five hours' sleep a night, ate and drank little, never smoked and reluctantly consented to one week's holiday a year. Even the most loyal of her aides conceded that she had little humour or patience.

Culture and the arts seemed to bore her. On a trip to Istanbul, she swept past the treasures of the fabled Topkapi Palace without

> She had a razor-sharp brain that reminded me of a card index …

stopping and was in and out within 30 minutes. 'That was a bit quick,' I remarked to an aide.

'It was as much as we could do to get her to even set foot in the place and we had to tell her the Turks would be very offended if she didn't,' he replied.

The Istanbul municipal sewage works came next. She spent more than an hour, expressing great interest in the machinery and asking probing questions of the engineers.

SHE DOMINATED HER OTHERWISE MALE CABINET and her Conservative Party with a hectoring style and could be openly scornful of colleagues she had decided weren't up to the job and brutal when she fired them. When she sacked John Biffen – former leader of the House of Commons – he called the regime in which he had served for seven years 'Stalinist' and described her press secretary and trusted lieutenant, Bernard Ingham, as a 'rough-spoken Yorkshire Rasputin who is manipulating government and corroding the standards of public morality'.

She was wary in her dealings with Party heavyweights, although she told Chancellor of the Exchequer Nigel Lawson at a cabinet meeting to get his hair cut, and the only man who really seemed to me to stand up to her was her defence secretary, Michael Heseltine. He stormed out of a cabinet meeting at No. 10 Downing Street in 1986 and announced his resignation to reporters outside. Heseltine quit after a bruising battle – characterized by leaks and mud slinging – over the future of the loss-making Westland company, Britain's only helicopter manufacturer. Heseltine favoured a European consortium to rescue it, while the staunchly anti-Europe Thatcher wanted an alliance with Sikorsky, a US firm.

The affair was nearly a Thatcher Watergate. When the question of whether or not she played a role in the leak of secret documents to the press discrediting Heseltine was raised in the Commons, she was sufficiently worried to tell associates before the debate, 'I may not be prime minister by six o'clock tonight.' But she survived, helped by a fumbling verbose performance by the opposition Labour Party leader, Neil Kinnock.

**The affair was nearly a Thatcher Watergate.**

It was not her only slice of political luck. She was returned to power in 1983 on a wave of patriotic fervour over the recapture of the Falklands and her third victory, in 1987, owed a lot to public distrust of 'windbag' Kinnock.

THROUGHOUT HIS EIGHT YEARS in the White House, Thatcher worked closely with President Ronald Reagan. They were soul mates, deeply conservative, Cold War warriors standing together against the 'evil empire' of the Soviet Union, despite vastly different personalities – Thatcher, who fussed over every nut and bolt of detail, and Reagan, who tended to seem happiest seeing the big picture rather than much else.

In November 1988, she flew to Washington to say goodbye to him, as he was about to leave the White House. The official British farewell gift was an album of recently discovered black and white photos taken when he was in Britain making films in 1940. She presented this to a surprised Reagan in the Oval Office, then patted him on the knee, saying, 'And he's as handsome now as he was then.'

On the flight home, Denis again came to the press section on the plane. In amiable mood over a tincture and playing up again to his satirists' image, he said to me, 'Can't understand what all that fuss was over Ronnie Reagan. Wasn't he supposed to be an actor? Can't say I remember him in anything.'

'What about *Bedtime for Bozo*?'

'Never heard of it,' he sniffed. 'They certainly didn't show that when Margaret and I used to go to the one-and-nines at the Gaumont in Chelsea.'

WITH MY FAMILY AND SOCIAL LIFE suffering from her punishing schedule, I told her at a reception once that I had a serious question to ask, 'When are you going on holiday?'

Came the reply, 'Don't be silly, Peter. We're going to Australia.'

It was one of the most gruelling journeys I ever made – a dozen cities in 14 days, plus side trips to a Cambodian refugee camp in Thailand and a helicopter ride to be winched down on to a British frigate on patrol in the Gulf. Just before we set off, I was settling in my seat in the VC10 when I looked up to find Mrs T standing there. 'Don't get up,' she said, 'I've just come to check that everyone's comfortable, as it's going to be such a long trip.'

On the final leg of the Australia trip, the press corps performed a skit in which I sang a satirical ditty I'd written, called 'We won't go waltzing Margaret Hilda with you'. Thatcher, who hated being reminded that her middle name was Hilda, joined in the chorus and told me afterwards over the champagne, 'I did so enjoy the show.'

MOST OF THATCHER'S CONTACTS with the media were influenced by the redoubtable Bernard Ingham, whom she once praised as the 'best press secretary in the world'. Fiercely loyal, blunt, tough and widely feared, he came to be described as the 'most powerful man in Britain', such was his reputation for making and breaking the careers of ministers in off-the-record briefings to journalists. The dismissal of Biffen had been signalled for months, on the basis of no more than a remark by Ingham that he'd become a 'semi-detached member of the cabinet'.

A burly bushy-browed redhead with a glare that could kill, Ingham didn't suffer fools at all, let alone gladly. But I got on with him, at first due to our shared northern heritage. He once told me, 'In all my years, you're the first lobby correspondent who's ever mentioned Rugby League to me.'

When I was moving on from the lobby, he sent me a hand-written letter on 10 Downing Street notepaper: 'I don't often write to journalists on moving onwards and upwards because I fear that in this conspiracy-ridden world it might be misinterpreted and conceivably damage them.' Flatteringly describing me as 'a consummate, straightforward professional', he added, 'Thank you for putting up with my temper and idiosyncrasies so easily.'

During her years in office, Thatcher was under a permanent death threat from the Irish Republican Army. As leader of the opposition, she had lost one of her closest political friends, Airey Neave, to a car bomb in the grounds of the House of Commons. Later, another, Ian Gow, was killed by a car bomb at his home. She herself only narrowly escaped being blown up by the IRA at the Grand Hotel in Brighton during the Conservative Party annual conference in October 1984. Five people were killed and 32 injured, some crippled for life, including the wife of her cabinet ally, Norman Tebbit. Thatcher insisted the conference went ahead as scheduled and delivered her usual rousing closing speech. Only the next day, in the privacy of family and friends, did she break down and weep.

**During her years in office, Thatcher was under a permanent death threat from the Irish Republican Army.**

Her waning days in office were marked by riots against her unpopular new Poll Tax, a levy on individuals that replaced rates on houses as a form of local taxation. Thatcher refused to phase it in gradually, as her advisers wanted, and it was this lapse of judgment, and sliding opinion polls, that led to rebel ministers' deciding they'd have a better chance of winning the next election led by somebody else. The rebels won the day and a divided Conservative Party ousted Britain's longest-serving prime minister of the twentieth century on 22 November 1990.

Thatcher rarely showed her emotions. She had only wept publicly in office, to my knowledge, when son Mark went missing for six days in 1982, while competing in the Trans-Sahara motor rally. So, a week after her downfall, I read a Reuters story about the woman I'd come to respect, but could never really warm to, that made a poignant footnote:

**Margaret Thatcher bowed off the world stage on Wednesday, drove to a new home in the suburbs and said, 'The first thing I want is a hot bowl of soup.' The former prime minister, 65, blinked back tears when she said goodbye to No. 10 Downing Street, the official residence in London that she and her husband Denis had occupied for 11½ years.**

# THE CENSOR USED A SILENCER

BERND DEBUSMANN

## THE CENSOR USED A SILENCER | BERND DEBUSMANN

# When all else fails to suppress news

that they consider harms their interests, ruthless governments resort to the most effective censorship of all – murder. In 1980, a dark year for freedom of reporting from the Middle East, three prominent Lebanese journalists were killed in Beirut. The BBC withdrew its correspondent and a freelance colleague after they had received death threats. The correspondent of *Le Figaro* of France received one too, and his editors ordered him to leave a city that had for so long been a window on the Middle East. I was Reuters chief correspondent and I was wounded in an attempt to assassinate me.

**Street scene in Beirut:
the debris of a civil war**
03 December 1990

© AP photo

THE PHONE RANG just before afternoon cocktail time at the Nicosia Hilton in Cyprus. 'Sorry to interrupt your holiday,' said Elias Nawas, my number two in the bureau back in Lebanon. 'But there is something you had better know before coming back.' He paused, choosing his words carefully. Telephone conversations from Beirut often attracted uninvited listeners. 'The bureau chief of SANA paid us a visit today, accompanied by two men who didn't introduce themselves. They asked for a photograph of you, a headshot. They said they needed it for their files in case they ever ran a story about you.'

**'They asked for a photograph of you, a headshot.'**

This was chilling news. SANA was the Syrian Arab News Agency, a state organization that faithfully reflected the views of its government. But it did not offer a picture service, nor was it known for writing about foreign correspondents in the Middle East. 'Perhaps it would be better if you postponed your return,' Elias went on. 'Or one might consider not returning at all, in light of recent incidents.'

THERE WAS NO NEED for a more detailed explanation. I knew that those 'recent incidents' included telephone calls to the bureau and to myself expressing displeasure with many of my reports from Syria. The media there were tightly controlled by a government that saw the free flow of information as a threat to its iron-fisted rule. On one occasion, a late-night caller let me know that my coverage of Syrian affairs had so angered the populace that its spontaneous anger was becoming uncontrollable.

The recent incidents also meant the abduction and murder of Selim al-Lawzi, the publisher and editor of the weekly *al-Hawadess*, not long before I left Beirut for my Cyprus holiday. Al-Lawzi had moved his magazine from Beirut to London after Syria sent 20 000 troops to Lebanon in 1976 to quell the civil war there among dozens of rival factions. *Al-Hawadess* had been sharply critical of Syrian rule over large parts of Lebanon. Al-Lawzi flew to Beirut in February to attend the funeral of his mother. On his way back to the airport, gunmen forced him into a car within sight of a Syrian military checkpoint.

A shepherd discovered his body on 4 March in the forest of umbrella pines south of Beirut. He had been shot twice in the back of the head, not an unusual form of death in Beirut. What was unusual was that the flesh of al-Lawzi's right hand had been burned off with acid. The act needed no explanation in a culture rife with symbolism. The right hand is the writing hand and al-Lawzi had used that hand to write articles critical of Syria.

The call from Beirut left me both frightened and furious. Fury won over fear. After a few days of pondering my options, I decided I would not let myself be intimidated by threats and even less by threats about reports that had filled me with professional pride. Since fulfilling a boyhood dream of becoming a foreign correspondent, my motto had been that a story is a story is a story and once you have it from good sources, you file it. No 'if's or 'but's and no self-censoring considerations about whether or not it might offend one side or another, inflame passions, change the world. You get your facts together. You report them.

The two recent stories that had prompted most reader feedback, so to say, from Syria, were datelined Latakia and Hama. The Latakia report described a normally boisterous port city shut down by fear, as explosions and the rattle of automatic fire after nightfall made citizens huddle behind closed doors. The clashes, between government forces and dissidents, were never officially acknowledged by the administration of Syria's president, Hafez Assad.

Even more offensive, in the eyes of the Syrians, were stories from the central city of Hama, reporting on widespread anti-government feeling, protest strikes and riots. One report described how rioters, chanting anti-Assad slogans, ran past the ancient creaking waterwheels on the Orontes river, hefting television sets looted from burnt-out shops. Such news would never be published in the controlled Syrian media, all owned and operated by the government. But Arabic-language radio stations based abroad would broadcast news from agencies like Reuters back to the countries that were under censorship.

ON ARRIVAL IN DAMASCUS from Hama, I was summoned to the office of the Syrian minister of information, Iskander Ahmed Iskander. I had got it all wrong, he informed me. What I had seen in Hama had nothing to do with dissidents of the Moslem

Brotherhood, even less with a loss of control by the government. Some 'criminal elements', the minister said, puffing on his customary Cuban cigar, had been responsible for an outbreak of thievery. Order had been swiftly restored. At the time, the Hama story was barely noticed. Two years later, Hama captured worldwide attention when the *Washington Post* and *The Times* of London reported that hundreds of citizens had been killed in another crackdown on the Moslem Brotherhood that involved tanks, troops and artillery, and reduced much of the city to rubble.

I left Cyprus and returned to Beirut on a Middle East Airlines flight on 15 May 1980. Stubbornness, some of my colleagues would later say, won over common sense. Perhaps, but the Beirut assignment had been the realization of a dream. It had everything I ever wanted – excitement, variety, danger, travel to exotic places, bylines in publications the world over. Since arriving in Beirut from Cairo early in 1975, soon after the civil war started, I had covered a series of big events. One was the hostage drama, when Islamic revolutionaries in Tehran seized the US embassy there. Another was Saddam Hussein's rise to absolute power in Baghdad.

LEBANON ITSELF PROVIDED ENDLESS MATERIAL for news stories. The civil war was officially declared over in 1976, when Syrian tanks rolled into Beirut to enforce a peace agreement signed by the Arab states, most of which had backed one warring faction or the other by supplying money or weapons or both. But the peace was never more than a fragile truce and it soon became clear that none of the political and social problems that had torn Lebanon apart in the first place had been solved, despite a death toll of at least 60 000 in 19 months of anarchy. Instead, new problems were being added – chief of them the ever-growing involvement of Israel – and over the next decade thousands more would die.

The Beirut assignment fitted me like a tailor-made suit. I had just persuaded Ian Macdowall, the chief news editor, to let me stay on for two more years. Back in 1976, I had also firmly rebuffed suggestions that I should leave Lebanon after being shot through the foot and hand while covering a battle in the commercial centre of Beirut. My argument against leaving

for medical treatment in Europe: who had as much experience in treating bullet wounds as Red Cross surgeons in a country at war?

Now, I would not allow threats to dislodge me from a city and a society that inspired a mixture of horror and fascination. Where else could you see people happily sip poolside cocktails served by smartly uniformed waiters in one part of their city, while mortar duels were being fought in another? Where else could you find a pet parrot that imitated the sound of an incoming shell so accurately that newcomers to the bar of the Commodore Hotel would dive for cover? Where else would you complain that your car had been stolen, not to the police, but to the leader of the teenage militia at the roadblock near your office? Where else would it be returned in a convoy led by a tank that once belonged to the Army? Where else could you have dinner-table conversations in three languages with worldly educated people who insisted on calling their fratricidal war 'les événements', as if these events had been wrought by *force majeure* rather than by people? Life in Lebanon had a tinge of surrealism that I found seductive.

> Life in Lebanon had a tinge of surrealism that I found seductive.

The Lebanese capacity for self-delusion must have rubbed off on me after five years in the country. Nothing happened to me on arrival at Beirut airport and nothing on the way to the city, where my then wife, Susan, and I lived in a penthouse atop a building overlooking the port. After a few days without incident, I began to reason that those who had issued the warnings must have decided that killing the bureau chief of an international news agency might reflect badly on the killers. Gradually, the knot of tension in my stomach dissolved, as I walked every day the few blocks from my apartment to the Reuters office on Sanayeh Square. During the height of the fighting, the office had been an island of sanity in a sea of madness. The 30 staff represented almost all of the communities who mortared, shelled and shot each other in the streets. Inside the Union Sanayeh building, they worked in a harmony found almost nowhere else in their tortured and splintered land.

Just three weeks after returning from Cyprus, I found out how false my growing sense of security had been. On 6 June we celebrated the fortieth birthday of Tim Llewellyn, the BBC correspondent for the Middle East. Almost the entire Beirut press corps crowded into Tim's apartment in the Raouche district. The music was loud and the drinks flowed freely. In Beirut, correspondents worked hard and partied hard. The party was still gathering steam, but Susan and I, with Elly Darley, an American who worked in Cairo and had arrived on her first visit to Beirut earlier that day, said our goodbyes about half an hour after midnight.

WHAT HAPPENED NEXT IS ETCHED ON MY MEMORY.
The three of us walk into the street and towards my car, a blue Fiat, parked outside Tim's apartment building. I open the front and rear passenger doors to let Susan and Elly get in. I walk around the car, open the door, climb in, shut the door and bend down to insert the ignition key. Out of the corner of my eye, I see a white car draw level. I turn towards the white car and see the long barrel of a silencer come up. The gun makes a soft popping noise. Pops again, and again. I feel as if a big fist has hit me in the back. The vehicle carrying the shooter accelerates down the road. I get out of my car, stumble across the sidewalk, shout, 'I've been shot,' and collapse.

At the American University Hospital, where I regained consciousness, doctors debated whether or not they should try to extract the bullet that had shattered a rib and was then deflected downward so that it came to rest near the spine. The marksmanship, one surgeon remarked, could not be faulted. Had it not hit the rib, the bullet would have pierced my heart. The sense of place and timing of those who decided to kill me in front of Tim Llewellyn's apartment block could not be faulted either. None of the birthday celebrants missed the message.

I left Beirut a week after the shooting, the bullet still in my back. Llewellyn left a month later, after receiving threats that what happened to me could happen to him, too. That warning came after he reported that President Assad had escaped an attempt to assassinate him. The long-time BBC stringer in Beirut, Jim Muir, also packed up. So did Jorg Stocklin of *Le Figaro*. Censorship by bullet and death threat was working.

I get out of my car, stumble across the sidewalk, shout, 'I've been shot,' and collapse.

# MR SHAKE YOUR MONEY

NICHOLAS MOORE

FRONTLINES 32

**MR SHAKE YOUR MONEY** | NICHOLAS MOORE

# Early in 1980, Reuters was wiring

the world's dealing rooms with its computerized Monitor screens. 'Russia has invaded Afghanistan and we want you to help cover that story,' the editor, Manfred Pagel, told me, 'but then you have a new job – reporting the oil shock.' The Organization of the Petroleum Exporting Countries was holding the world to ransom as it began to ratchet up the price of a barrel towards $40, a record for the century. Refiners were panic buying for fear that the Islamic revolutionaries who'd overthrown the Shah of Iran would throttle supply. Motorists queued at the pump. The crisis ravaged the world's poorest nations with an abiding legacy of debt to the Western banks. Inflation buoyed gold, rattled the dollar and hit stocks. OPEC was cast as the croupier, throwing the dice in the electronic casino of a global exchange.

**Saudi oil minister Sheikh Yamani,
symbol of Arab oil power**
1975

© Hulton Getty

I MADE A BRIEF FORAY UP THE KHYBER PASS to Kabul, where the Red Army had dug in in the Afghan snow, then I was on the road again in another exotic land, driving on a starlit desert night in Saudi Arabia around the edge of the holy city of Mecca to Taif. My companion was a Reuters Middle East veteran, Youssef Azmeh, and he was taking me to meet the man who the tabloid press had demonized as 'Mr Shake Your Money' – the Saudi oil minister and OPEC linchpin, Sheikh Ahmed Zaki Yamani.

I'd worked for Reuters since 1964 but no story could prepare an agency reporter for an OPEC meeting. You never knew, day or night, when a minister might emerge from a cabal in his smoke-laden hotel suite to announce a new rise in the price of petrol, often in terms so cryptic that the Delphic Oracle would have blushed. Agency rivalry to decode and flash these utterances was, as people used to say of rugby football, the ethical equivalent of trench warfare. Dealers timed the competing headlines in seconds.

'If you are the kind of reporter who relies on a communiqué you are going to die,' said Youssef Azmeh, an Arab journalist

**'If you are the kind of reporter who relies on a communiqué you are going to die.'**

with an array of inside-track contacts who had just been named Reuters financial news editor. Soon he and Yamani, in gold-edged robe and flowing headdress, were swapping oil industry gossip as old friends there in Taif.

Anyone less like a demon than Yamani, I observed, was hard to imagine. Born in Mecca and now in his fifties, he was a devout soft-spoken man of elegance. For civility to a correspondent, if he knew you, I'd set him alongside the impeccably courteous Muhammad Ali. Like a Homeric god at Troy, he would sometimes descend to the lobby and lead you aside to confide a hot tip, if he thought that your competitors had wounded you too badly.

'I dream of being a fly on the wall at OPEC,' Youssef said. 'I am told that Yamani draws rings around many of the others, as he munches on pistachio nuts or plays with his worry beads. He is clever and manipulative and in a class of his own. It is ironic that the man caricatured in the West as a greedy shifty oil sheikh is widely seen in the Arab world as an American lackey.'

The truth was that the architect of the 1973 Arab oil embargo against the West – imposed because of its support for Israel – was no longer quite the scourge of the consumer that he'd been then. Unsheathing the oil weapon wasn't in the Saudis' interest now. They were afraid of Communism, and they could also see that high fuel prices simply stampeded the advanced economies to turn down the thermostat and find alternative sources of energy. If you had as much oil as they did, that was crazy.

NEXT TIME I MET YAMANI, he was counselling price moderation in talks at cartel headquarters in Vienna. He wasn't at ease there. Vienna was where a Venezuelan terrorist called Carlos, or the 'Jackal', after the hit man in Frederick Forsyth's novel, had held the OPEC ministers to ransom back in 1975.

The gang shot its way into a meeting and singled out Yamani to die, before Austria cut a deal for them to fly to Algiers, where he was set free. That year he'd also witnessed the murder of his royal patron, King Faisal, by a deranged nephew of the Saudi monarch. I remember that I asked him once about those experiences, when he reminded me that he was a Moslem. 'Was my belief shaken? The opposite. Violent death comes from the bad side of human nature. God gave us freedom of choice.'

**The gang shot its way into a meeting and singled out Yamani to die …**

In Vienna again at the Hofburg Palace, in September 1980, Yamani struggled to end an oil price free-for-all with a new strategy to make things easier for the consumers by indexing gradual price rises, beyond the current $30 per barrel, to inflation and economic expansion. He was soon stymied. 'Nice idea,' said the militant pricing 'hawks', led by Iran and Libya, 'but let's base at $40 and go on up from there.'

'Back to the bazaar,' sighed Yamani. Later, the talks collapsed. Colin Macintyre of the Austria bureau saw Yamani race away in a limousine around the Spanish Riding School and then some aides carried out the red-headed Iraqi, Tayeh Abdel Karim, fearing that he'd had a heart attack in a blazing row with the Iranians, and that night, we learned, their nations had begun mobilizing for their Iran–Iraq war that would last a decade and kill a million people.

WHEN OPEC MET NEXT, marvelled at by bemused Australian surfers on the island of Bali in Indonesia, in December 1980, the Iranian minister had been listed missing, believed killed in battle, so his delegation arranged for a portrait of that unfortunate man to glare at Abdel Karim from his empty chair. Ministers were kept inside a bamboo stockade that was guarded by paratroopers from terrorist attack, and also from the press, although there was a gap. Just a fishpond stood there. After a gala evening of Balinese folk dancing, Yamani was espied on the far side and reporters asked him to call the news across the water lilies.

Tom Thomson was up in the media scrum for Reuters. Yamani esteemed Tom, an intrepid Glasgow Scot who once hid in a dustbin to dodge competitors on a stakeout, and he rewarded him with a bombshell. 'I just raised my price,' he said, 'and you may say that it was by $2 a barrel.'

We had a nice beat. Our Jakarta bureau chief, Colin Bickler, had set up our logistics and he'd seen how a tin shed where the agencies had their telecomms was located 500 yards from the stockade. No walkie-talkies or mobile telephones in those days – so he'd hired us a bicycle.

Next day OPEC announced something that it called the 'deemed marker'. Nobody had heard of anything like that before, nor did the cartel explain. It was my turn to bike the newsflash and I saw to my horror that competitor Bushan Bahree now had wheels too. We both set off for the telecomms shed, pedalling furiously. Then we braked. Soon we went so slowly we nearly fell off. We dispute to this day who blinked, but one of us turned to the other. 'What the —— is a deemed marker?'

I forget what we agreed we'd tell the world, but it was about right. The Saudi price at that time was supposed to be a marker or benchmark that the others, with varying assigned premiums, all aligned their quotations on. Yamani considered his new jump to $32 made a peg to unite around and restore order, but the 'hawks' said he wasn't high enough yet, so cartel spin doctors had tried to paper over the cracked façade. The 'deemed marker' was a polite way of saying that you were free to dream up your own notional value for Saudi Arabian oil to use as your base, and that was how some of the 'sweet' petrol-rich kinds of crude

hit $40 a barrel and even a bit more in that year. The OPEC script was rich in farce.

These record prices soon depressed oil consumption and thereby created the glut that Yamani had predicted. The cartel pricing system collapsed in an orgy of discounting and today's volatile era began, when traders determine what you pay for your fuel in a free market. OPEC changed tactics and tried to steady things by using output curbs to mop up the surplus, but that didn't work too well either, because there was always someone who called his quota unfair and felt free to cheat.

It also needed sellers who were outside it to help curb supply and retrieve prices from as low as $10, but Margaret Thatcher crucially refused in the name of free trade to cut North Sea production. It was another irony, therefore, when Texas felt the pinch, that we heard from diplomats that America was hinting that OPEC should do a proper job of regulating production. I've always suspected that Yamani, were it his call alone, might have let the Western oil companies continue to suffer until the pain got so bad that even the Iron Lady had to buckle.

In the event, however, he arrived at a 1986 conference with proposals for some new criteria to assign fair, enduring cartel quotas. Like a vexed headmaster, he kept the ministers in a Geneva hotel for 17 days, discussing a formula based on output capacity, reserves and – problematically – population. Nations with too few people disagreed with those who had too many, on a weighting to assign to that factor in terms of barrels. 'Do we reward them for copulating?' snapped an Arab, before everyone despaired and, in secret session, scribbled out another set of arbitrary quotas.

THAT FLAWED SUPPLY PACT erased some of the glut and buoyed oil above $10 a barrel, but renewed quota violations kept it weak and volatile. I met Yamani briefly that day. His post-Carlos British bodyguard shook his head as he let me ride the elevator. 'He's very tired,' he said. He was pale. Downcast. Ill. His patrician dream of a long-term stability for world energy was over, and a royal decree a week later when King Fahd dropped him had a bleakness that chimed for me with the cold logic of a new epoch of raw market forces.

'Mr Ahmed Zaki Yamani is relieved of his post.' A saddened press corps, with apologies to Jerome Kern, saluted him with its cartel anthem of 'Ol Man Zaki' that we used to sing late at nights around the bar piano – and oil languished in the bargain basement until 1990 when Saddam Hussein of Iraq invaded Kuwait, part of his *casus belli* being his fury over its flagrant violation of its OPEC quota.

'Mr Ahmed Zaki Yamani is relieved of his post.'

AS SADDAM MASSED HIS TANKS, oil ministers had an ugly meeting back in Geneva again, when Philip Shehadi, a gifted young Arabist and a terrier to get the inside story, told how the Kuwaiti delegates sat petrified in their suite, dreading that anything they said might trigger the Iraqi onslaught.

The new Saudi minister, Hisham Nazer, was taciturn among reporters, but his spokesman Ibrahim al-Muhanna was gold dust. He never lied. After Iraq invaded Kuwait, I trusted him on a story that the Saudis had enough spare capacity to prevent any shortage of oil now that the West had banned Iraqi-controlled exports. Some pundits said I'd gone mad, but it had. Petroleum futures flirted with $40 again, but the speculators dumped them as soon as they saw that US air power could defend those brimming Saudi wells in the Gulf War.

About a year later I was on the road in Saudi Arabia again. This time my companion was Ibrahim. We pulled in at a café for some coffee during a sandstorm and it was time to say that I was too old now to do OPEC. He needed no introduction to my successor; an American journalist called Karen Matusic. She was a tall blonde who played basketball and had reported oil for the competition. By then the agencies were equipped with walkie-talkies in the lobbies and a lot of the Reuters air chat was about who she'd interview next so as to burn us with another rival scoop. 'Sorry, Nick. We can see Neil and Tim, but we lost the Head Girl again. Over.'

At Reuters, Karen would chronicle how the global economic expansion of Bill Clinton's presidency drove up consumption of oil and, as new tension smouldered in the Middle East, there was not too much spare emergency supply on tap this time around. In a new millennium, another colleague, Dick Mably, interviewed Sheikh Yamani at his London consultancy, the Centre for Global Energy Studies. Excessive prices now – he said – would hasten a day when technology dispenses with a need for oil. 'The Stone Age didn't end because people ran out of stones.'

# POLITICS – THE NAME OF THE GAME

CLARE McDERMOTT

FRONTLINES 33

## POLITICS – THE NAME OF THE GAME | CLARE McDERMOTT

# I grew up in Edmonton, Canada,

playing basketball, watching ice hockey and dreaming that one day I'd be a sports writer. That boyhood dream survived an apprenticeship on the nightshift of the *Ottawa Journal* and it came true for me at Reuters. It turned to ashes when, as the sports editor, I reported the 1980 'joyless Olympiad' in Moscow, where America led a boycott by 40 countries in protest against the Russian invasion of Afghanistan. In the half century since I became a journalist, politics gnawed at the Olympic ideal like a hungry rat and, when the politicians stayed away from world sport, it was the turn of money and drugs.

**Flo Jo, who died of a heart seizure on
20 September 1998, ten years after her
victories at the Seoul Olympics**
29 September 1988

© Reuters. Photo by Gary Mershora

NOT THAT I SHOULD HAVE BEEN SURPRISED at how sad I was in Moscow. There'd been other, and uglier, Olympics. I had my background brief to remind me that, in Berlin in 1936, Adolf Hitler refused to congratulate the triumphant black American athletes, among them Jesse Owens, who won the 100 and 200 metres and beat Germany's Lutz Long to take the gold for the long jump.

At least, too, at those unhappy Moscow Olympics, nobody was killed. In 1968 at Mexico City, the Army opened fire on the students who were demonstrating in the main square and more than 260 people died. Then bloodshed ruined the return of the games to Germany at Munich in 1972, when Palestinian terrorists broke into the Olympic village and kidnapped Israeli athletes. Eleven of them died in an airport shootout. Despite revulsion around the world, Avery Brundage, the American president of the International Olympic Committee (IOC) declared, 'The games must go on.'

**'The games must go on.'**

Stephen Parry was the Reuters reporter at the memorial ceremony that was held for the Israelis in the stadium the next day. 'I just choked,' he recalled. 'I had to break off dictating my report. I was full of personal fury that commercialism and political interference had reached the state where murder was condoned.'

I REFLECTED HOW DIFFERENT it must have been back in the pre-war days, in the era of the gifted amateur.

The first sports editor at Reuters, appointed in 1933, was the legendary Vernon Morgan, just such an amateur sportsman, educated at Oxford, who had run for Great Britain in the 3000 metres Olympic steeplechase at Amsterdam.

Morgan, who also played football once for Manchester United, always said that he was inspired as an athlete by the 1924 Paris Olympiad – the games that, in the film *Chariots of Fire*, would immortalize the amateur ideal that he cherished. Known as 'Baron Reuter' to a generation of sports writers, he travelled the globe to report every Olympic Games from pre-war Berlin to Mexico City and, when he retired, he was among the first ten people to be awarded the IOC Diploma of Merit.

Each year, Morgan also decamped to France for the Monte Carlo rally, then to the English classics of the turf at Epsom, Newmarket and Royal Ascot. A jovial Irishman called Claude Richardson, a shrewd judge of form, ran the English racing wire at that time. 'I seldom got much closer to the horses than my bookie's shop behind Fleet Street,' he said.

That was before television helped turn sport into a mass-entertainment industry, propelled by the riches of commercial sponsorship. Up until World War II, Reuters used to classify most sports news as a 'special service', charging newspaper clients at a farthing a word, and later on, I remember, there were some ingenious efforts to get the sports journalists – the 'sweaty literati' as they were called on Fleet Street – to generate some revenue for an impoverished editorial budget.

One such innovation was a racing service from the English racecourses that was delivered to bookmakers in a few of the far-flung corners of the globe over a teletype wire. Nobody had a mobile then, and the law banned telephones of any kind from the race meetings. A clerk tapped in a series of betting 'shows' ahead of each race and the bookie in Africa or Bermuda ripped them off the Reuters ticker, so that he could chalk up the odds. Later it flashed him the 'off', so he knew when to stop taking bets, and then the result.

Improved public telecommunications did away with it in the end. The bookies feared that there might be a 'pirate' out there with a pair of binoculars, who'd hold an open international trunk line to a local punter from some place that overlooked the course. The dread was that, in the flat season, he could call the result of a sprint before the telegraphist had even keyed in the 'off'.

**The bookies feared that there might be a 'pirate' out there with a pair of binoculars …**

I WASN'T HIRED AS A SPORTS REPORTER, but I grabbed many chances to write about sport and early on in my time as a foreign correspondent: and – no – looking back, I know that there really was no excuse for being so sadly surprised at the way that politics intruded on those 1980 Olympics that I'd eventually cover as an editor under a sunny blue sky in Cold War Moscow.

In the early 1960s I was based in Beijing, when we had a

foretaste of what would later be called 'ping-pong diplomacy'. Mao's China built a magnificent new arena to stage the twenty-sixth World Table Tennis Championships. Britain and Australia competed, but the United States and many others boycotted the event.

It was a bizarre moment. I was out there writing about ping-pong, yet at the same time – forbidden to travel beyond Beijing and facing a wall of silence from Chinese communist officialdom – frantically trying to piece together scraps of information about the horrors of drought, famine and the chaos of Mao's Great Leap Forward, when perhaps as many as 20 million people perished.

When Americans eventually did play table tennis in China, in 1971, it was headline news – a signal that the ice was breaking in US relations with the Chinese in a thaw that led, the next year, to President Nixon's trailblazing visit to Beijing.

**The Chinese didn't want Taiwan there and the Arabs sought the exclusion of Israel.**

At an Asian Games in Jakarta, politics kept me up all night, after I'd reported the results during the day, as I doorstepped the hotel where officials were trying to prevent the breakdown of the whole event. The Chinese didn't want Taiwan there and the Arabs sought the exclusion of Israel.

Two veteran journalists, John Davis and tennis writer Aubrey Higgs, led the sports wire at Reuters after Vernon Morgan retired – then it was my turn, with the indefatigable Steve Parry to support me. 'It is jet travel that has led to the tremendous increase in international sport,' Higgs observed as he reflected on a period when the boom in sports news began to take off.

THERE WAS NO ESCAPING THE POLITICS. My first Olympiad in the job was at Montreal in 1976, when the African nations packed up and flew home on the eve of the games in protest at the participation of New Zealand. That country had allowed a rugby team to tour South Africa soon after the massacre at Soweto, in June of that year, when police fire killed some 100 blacks who were protesting against apartheid.

So to Moscow in 1980.

President Jimmy Carter was facing an election. In the revolutionary Iran of Ayatollah Ruhollah Khomeini, militant

students had occupied the US embassy and were holding the Americans there hostage. Then, at the end of 1979, Kremlin ruler Leonid Brezhnev invaded Afghanistan to buttress a shaky new communist leader called Babrak Karmal.

The Winter Olympics went ahead as scheduled at Lake Placid in the United States and they were, I recall, interesting because they were the last Olympic meeting before satellites ushered in an era of real-time television cover.

The Americans were jubilant when they beat the Russians in a semi-final in the ice hockey, but Carter had refused to go and open the games. Instead, he sent his secretary of state, Cyrus Vance, to make a political speech declaring that the United States would not go to Moscow in the summer if Brezhnev didn't withdraw from Afghanistan.

His position hardened as the year went by. In April, a daring US military bid to rescue 53 American diplomats who were still held in the embassy in Tehran ended in disaster, when a helicopter and a tanker plane collided and caught fire in the Iranian desert. This would be one of the reasons why Carter eventually lost the White House to Ronald Reagan.

Carter reiterated his threat that there would be no US team at the Moscow summer games and he stood by it, although he was violating the rules that said that such a decision belonged to the American Olympic Committee, while the IOC stood by its contract with the Russians. The United States lobbied hard and, when we got to Moscow, only 81 nations out of the 120 who had been invited were there to compete.

**So much hard work, and such a damp squib of glory.**

Absentees included West Germany and France, although the British Olympic Association defied Margaret Thatcher and voted to send a team. It was, incidentally, Lord Killanin of Ireland, who succeeded Brundage at the IOC, who declared that 'the Games were joyless'. So much hard work, and such a damp squib of glory. As I say, I should not have been surprised, but how sad it was to be there.

THE END OF THE COLD WAR and of apartheid in South Africa would take a lot of the politics out of sport and – in my retirement – I would watch with delight as the glory of Sydney in 2000 seemed, for a new millennium, to redeem the Olympics from a lot of their recent past. If, though, there wasn't so much politics, so often, now, it was the big money that seemed to dominate sport and, with it, new pressures on the athletes and, inevitably, doping scandals.

I was never, like Vernon Morgan, a deep-dyed believer in the ideal of the pure amateur. Yet the pressures seemed to have got so big.

There was just a terrible pathos in the death in 1998 of Flo Jo, only a decade after she won her triple gold medals at the Olympic Games in Seoul. Only hours after Florence Griffith Joyner died, aged 38, of an apparent heart seizure, there were other athletes who were already reviving rumours that the sprint queen, with her grace and beauty, dazzling body suits and long fingernails, had been 'on something' when she entranced the world with her superhuman speed. She had denied taking steroids or growth hormones and no test ever found that she had been guilty of doping. But in the world where sport had got to, Flo Jo could not go to her grave without controversy at her heels.

# HOW A BUDDHIST LAMA OPENED MY EYES

BERNARD MELUNSKY

FRONTLINES 34

## HOW A BUDDHIST LAMA OPENED MY EYES | BERNARD MELUNSKY

# Some people have stumbled

across God in the Himalayas, or at least meditated their way towards
enlightenment. In my case, there was no flash of divine intervention, but I was
lucky enough one day, on a hilltop close to Tibet, to meet someone whose career
was in making miracles. Our paths crossed briefly. He was doing his job, and I was
trying to do mine, and maybe that was why I was graced with a touch of kindness.
It didn't turn me into a believer, but it confirmed an agnostic in a lingering
suspicion that there are indeed more things in heaven and earth than are
dreamed of in our philosophy.

**Chu Thing, miracle-maker**
February 1982

© author

I TRAVELLED TO SIKKIM in February 1982 to report on the funeral of the deposed *chogyal* or king of that Himalayan land that had not long been merged with India. It was to be an occasion of high emotion, national grief and political expression in this ancient mountain kingdom.

Despite the damp and miserable weather and the fact that the mighty Kanchenjunga, the world's third-highest mountain, was hidden behind storm clouds, it was good to be in Sikkim, a long way from the urban grind of Delhi – though I was still worrying about problems at home, involving a health risk to the household and the deprivation of our only means of listening to Mozart, Beethoven and the Beatles. More of that later.

Sikkim was in mourning and the weather worried its people. It was cold, grey and sodden. Popular belief was that this was due to the *chogyal's* death – in a New York hospital three weeks earlier – but that the skies would be clear and blue for the funeral. Anything else would be extremely inauspicious for the cremation of one who was regarded as a reincarnated lama.

At the moment, it was dismal, and had been so since the former ruler's body had returned to his homeland. The *Sikkim Herald* newspaper reported it was 'as if Nature itself is sharing the grief of the people'. The only variations on the bleak and drizzly days had been some dramatic hailstorms and snow on the invisible heights above the capital, Gangtok.

Devout Buddhists were confident that the weather would lift in time for the funeral, but would it? Just to make sure, the royal family took the precaution of hiring some monks, known as 'weather lamas', to bring out the sunshine. I was told that Sikkim had a number of such lamas to control the climate for big occasions through prayer and meditation.

> Just to make sure, the royal family took the precaution of hiring some monks, known as 'weather lamas', to bring out the sunshine.

Sure enough, the weather began changing on the eve of the funeral. The day itself dawned bright and virtually cloudless, though bitterly cold. The whole scene seemed as clear as a miracle in stained glass. At last, the sun reflected dazzlingly from the five gleaming snowy peaks of Kanchenjunga, a sacred place for the Sikkimese and a spectacle of breathtaking majesty.

Thousands of Sikkimese, including members of the royal family and monks, trudged steeply up from Gangtok to the 8000-foot-high cremation site, while pipes and cymbals sounded in the mountain air. Then I felt impelled, as a reporter, to speak to a weather lama and ask exactly what it had taken to push the clouds to the periphery. I was taken to meet one, outside a tent reserved for him and his fellow oracles. Would one, I wondered, have dared seek an interview with Moses the day he divided the Red Sea?

THE LAMA WAS A SMALL MAN with a pencil moustache and eyes that twinkled behind plastic-framed spectacles. He wore a grey shawl over ochre clothing. Through an interpreter, he told me his name was Chu Thing, that he was 63, had originally come from Tibet and now lived in Gangtok. He had been retained at a fee of 50 rupees – then about £5 – and he had begun praying at the cremation site two days before. He said he'd been studying his calling for 21 years.

'Not everyone can do it,' he said. 'A person has to be blessed by so many incarnate lamas, and read so many holy books.'

> We smiled at each other and he seemed to search my mind.

He couldn't talk long. He had to keep an eye on the weather. The clouds were trying to creep back. We smiled at each other and he seemed to search my mind. When I asked a friend of the royal family about the powers of the weather lamas, she said in a matter of fact way, 'You might find it difficult to believe, but we take it so much for granted. For us, it's a normal thing.' Up there, however, I didn't find it hard to believe in miracles. Especially in the shadow of the Kanchenjunga, revered as the abode of Sikkim's protecting deity.

But the rest of my stay in Sikkim was tied up more in political than in spiritual reporting. India had annexed the land of 300 000 people in 1975, following a vote in the Sikkimese legislature and a controversial referendum approving the merger and the abolition of the monarchy. The *chogyal*, Palden Thondup Namgyal, went into exile alleging the annexation was illegal and unconstitutional. By the time he died in New York, aged 58, on 29 January 1982, he was a tragic and, it seemed, irrelevant figure. Sikkim was the newest Indian state and a very visible Indian Army presence drove home the point both of that and of its strategic importance in bordering Tibet. India's governor in Sikkrim said that, even in the remotest places, he found people were fully aware of the benefits of integration and had been 'clamouring' for that status. But sentiment for the 340-year-old royal dynasty had not faded – and the cremation was followed by an emotional scene, as crowds at the palace called for his son to be crowned. Monarchists said an agitation that began the move to merge with India had been engineered from outside and that voters were barely aware of the issues.

I FILED STORIES ABOUT THE FUNERAL, and the politics and the geopolitics, although I also wrote a feature on the weather lama. Then, very sadly, I left this remote place of such beauty and returned to the densely peopled plains of India and the bustle of New Delhi. For a busy journalist covering South Asia, that should have been the end of the episode. The Sikkim story was done. New flashpoints and tragedies would demand attention. But there was a postscript.

The problems of my own that I'd carried there in my mind were obviously trivial compared to the human suffering wrought by flood, famine and poverty, if of importance to my wife and myself.

In the previous few weeks, swarms of angry bees had taken up residence in our Delhi garden and they refused to leave. Neither family, staff nor dogs could venture outdoors, especially not our elder son, aged eight, who was very allergic to stings. One solution, we'd been advised, was to use some sort of spray. We had baulked at that. It would have made the garden even more of a health hazard for children and animals, and we had environmental concerns. We didn't want the bees dead. We just wanted them far away from us.

Another worry was that our hi-fi set had gone on the blink. No problem if you lived in the West or in many other parts of Asia, but the India of that day discouraged foreign imports and spare parts were hard, if not impossible, to get. Indian radio stations rarely played the music we loved.

As I say, such concerns were scarcely of cosmic import and I probably should not have had them on my mind that day below the snows of Kanchenjunga when I trudged up to the *chogyal's* cremation site, but they were there – and I am in no doubt, too, that the weather lama knew that.

I returned home to Delhi, bursting to talk of Sikkim's scenery, the poignancy of the funeral and the triumphs of the weather lamas. My wife indulged me for a minute or so and then told of some miracles that had happened to *her*.

An old man had appeared at our Delhi home from out of the blue, asking if some bees needed removing. He'd be happy to take them away in exchange for the honey. Deal agreed, he wandered off with swarms of bees following him as though he were the Pied Piper.

Then my wife went inside and noticed that the hi-fi lights were on and that the previously immobile LP was revolving, playing Beethoven's 'Pastoral' Symphony.

We did some calculations and realized that these things had happened at about the same time I was listening to Mr Chu Thing on a hilltop in Sikkim. Coincidence? Maybe. I tend to a belief that we were the recipients of a favour by a kindly oracle, done for a bemused heathen who took the trouble to seek him out and tell the world about the power of faith and the winter tears shed for a toppled throne.

My wife indulged me for a minute or so and then told of some miracles that had happened to *her*.

## APOCALYPSE IN AFRICA

JOURNALISTS who reported the plight of the world's poor in the Cold War era rarely found it easy to wake the conscience of the rich. Some were to succeed. They included cameraman Mohammed Amin and BBC correspondents Michael Buerk and Mike Wooldridge who in 1984 broke the story of the famine in Ethiopia. Amin shot the film that led the Irish pop star Bob Geldof to stage Live Aid and record the hit song 'Do they know it's Christmas?' to help raise millions to send food and medicine to the Horn of Africa.

Mo Amin was killed in 1996, aged 53, in the crash of a hijacked airliner in the Comoro Islands. A Kenyan of Asian descent, he filmed for some three decades for Visnews, the television agency created by the BBC and Reuters, driven by his own passionate belief that Africa's story had to be told. On another assignment in Ethiopia, a rocket explosion killed his soundman, John Mathai, and Amin lost part of an arm. He was soon filming again, with an artificial limb and an adapted camera. President George Bush paid homage to him as 'a man who mobilized the conscience of mankind'. Mother Teresa once told Amin, 'God sent you for this hour.'

To the war and the famine that journalists like Amin travelled Africa to report, the later twentieth century added its new plague of AIDS. Reporters quoted Lester Brown, the chairman of the Worldwatch Institute and a man with an eye for the kind of statistic that, like a picture, can tell a story even in an age that has been made numb by headlined horror. He observed that AIDS was killing 250 Africans each hour, or as many people as would die if 15 jumbo jets were to crash every day. The schools of Africa became orphanages. There never were enough hospitals. Now, in some cities, victims of AIDS occupied more than half the few beds.

If Africa was a cockpit of misery, as the population of the world rose through 6 billion, it had no monopoly on distress. Even as the poor went hungry to bed, the rich choked on the fruits of affluence. Another of those graphic statistics that reporters quoted from the Worldwatch Institute was that, for the first time in history, the planet had as many overweight people – or 1.1 billion of them – as there were underfed.

**This photo, taken in Korem, Ethiopia, was among those that alerted the world to the famine in Africa**
16 October 1984

© Mohammed Amin

# 'MRS GANDHI IS NO MORE WITH US'

BRIAN WILLIAMS

FRONTLINES 35

## 'MRS GANDHI IS NO MORE WITH US' | BRIAN WILLIAMS

# The news outlook that we sent from

New Delhi on 31 October 1984 was brief and routine. 'Very quiet day. Only news likely to be from visiting England cricket team.' The message would hang on the wall in the Asia newsroom in Hong Kong for years to come as testimony to how – even if the England cricketers are in town – you never know when news is going to break. About an hour later, Sikh bodyguards assassinated Prime Minister Indira Gandhi. More bloodletting followed, as Hindus took revenge on India's minority Sikhs, then a poison gas leak at Bhopal turned out to be the worst industrial accident the world had yet seen.

**Indira Gandhi's funeral pyre is lit by her son, Rajiv**
03 November 1984

© AP photo

LOOKING BACK ON THE PAIN OF THOSE DAYS, the image in my mind is of the opening scene of a 1950s Hollywood historical drama, where the screen is filled with a map that slowly dissolves into blood or flames.

I'd arrived in India a year earlier, an Australian with 15 years' experience of Reuters under my belt, to the new post of chief correspondent for South Asia, to be wakened in my hotel on my first night there by a telephone call. Najmul Hasan, a journalist from my bureau had been killed by a land mine on an assignment in Iran to cover the war with Iraq. Najmul left a wife, Barbara, and two young children, who, when I knocked on their door with his distraught elder brother to tell them he was dead, instinctively rushed into each others' arms as if to ward off the evil news.

The memory of Najmul, a gifted reporter, the gentle thoughtful son of a leading Moslem historian, and the strength of Barbara and her family, were, I believe, a source of support for me and my young bureau in covering the tragedies that lay ahead.

Another memory spurred us on. In 1948 the doyen of Reuters foreign correspondents Doon Campbell, and an Indian reporter, P. R. Roy, had broken the news to the world of the assassination of Mahatma Gandhi. Indira Gandhi was not, incidentally, a relation. She was the daughter of Prime Minister Jawaharlal Nehru.

Ours was an untested bureau. Indian journalists Ajoy Singh, Moses Manoharan and Chaitanya Kalbag had never reported abroad for Reuters, and my expatriate colleagues – John Fullerton, Frances Kerry and Mark O'Neill – were on their first assignments. But in the end I think that lack of experience was a strength. India is a country that needs boundless energy, and almost innocence, to report.

NOTHING TO ME SUMS UP THE DISBELIEF and shock at Indira Gandhi's death better than the way India announced it. 'Mrs Gandhi is no more with us,' said the flash on the Press Trust of India news agency. Not 'Mrs Gandhi dead' or 'shot' or 'assassinated'. 'Mrs Gandhi is no more with us.' It was as though the enormity of it was just too dreadful to say the words

> It was as though the enormity of it was just too dreadful to say the words outright and aloud.

outright and aloud. It was a hearkening back to ancient times, when the bearer of ill tidings was also cursed or put to death.

She had herself, just weeks earlier, spoken of how threats to her life were part of governing the world's second most populous nation. 'I am not afraid,' she said. 'I am frequently attacked. Once, a man poked a gun at me. Another time someone threw a knife. And then of course there are always the stones, the bricks, the bottles – especially at election time.' But perhaps she had seen an evil omen of her own, because she had also, aged 66, just made her first will.

IT WAS AJOY SINGH who alerted the world to the seriousness of the initial reports that had come in about an incident at Mrs Gandhi's home. He managed to corner a doctor friend in the crush of journalists besieging the hospital where she had been taken, who told him that Mrs Gandhi had been struck by seven bullets – four in the lower stomach and three in the chest. She died two hours after the shooting.

We would learn that she was shot down by two of her trusted Sikh bodyguards, while she walked serenely through a flower-laden garden to her office to meet British actor Peter Ustinov. Without a word, as she approached a garden gate, one opened fire with a pistol and the other with a Sten gun. They then quietly – almost contemptuously in the words of one witness – surrendered to other bodyguards.

Nearly every morning, I had driven past the prime minister's residence, at almost the time she was shot, to drop my young children, Joe and Lily, at their school. From that fateful day until I left India three years later, I never used the same route again, instead taking a road that avoided any sight of the place, because of an irrational fear or superstition that evil still lurked there.

Mrs Gandhi wrote her own death warrant four months before the shooting, during a rebellion by Sikhs who wanted an independent state in the Punjab, when she ordered troops to attack the Sikh faith's most holy shrine, the Golden Temple in Amritsar, to root out extremist killers who'd been offered sanctuary there. It was like ordering a battalion of British soldiers from Northern Ireland, all chosen because they were Protestants, to storm the Vatican.

I think we all knew that there would be a terrible retribution, but most people thought the target would be her older son, Rajiv, reluctantly drawn into politics after his younger brother, Sanjay – her chosen heir – died in an air crash. The popular wisdom was that Rajiv, a 40-year-old airline pilot married to an Italian, had persuaded his mother over her misgivings to attack the Golden Temple.

The attack led hundreds of Sikhs to desert from the army, but Mrs Gandhi went out of her way to offer an olive branch to that most warlike of the offshoots of Hinduism, rejecting advice from security chiefs to replace Sikhs in her bodyguard. Months later a well-placed Indian official told me of an incident, several weeks before her murder, when she flew by helicopter to an Army outpost in the glaciers of Kashmir, where Indian and Pakistani troops faced each other on a tense frontline. The commander of the unit radioed the pilot that she should not land, because he could not guarantee the loyalty of his Sikh soldiers. An incensed Mrs Gandhi ignored the advice, then ordered the officer to be replaced.

WITHIN HOURS OF HER DEATH, Hindu mobs began attacks on the Sikh minority across India. The toll in several days of madness was nearly 1500 killed, thousands injured and 25 000 Sikhs turned into refugees. They were the worst communal riots since the Hindu–Moslem slaughter at the time of the partition of the India of the British Raj into present-day India and Pakistan. The Sikhs had then sided with the Hindus. There was even an echo of that mayhem in the story we were told, by a British woman doctor on holiday in India, of how a train in which she was travelling was stopped and ten Sikhs singled out from the passengers and hacked to death with knives and hoes.

Communal clashes were never far below the surface in such a huge and overpopulated nation, where religion was a defining way of life, but what seemed terrifying was that, for days, the mainly Hindu police and other authorities seemed either powerless to act or ready almost to turn a blind eye.

Our reporters were on the streets 24 hours a day in the thick of the fighting and looting in Delhi, while police stayed away. We kept a staffer day and night on the office roof with a pair of binoculars to spot the latest clashes. A puff of smoke would rise from a section of the city, or at night a pinpoint of flame as property blazed. I remember looking out and counting 30 'hotspots' at once in the general breakdown in law and order.

Chasing the smoke, our reporters, a fit bunch, used hired bicycles to enter narrow alleyways and weave their way round police roadblocks. Office manager, Surinder Chugh, a Sikh, telephoned to say how his community had formed vigilante groups, armed with bottles of petrol, shotguns and cudgels. I remember the fear I felt when I made a quick trip home for a change of clothes after several days sleeping at the office and found myself on a street littered with rocks and burning tyres yards from my door. I have never felt such relief as when I saw my children playing unconcerned in the garden.

> We kept a staffer day and night on the office roof with a pair of binoculars to spot the latest clashes.

WE ALSO HAD TO FIGHT on another front. The government hinted we should tone down our reports and I got a blunt warning from an information ministry official, who hinted that our communications could be cut. It was not unexpected. Indian governments fear that media reports about communal violence can lead to revenge killings, and I understood the sensitivity. I'd laid down rules that we would only report what we saw or learned from credible witnesses, and I now read all our stories again to be sure we'd kept those rules. But these were passion-laden times and I wanted to be happy we were cleaner than clean, so I decided to call the Asia editor, Ian Macdowall.

Ian was a legend, a journalists' journalist in a great tradition of Scottish newsmen. A man of few words – many unintelligible because of his Highland accent – he was loved and feared for his intellectual and personal honesty, as well as his passion for Reuters. You could disgrace yourself getting tired and emotional at a company function and just earn a wry shake of his head next morning, but spoil a story by laziness or bad writing and there'd be an acerbic Macdowall thunderbolt on the message wire.

Another thing about Ian was that no one – in or outside Reuters – was allowed to mess with his correspondents in the field. He'd been there himself in places like Beirut. He flew into Delhi that evening! 'The file looks good to me,' he said.

Next day we met India's top foreign ministry official when, once again, there was the indirect threat of possible 'unavoidable' communications problems. Ian spoke with as much care as any diplomat. He said he realized how difficult things could be. Then he added, 'Of course, Foreign Secretary, if communications became totally unreliable, we would have to move our reporting of events in India as well as our South Asian headquarters to a neighbouring country.'

He never said 'Pakistan' – and I think he was bluffing, although you never knew with Ian – but the message was taken on board and the meeting ended with the official accepting that perhaps there had been an overreaction by the government.

Mrs Gandhi was cremated a week after her death, with barely a Sikh turban to be seen among the millions who mourned her. The handsome widow with the white streak in her dark hair had led India for most of two decades, during which it exploded a nuclear device and put a rocket in space, and saw off Pakistan in a 1971 war, when she helped its Bengali eastern part become the independent Bangladesh.

Her son Rajiv succeeded her and soon called an election, and it was when we were covering the campaign that, on another glorious Indian summer day, the tragedy of Bhopal happened.

I WAS TRAWLING THROUGH the Indian news agency file, when my eye was caught by a short routine story that said several people were in hospital with breathing difficulties after foul fumes spread over the city. Some sixth sense nagged at me to read it again. The last paragraph mentioned, almost as an aside, that several hundred people were awaiting treatment in the grounds of the main hospital. I got a reporter to call the Bhopal police, while Ajoy Singh said he knew a woman doctor at the hospital there.

The police dismissed the report as a routine pollution scare, and I'd gone back to writing about the election, when Ajoy gestured wildly from the telephone as he spoke to the doctor. 'Scores of people dead ... poison gas leak from Union Carbide plant,' leapt at me from his scrawled notes. Sourcing is everything in

**'Scores of people dead ... poison gas leak from Union Carbide plant'**

Reuters and we had the perfect source: a named expert witness who was known to us. We ran an urgent story.

Two hours later, though, I began to get nervous. There was still only the brief early report on the Indian wires and then I got a call from my good friend Mark Tully of the BBC. 'Brian, are you sure this Bhopal story is right? Is it really as big as you guys are saying? I'm not getting anything on it,' he said. We had to wait another hour before the Indian news agencies matched our report. They'd been silent, we learned, because their own staff were affected by the gas leak.

The gas that escaped from the Union Carbide insecticide plant in Bhopal, a city of nearly one million people, was methyl isocynate. It killed nearly 3000, and more than 10 000 needed intensive hospital care. Investigations showed the escape happened while unskilled workers were cleaning a tank that was two-thirds full of the gas and damaged an escape valve. Gas escaped for nearly two hours, as workers fled, and nothing was done to shut off the leak until senior managers arrived.

In the race to get to the scene, the first flight from New Delhi to Bhopal was at 6.30 the next morning. India's railways may be grimy and old, but they run on time, so we put Moses Manoharan, a street-wise journalist who I knew would get through, on a train – and he reached Bhopal early next day, before the rest of the foreign press, to write a story that got a front-page splash in the *New York Times*.

'It is a nightmare Brian,' he shouted down the telephone from the station. 'There are people dead on the platforms and there is vomit everywhere.' It was a horrific story. Before Bhopal, I think, and then the Chernobyl nuclear catastrophe in the Ukraine, we simply couldn't guess at the scale of the kind of disaster that can happen when you put science in a factory and then somebody makes a mistake.

MAYBE IT'S JUST A FUTILE ATTEMPT to see something positive in the thousands of senseless deaths after Indira Gandhi's assassination and at Bhopal, but I believe India came of age in those days. There had been a belief that it could only be held together by the force of a powerful personality. There'd been Mahatma Gandhi, then Nehru and then his daughter, the woman known as 'Mother India' herself. In the end, India's institutions held together – parliament, the army, the police, and the bureacracy reasserted themselves, in the name of law and order. It seemed that Indians learned that it was not who led the country that mattered, but that the nation should go on.

# FEAR AT THE WHEEL

ALLAN BARKER

FRONTLINES 36

## FEAR AT THE WHEEL | ALLAN BARKER

# The 1980s belonged to Ronald Reagan

and Margaret Thatcher. It was the decade of the ascent of the free market. But a spectre would haunt the West's affluent 'baby boom' generation, as its pension fund and other life savings sloshed around the exchanges in quest of a safe inflation-proof haven. Could there be a replay of the 1929 Wall Street Crash? I'd been in Washington for Reuters when President Richard Nixon cut the dollar's link with gold in 1971 to loose the genie of fluctuating exchange rates, but nothing could match the drama of the collapse of share prices on Black Monday, 19 October 1987, when as editor of Reuters Business Report – a business wire for the media – I found I was in the eye of the worst storm to hit global finance in more than half a century.

**Dealers on the floor of the New York Stock Exchange are caught up in the frenzied selling on Black Monday**
19 October 1987

© AP photo

IT WAS A DAY WHEN FEAR TOOK CHARGE as the driver of the stock market and thrust greed to a back seat. The grim arithmetic that made history has been recalled every subsequent autumn as an admonitory tale of what can happen when optimism and trading excesses blend into an explosive cocktail.

On Black Monday, the Dow Jones Industrial Average of 30 leading US stocks dropped 508 points to close at 1738.74. As a percentage – a shocking 22.6 per cent – it was the biggest one-day slump of all time. It compared with 28 and 29 October 1929, when successive losses of 12.8 per cent and 11.7 per cent shattered confidence to herald the Great Depression.

'It's the nearest thing to a meltdown that I ever want to see,' said John Phelan, the chairman of the New York Stock Exchange.

The shock waves rippled out from Wall Street. Exchanges around the globe took their cue from New York, as they usually do, and also suffered huge drops. Big losses hit Wall Street brokerages that had got into a lucrative habit of trading for their own account, even as small investors were stunned to see the value of their portfolios halved or worse. When they tried to call their brokers with sell orders, they were often met with engaged signals from overloaded telephone systems. The little guy couldn't even bale out.

**The shock waves rippled out from Wall Street.**

'Don't panic – the economy is fine!' So went the message to him from the Reagan White House on that desperate day. Experts assured us that 1987 did not equal 1929. But it has since been revealed that it was very much touch and go – certainly on the day after Black Monday, before the market suddenly turned up.

Market insiders, we have also learned since then, knew at the outset that it was going to be a terrible trading session after months of severe volatility. But predicting the stock market is hazardous, so as 19 October dawned, few would bet on a fall rather than bounce from the recent setbacks. Still, the previous week had seen heavy selling and we were apprehensive as we arrived at our office in midtown Manhattan on that fine Monday morning, under a blue sky and in the crisp air of New York in the autumn. It had been a blue sky like that for the Cuban missile crisis 25 years earlier, I recalled.

As an editor, I was several steps back from the frenzy that broke out on the floor of the Stock Exchange and in the pits of the Chicago futures and commodity exchanges, but with the Dow sliding as we had never seen before, it needed strong nerves to stay calm. It was going to be an acid test of our reporting resources in New York and also in such other financial centres as London, Tokyo and Frankfurt. Reuters Monitor screens carried headline news, stock quotes and indices to thousands of traders in dealing rooms around the world. The copy that we also filed on wires to the newspapers, radio and television media helped tell the story to millions of other people – including those stricken small investors. Money news on television was in its infancy. To help our writers, we tried to keep the office quiet. There was none of the hubbub of the trading floor that maybe helps ease the tension.

AFTER HEAVY FALLS IN TOKYO and in Europe before New York opened at 9.30 am, and a negative story in that day's *Wall Street Journal*, drawing some parallels with 1929, the market was soon in deep trouble. It was down 200 by 11 am. Today's electronic exchanges often see volatility like that. Back in 1987, it was drama.

Sell orders were so heavy that by 10.30 am a total of 175 NYSE stocks, including IBM and Exxon, were not trading due to stock imbalances between sell and buy orders. Specialist firms assigned the task by the Exchange of ensuring orderly marketing in assigned stocks were overwhelmed. Then confirmation that this was no ordinary slide came around noon. The chairman of the Securities and Exchange Commission, David Ruder, disclosed in response to press questioning that the idea of a brief halt in trading to see if things would calm down had been discussed with NYSE officials. That alarmed traders, who feared their business would be halted, possibly indefinitely.

A factor that added to the jitters was news from the Middle East that the US Navy had shelled two Iranian offshore oil platforms in retaliation for what it called unprovoked attacks on American-registered Kuwaiti vessels in the Persian Gulf. The move was seen as a warning to Iran, at war with Iraq and becoming increasingly dominant in the Gulf region.

The markets deteriorated rapidly as the 4 pm end of the trading day approached in New York, with the deficit on the Dow growing by more than 200 points in the last hour.

The futures stock index trading pits in Chicago were in chaos.

'It is out-and-out panic. I have never seen anything even close to this,' said Trude Latimer, a stock expert at Josephthal & Co.

At 3.42 pm Eastern time, we reported the Dow was down 390 points. Ten minutes later it was down 400. The index fluttered erratically for several minutes at the close and at 4.07 pm a Business Report bulletin said the Dow ended down by a record 507.99.

THE STOCK EXCHANGE TAPE that records trades was running two hours late at one point, and the day's volume hit an unprecedented 604 million shares, so it was early evening before the fall was settled at 508 points. Even that was not officially confirmed until next day. Blue-chip stocks ended with dramatic losses. IBM was down $31 to $104, General Motors down nearly $14 at $52.25 and Exxon down $10 to $33.50. Bank of America was down to almost $8 and Citibank was around $20.

For Reuters, Mike Clancy reported 'bedlam on Wall Street' from Manhattan bars, as analysts told Arthur Spiegelman it was now a bona fide crisis. London anchor Ron Howard, a cautious chief sub, pursed his lips at a headline that spoke of 'carnage' in world markets. Then he looked again at the indices. He hit the transmit button on it.

Says top financial writer Dick Satran, 'It was the closest I ever came to covering a war in 18 years at Reuters.' Our job now was to set events in perspective.

Americans are an optimistic people, but every decade, or so it seems, their faith in the stock market can build up a head of steam that worries central bankers. That happened again in the mid-1990s, when Federal Reserve Chairman Alan Greenspan warned investors against 'irrational exuberance'. Economist John Kenneth Galbraith, chronicler of the 1929 Wall Street Crash, sees a tendency for stock prices to get ahead of economic reality.

THE 1980S HAD BEGUN BADLY when Paul Volcker, who was then the head of the US central bank, used monetarist policies, with interest rates that at one stage exceeded 21 per cent, to throttle rampant inflation. OPEC had just hit consumers with a $40 barrel 'oil shock'. But Volcker later eased up and a bull market in stocks began in August 1982.

Wall Street was soon making big money. A wave of corporate mergers saw top firms plunge into risk arbitrage, which paid off handsomely when takeover targets were correctly identified in advance. Michael Milken exploited low-yield high-risk junk bonds that financed corporate leveraged buyouts, but saddled the new owners with heavy debt. In 1987 Milken earned $1.5 million a day. Insider-trading scandals and the disgrace of arbitrage king Ivan Boesky, who paid the government $100 million to settle charges against him, took the cream off the story, but Wall Street brokerages continued to make profits trading stocks for their own account. They discovered program trading, using computers to buy and sell portfolios of stocks. This was widely blamed for the excesses that contributed to the market crash.

THE STOCK MARKET HIT A RECORD 2722.42 on 25 August 1987. Then selling began. People were unnerved by huge US trade and budget deficits, a weak dollar and rising interest rates again in the US and elsewhere. In early September, Greenspan, new to the top job at the Federal Reserve, raised a key rate by half a percentage point, which was seen as a warning shot that he would not provide cheap money to ensure a Republican victory in the 1988 presidential election. Stock markets are usually vulnerable when interest rates are rising.

In the week before Black Monday, the yield on 30-year US Treasury bonds had for a time exceeded 10 per cent – historically very high – reducing the investor appeal of stocks versus bonds. Stock market confidence was then further battered when data on Wednesday 14 October showed the US monthly trade deficit

'It is out-and-out panic. I have never seen anything even close to this.'

They discovered program trading, using computers to buy and sell portfolios of stocks.

had narrowed by less than had been expected to $15.68 billion. There was talk in Congress of drafting a retaliatory trade bill to stem imports from other countries and a nervous market saw shades of 1930s-style protectionism.

On Sunday 18 October US Treasury Secretary James Baker called vigorously on television for a cut in German interest rates to help the weakened dollar – comments that raised fears that international monetary cooperation was breaking down and were later to draw criticism that he had helped to precipitate Black Monday and that stomach-churning 22.6 per cent drop on the Dow.

ALTHOUGH BLACK MONDAY made the biggest headlines, it was really the next day – the Tuesday – that produced the most drama behind the scenes. That was the moment that could have brought the market to its knees. Few people knew then how dangerous it all was.

Greenspan had been in Dallas for a speech on Black Monday, but headed back to Washington. A major central bank figure in the crisis, we now know, was E. Gerald Corrigan, the chairman of the Federal Reserve Bank of New York. He was in close touch with the NYSE and with the key banks to ensure that the credit taps were not turned off as they had been, with disastrous consequences, in 1929.

Everyone was certainly looking for a Wall Street bounce on Tuesday morning – and an hour before the opening bell, the Fed boosted confidence with a statement in Greenspan's name promising to supply the market with the liquidity needed to overcome the crisis.

**Everyone was certainly looking for a Wall Street bounce on Tuesday morning ...**

But the backdrop elsewhere was bleak. The shock from Black Monday had spread rapidly around the world. The price of gold, a refuge in tough times, soared to $481 an ounce in London. Among stock exchanges outside the Americas, the London 100-share FTSE index had dropped 10 per cent on Monday and was down 11.6 per cent on Tuesday. Tokyo was down 14.7 per cent. Hong Kong had closed for the rest of the week after a slide on Monday and would plunge 33 per cent

when it reopened. That would later be cited as proof that the NYSE was right to keep on trading despite the bad omens.

The Dow swung violently in the morning. It soared 100 points in an early buying spree, then it faltered and hit a low for the day of 1708 at noon. Buying by New York firms in the Chicago futures pits had also failed to stop an alarming slide in futures prices.

Around 11 am Eastern time, the NYSE asked member firms to refrain from using its order system for computerized program trading, and brokerage firm Goldman Sachs said it would make $1 billion of its capital available to ailing mutual funds. Then the stock and commodity exchanges halted all trading in index options, a key element in program trading.

Tim Metz, in his book *Black Monday* (William Morrow & Co. 1988), says the crisis was at its worst around 12.30 pm on Tuesday. Several specialist firms, entrusted with ensuring an orderly market in specific shares and whose finances had been hard hit, pleaded with John Phelan, as chairman of the New York Stock Exchange, to close the markets. Some specialists trying to draw down new credit later reported they were then getting scant help from their bankers. Ten of the Dow 30 stocks were not trading as market activity slowed.

The turnaround that saved New York came out of the blue at around lunchtime. The Dow began to move, at first very slightly and then more positively. By 12.40 pm several big stocks like Philip Morris, American Express and General Electric had gained several dollars, while General Motors shot up more than 15 per cent between 12.30 and 1 pm. The Dow gained more than 115 points in that half an hour.

WHAT THE TRIGGER WAS has never been clear. Metz suggests the turnaround was orchestrated in the Chicago futures pits. The market authorities later said they could not explain the trading and it was just a natural market turn. A *Wall Street Journal* study of the crisis said that, by 1 pm the banks had finally pledged their support after reassurances from the Fed, giving specialists and other firms the confidence to execute orders. Soon a series of share buybacks by major companies, flashed on Reuters and Dow Jones after their chairmen had been encouraged to act by White House Chief of Staff Howard Baker, provided a fillip to

**Public pressure soon led the big brokerage firms to abandon or curtail computer program trading.**

fragile confidence. The blue-chip Dow industrial index ended Tuesday up 102 points. On Wednesday it rose 187. Lessons were learned from the crisis. Public pressure soon led the big brokerage firms to abandon or curtail computer program trading. Market circuit-breakers were introduced to slow or interrupt trading when the Dow falls, or rises, sharply. The market remained nervous and highly volatile into November after the crash, and few small investors who snapped up bargains in the crisis saw much of a return for a long time – but they did benefit later and, for those who were patient, the crash was a golden buying opportunity.

Many Wall Street firms later reported hefty losses in October. E. F. Hutton was so badly hurt it was soon taken over and L. F. Rothschild & Co. posted a fourth-quarter loss of $128 million before being acquired by a Kansas savings institution. Job losses on Wall Street totalled 12 000 by the following January and the New York economy was badly dented for a year.

From a longer perspective, the crash of '87 was just a blip in the upward curve of a bull market that lasted from 1982 through the dawn of a new century. On the charts it can be seen merely as a violent correction. It did not lead to a world recession – and by January 2000 the bulls had taken the Dow as high as 11 722. Technology shares of the new economy soared to the stratosphere and the lessons of the crash of 1987 were forgotten or ignored as speculators created a classic bubble.

The bubble burst in March 2000 and the bears were still on the rampage a year later.

# RED GUARDS TO TIANANMEN

VERGIL BERGER

FRONTLINES 37

**RED GUARDS TO TIANANMEN** | VERGIL BERGER

# Mao Tse Tung launched his

'Great Proletarian Cultural Revolution' in 1966 to oust pragmatic opponents in China's communist leadership, secure his position as unfettered ruler of a quarter of humanity and enforce a spirit of continuous revolution. His ten-year dream of creating an egalitarian self-reliant nation, devoid of individual aspirations and untainted by ancient tradition or modern Soviet influence, cost thousands of lives, wrought untold suffering and did huge damage to the economy. Neither the Cultural Revolution nor the fanatics who helped to lead it outlasted Mao's death in 1976 at the age of 80.

Surviving moderates, led by Deng Xiaoping, came back to power after years of ostracism at best, and for many far worse. Even the millions of young Red Guards, the Maoist shock troops, were betrayed, discarded and sent to toil for years in remote farming areas. In a desperately poor country, the education of a whole generation was lost; thousands of able officials, scientists and teachers were purged. I was one of just four Western correspondents in Beijing when the Cultural Revolution began. I would be based there again in the 1980s as China recovered from it.

**Red Guards wave their 'Little Red Books'
as Chairman Mao drives past during a Beijing
rally**
c. 1966

© Hulton Getty

MAO RESEMBLED THE REBEL FOUNDERS of some imperial dynasties of China's distant past, whom he openly admired, in his writings, for toppling decaying previous regimes and ruthlessly imposing their own ways. More emperor, visionary and poet than Marxist or communist ideologue, he was determined to stamp his personal ideals on the country forever. But the ultimate result of his Cultural Revolution was the opposite of all he stood for. It destroyed the authority of the Communist Party and left his successors with no option but to seek legitimacy through economic progress and widespread reforms. What followed was a China far more liberal than it had been before Mao launched his cruel crusade, with probably greater personal and social – but not political – freedoms than most Chinese had known for centuries.

When the Red Guards first swept into the streets of Beijing in the summer of 1966, proclaiming Mao's campaign to abolish all old things, customs, traditions and also anything redolent of Soviet 'revisionism', they seemed more amusing than threatening – just adolescent ideological pranksters.

People laughed when, without briefing the police, they declared red the colour of revolutionary movement and green for static rural calm, so traffic must stop at green lights and move at red. Journalists enjoyed the spectacle as some drivers and cyclists obeyed the Red Guards and others the usual rule of the road. It looked like a political joke to see them waving their Little Red Books of Mao quotations, as they tore down the street sign of the road leading to the Soviet embassy and replaced it with a huge sign that said 'Fight Revisionism Street'. A road outside Western embassies became 'Down with Capitalism and Imperialism Street'. They even banned the national anthem, detecting a malign Soviet musical influence in its stirring tune. Anyone caught even humming it was in for trouble.

But within weeks, as the Maoist leaders recruited almost everyone in schools and universities, first in Beijing and then across the country, and as their numbers swelled to more than 22 million, the Red Guards ceased to be in any way funny. We began to hear credible reports of how they were humiliating and tormenting their teachers and in some cases their parents, forcing respected professors previously considered communist loyalists to attend day- and night-long 'struggle meetings'. Even when these did not include physical torture and beatings, though very many did, the treatment was agonizing in a land where 'face' is all-important, and drove many to suicide. Soon the Red Guards were making no secret of their persecutions and often journalists could see for themselves how by sheer force of numbers they bullied and oppressed.

Before long, they fanned out from schools and colleges into streets, offices, and factories. By now everyone, from Mao to the corner shopkeeper, was dressed alike in baggy blue boilersuit or military-style olive-green fatigues, adorned only with a metal button or badge showing either Mao's chubby countenance or a quotation from the Little Red Book of his thoughts, or both. In that hot summer, I saw a Red Guard who had pinned his Mao badge into the bare skin of his chest in a display of zeal. Newspapers recounted how Mao's thought could work miracles and patients refused anaesthetics for surgery, convinced that fixing their minds on Mao would see them through. According to the official press, it did. Even Stalin's personality cult lacked this element of magic. Kim Il-Sung's in North Korea came close.

There were endless demonstrations. Mao would review from the balcony of the ancient Tiananmen – the Gate of Heavenly Peace – more than a million Red Guards on the huge square below. They screamed with adulation, many shedding tears of joy, though for most he was a tiny distant figure. It was enough for them to be in the same place at the same time.

ONE BY ONE, MORE MODERATE LEADERS, including President Liu Shao-chi and Communist Party Secretary-General Deng Xiaoping were publicly humiliated – many in kangaroo trials – and ousted. Some were beaten. The army chief of staff Lo Ruiching broke his leg jumping from a window to try to escape his teenage tormentors. Mocking cartoon posters then depicted him in a plaster cast uttering 'revisionist' cries from contorted lips.

I saw another general, Yang Shangkun – later to become president of China and a decisive figure in the June 1989 Tiananmen Square massacre – driven around Beijing in a truck

A road outside Western embassies became 'Down with Capitalism and Imperialism Street'.

by jeering Red Guards who forced him to bow abjectly. They pointed to a dunce's cap on his head and placard on his chest, proclaiming this lifelong communist and veteran of the Long March a traitor and enemy of the people. By the spring of 1967, the Communist Party Central Committee and the higher levels of the national and provincial governments had been decimated. Cultural Revolution fanatics took over the central government and, as chaos spread across the country, Mao called in army officers loyal to him to run most provinces.

Some victims, including the famous Marxist novelist Lao She, resorted to suicide, the traditional mandarin protest against oppression. Others disappeared into prisons or grim labour camps. President Liu, a dignified white-haired Party elder who had served as Mao's deputy in the hierachy since the communists took over in 1949, was branded 'China's Khrushchev'. Denied medical care, he died of cancer in 1969, alone and untended on the stone floor of a bare prison cell.

The general population also began to suffer as Red Guards turned on anyone they considered not sufficiently revolutionary. As their line kept changing, with leaders or ideas praised one day and demonized the next, it was hard for ordinary people to know how to stay out of trouble and give the 'correct' answers.

> ... it was hard for ordinary people to know how to stay out of trouble and give the 'correct' answers.

I LIVED IN NAN CHIHTZE, close to the Forbidden City, the vermilion-walled and golden-roofed complex of palaces and pavilions that for centuries was the home of Chinese emperors. At sunset one evening about a thousand Red Guards marched in with drums, red banners, placards and portraits of Mao. I did not see anyone beaten that night, but within minutes old furniture, books, pictures and household items, including porcelain vases, were hurled from the houses and carted off.

Next to my house lived a clearly cultured family, probably once wealthy, but already reduced by previous Maoist anti-bourgeois campaigns to poverty. I especially liked the ancient grandmother, with the tiny bound feet of the last dynasty, who used to enjoy sitting on a stool at her front door to brush her still beautiful long white hair in the sunshine. That seemed her only remaining pleasure. The day after the Red Guard invasion, she was sitting in her usual place – with a grotesque crew cut. The teenagers had deemed her long hair counter-revolutionary and forcibly shorn it. She glanced at me and then in an irritated gesture flicked her fingers where she had brushed before.

In what they called 'bloody August', more and more ordinary citizens were dragged before screaming audiences of up to 100 000 Red Guards, to be abused and often tortured for hours. Most were unaware of what they had done to incur Red Guard wrath until wild accusations were screamed at them and they were forced to confess, often to absurd 'crimes'. Some were victimized only because they, or their parents, or even their grandparents had worked in some capacity for the pre-1949 nationalist government or, later, were accused of being connected in some way with figures such as President Liu, or with Russians, Americans or other foreigners some time in the past.

Raw pork was forced in the mouths of Moslems. Many people were beaten to death. Most were imprisoned or sent to grim labour camps and remote state farms until the campaign ended in 1976. One professor whom I knew spent eight years in a tiny dark space under the stairway leading to his classroom, allowed out only for a few hours daily to clean lavatories or to confess yet again at a Red Guard rally. But thanks to some of his kinder-hearted former students, now Red Guards, he was regularly fed and told me years later his treatment had been better than most.

> Raw pork was forced in the mouths of Moslems. Many people were beaten to death.

Theatres, the opera and ballet, cinemas, bookshops, libraries and newspapers were either shut or allowed to present only dull Maoist propaganda fare ordained by the Cultural Revolution's draconian cultural tsarina, Mao's wife Chiang Ching.

A FORMER SHANGHAI FILM STARLET, Chiang had pushed aside Mao's respected second wife and was widely detested, but idolized by the Red Guards. Now she used her husband's campaign to pursue vicious vendettas, often against those she believed had slighted her in the past, from long-forgotten film colleagues of the 1920s to the wife of President Liu, Wang

Guangmei. Wang, taller and by general consensus far more beautiful than Chiang, survived and years later became a prominent member of a government advisory council. But many other victims were killed or hounded to suicide. One woman Chiang had denounced was said to have had her tongue torn out to stop her crying out 'Long Live Chairman Mao' as she was being put to death.

FOR CORRESPONDENTS, the Cultural Revolution cut off our previous fairly easy informal access to top leaders, except Mao, but served up a plethora of new sources of information. Posters were plastered on every wall. Our biggest headache was to decide which posters and Red Guard newspapers might be authentic and which represented mere aspirations, or even deliberate distortions.

During nationwide clashes between factions, posters went up declaring that 200 of the 'Great Helmsman's most loyal Red Guards' had been buried alive at noon one Sunday in Wangfujing Street. Some journalists splashed the story. My home was near the scene and I needed only 20 minutes to establish that nothing untoward had happened, with no sign of recent digging. So I concluded that the burial posters were the work of people loyal to one or several of the senior leaders who were being denounced, with the aim of discrediting Red Guard posters in general and thus casting doubt on the political attacks.

I was right that day. But I also recall expressing in my news cover similar doubts about reports in 1967 from the Red Guards and even in the official media about serious factional fighting in the large Central China city of Wuhan, with guns on both sides and numerous casualties. Later I was able to establish that I had been wrong to play it down. The reports were essentially true, though the clashes fell well short of full civil war.

Some places, even in Beijing, did however look as if they had been hit by something like civil war. Red Guards ransacked many ancient temples and desecrated cathedrals and burial places, including the old British cemetery, whose Victorian tombstones were smashed. The ancient Confucius shrine in the sage's birthplace at Chufu was badly damaged. The fact that Mao prided himself on his classical verse was neither here nor there,

although the government did lock up and guard the Forbidden City and a few other famous historical sites and temples in Beijing and elsewhere.

AS A FOREIGNER accredited to the government, I experienced no Red Guard raids. But loudspeakers were installed outside for me to hear Maoist hymns and propaganda at home day and night, some of the ballads considerately translated into English and French, in case my knowledge of Chinese was not good enough to get the message.

Some foreigners were less lightly treated. A French diplomat and his wife were surrounded, separately, by hundreds of Red Guards and harangued for many hours for the 'crime' of having inadvertently stepped on a Mao quotation chalked on the pavement. Curiously, the screaming teenagers politely allowed me through for brief interviews with their victims.

After about 11 000 Red Guards laid siege for 10 days to the walled compound of the Soviet embassy, Russian wives and children were sent home and had to run a Red-Guard gauntlet at the airport. I saw British, French, and Swiss embassy representatives, there in the name of diplomatic solidarity despite Cold War differences with Moscow, absorb plenty of blows. But they could not prevent the women being slapped as they ran across the tarmac, bowed

> Russian wives and children were sent home and had to run a Red-Guard gauntlet at the airport.

beneath the raised arms of ranks of Red Guards, to the safety of the airliner.

One winter morning in 1967, I received a rare phone call from the foreign ministry suggesting I go to the airport, but refusing to say why. On the tarmac, I was amazed to see a Soviet airliner carrying Alexander Shelepin, then high in the Moscow leadership under Leonid Brezhnev, land for a refuelling stop on the way to Hanoi. Possibly the Russians chose Beijing, of all places, in the hope of easing acute Sino-Soviet tensions through brief airport talks with a Chinese leader.

AS SHELEPIN AND HIS ENTOURAGE descended from the plane, a thousand Red Guards surged forward, whipped out canisters of strong-smelling disinfectant and sprayed it on the feet and legs of the Russians until their trousers were drenched. They unfurled banners proclaiming 'Protect China's Agriculture, Save our Cattle' and brandished Soviet newspapers with a tiny news item about foot-and-mouth disease in deepest Russia. Shelepin walked stoically to the airport building for talks with a Chinese minister before taking off an hour or two later, his trousers still damp.

Worse befell the British in August 1967, after I left China. Their embassy was burnt and its staff roughed up as they fled – Red Guard retaliation for measures against Cultural Revolution activists in the British colony of Hong Kong. My Reuters successor, Anthony Grey, recalls his two years' solitary confinement as a Red Guard prisoner elsewhere in this book.

WHEN I RETURNED TO BEIJING in 1984, first for a series of regular visits and then in 1987 for a further five years of residence, the city was in many respects barely recognizable.

Despite its horrors, the Cultural Revolution deserves some thanks from the hundreds of millions of Chinese who lived through it and whose lives for the most part improved beyond their wildest dreams in the subsequent decades. The sweeping reforms that followed Mao's death were, contrary to all his intentions, the direct result of his disastrous campaign.

Mao himself – the new leadership under Deng Xiaoping proclaimed – must be honoured for his decades of achievement, but not for the Cultural Revolution. They voiced formulas like, 'Mao was 70 per cent good and 30 per cent bad' and left it at that, while handing down suspended death sentences or long terms of imprisonment to leading lights of the Cultural Revolution, including his widow Chiang Ching, indicted in 30 000 murders.

'Mao was 70 per cent good and 30 per cent bad'

But Mao had hit the Communist Party so hard that it never recovered its authority. His early battle cry to the Red Guards spoke volumes: 'To Rebel is Justified. Bombard the Headquarters.' By first publicly ridiculing its leaders, then dismantling many of its policies, the Maoists destroyed the Party's credibility. So when the veteran communist and erstwhile Mao supporter Deng returned to power, after twice being purged for revisionism and for covertly 'following the capitalist road', he and his group of pragmatic 'immortals' had no choice. They either had to move far beyond even the 'revisionism' that Mao had accused them of in their drive to modernize, or cease to rule.

Deng's message was that while the Party must exercise sole political control, it would now encourage money-making and under its umbrella of 'stability' allow more economic, social, personal and cultural freedoms than most Chinese then alive had ever known. Bruised by the violence and unpredictability of the end of Mao's rule, most Chinese accepted the bargain with relief and relished their first taste of capitalism since 1949.

In foreign affairs, a turning point had been reached even while Mao still reigned. In his later years, tension with the Soviet Union led to border skirmishes. Fearing worse, he approved closer contacts with the 'enemy number two' in his mythology, the United States, and this led to President Richard Nixon's visit to Beijing in 1972. Deng then established full diplomatic ties with Washington within the decade and, in 1989, welcomed Soviet President Mikhail Gorbachev on a state visit.

NEW BUILDINGS RISING all over the capital and growing material prosperity, with far greater choice of goods in the shops and fashionable clothes, were the things Chinese friends expected me to comment on when they asked me what I thought of the post-Mao changes.

I always replied that what impressed me much more was the relaxed behaviour of the people on the streets. The fear, the constant quick glance round to check whether they were being watched, the everyday tensions of the Mao years, and the feeling of being among a terrorized and regimented people had simply vanished. I could talk freely to Chinese and invite them to my home. Those friends who were known dissidents told me no one troubled them if they aired their views in private, but public protest or attempts to organize meant trouble. The Deng years were marked by alternating tolerance and periods when active dissidents drew long terms in jail or labour camps.

Restaurants, theatres, opera and music, state-approved and supervised religious life, and other forms of social and cultural activity first returned to their pre-Cultural Revolution state and then rapidly moved in most cases far beyond it. Selected Hollywood blockbusters vied for popularity with the works of a newly vibrant domestic film industry, some of whose products unsparingly depicted Cultural Revolution excesses and even got away with some mocking digs at officialdom.

POLITICAL RELAXATION and public freedoms reached a peak in the two months of student-led demonstrations before the Tiananmen massacre on 4 June 1989. They were sparked by a public outpouring of grief after the death in April of a long-ousted, but still popular, Communist Party chief Hu Yaobang who was renowned for his personal probity.

Starting with demands for an end to corruption, in the spirit of Hu, and a more open, accountable government, the demonstrators progressed to outright calls for democracy without really explaining how it should work in China. Numbers ranged from thousands one day to more than a million the next, but the demonstrators clearly enjoyed wide support, at least in Beijing and other large cities.

For a time, especially when the liberal wing of the leadership was in the ascendancy, police let the marchers pass. Even the staid Party mouthpiece, the *People's Daily*, had kind words for them. The demonstrations were initially spontaneous, but there is little doubt that, as they grew ever larger, they were, in time-honoured Chinese fashion, increasingly used by liberal leaders for their own ends.

The public enjoyed the spectacle of student leaders arguing sarcastically on live television with hard-line Prime Minister Li Peng in the hallowed Great Hall of the People on the edge of Tiananmen Square. But Li, a pudgy Soviet-trained engineer backed by Party elders including Deng, had the last word with the removal of the liberals from top Party ranks and by declaring martial law, opening the way for the military crackdown. Nothing can excuse the shooting around Tiananmen that June night, in which a still unknown number were killed, certainly hundreds and possibly thousands. We saw, not only unarmed

**Nothing can excuse the shooting around Tiananmen that June night, in which a still unknown number were killed, certainly hundreds and possibly thousands.**

demonstrators, but many curious bystanders felled by ferocious and often indiscriminate fire. Nor can anything excuse the reversion to repression that followed, with many arrests, an unknown number of executions, and for a few weeks the daily televised parade of mostly young accused troublemakers being frog-marched to police stations or tribunals for questioning and arraignment.

But if nothing can excuse, perhaps to explain, a look back to the Cultural Revolution might make sense. I was the only Western correspondent in Beijing in 1989 who had also experienced the Red Guards more than 20 years before. That gave me an inkling of what must have passed through the Party elders' minds when they gave Li Peng the go-ahead to use force.

These so-called immortals, some relatively liberal, like Deng himself and also President Yang Shangkun, who was widely and credibly reported to have been a strong proponent of military action to clear the square, had all been victims of the Cultural Revolution. They had then been the moderates and they suffered greatly at the hands of the Red Guards. I remembered how Yang and former Beijing mayor Peng Zhen, seen as conservative now but treated by Mao as an especially dangerous revisionist, had again and again been physically assaulted and publicly humiliated by the Guards. Deng was not beaten up, but he was castigated daily as public enemy number two, after President Liu, and the chief accomplice of that 'renegade and hidden traitor' and sent to labour on a distant farm. Red Guards threw his son, Deng Pufang, out of a window and crippled him for life. I talked to Pufang several times in the 1980s when, in a wheelchair, he represented at official functions an association for the disabled.

THE SIGHT AND SOUND OF HUGE CROWDS of student demonstrators, from universities that had spawned the Red Guards, waving banners, putting up posters and mocking political leaders, must have horrified the elders and revived their worst nightmares. Possibly they genuinely feared a repeat performance of Cultural Revolution excesses unless firm action was taken, although if they had been closer to their people they would have known that the 1989 students were a quite different and incomparably milder breed.

No one in the Party or government has ever publicly admitted that the massacre was wrong or even a mistake.

No one in the Party or government has ever publicly admitted that the massacre was wrong or even a mistake.

Tiananmen was not mentioned when, several years later, Yang was replaced as president and Li as prime minister. For the authorities, it was a non-event. But not for ordinary Beijingers. Now and again the words 'everything must be accounted for' are painted on walls. They are removed. After a while they reappear somewhere else. A decade after the massacre, its impact continued to resonate.

'After the Cultural Revolution, the authorities did come clean after a fashion and even put the worst evildoers on trial,' a schoolteacher said to me on a late 1990s visit to Beijing. As for Tiananmen, she went on, 'Now, we are still waiting'.

# MOSCOW'S AFGHAN VIETNAM

HELEN WOMACK

FRONTLINES 38

## MOSCOW'S AFGHAN VIETNAM | HELEN WOMACK

# When an ageing Soviet ruler,

Leonid Brezhnev, ignored Politburo advice and invaded Afghanistan at the end of the 1970s, it was a last flail of the Soviet bear's paw. Nearly nine years later, in 1988, when a new reforming Kremlin leader, Mikhail Gorbachev, boldly ordered the withdrawal of Soviet forces, I went to Afghanistan to see them go. For Russians, the war was a trauma even greater than Vietnam had been for America. Defeat contributed to the collapse of their country, the Soviet Union. In Moscow for Reuters, I was 32, experienced enough to hope to survive a war zone, yet still enjoying just enough of the crazy courage that belongs to the young.

**Soviet forces withdraw from Afghanistan along the Salang Highway**
February 1989

© Hulton Getty

MIKHAIL GORBACHEV WAS PURSUING HIS POLICIES of *glasnost* and *perestroika* – or openness and restructuring. They were heady days in Moscow in the late 1980s and, as the ice of the Cold War melted, I fell in love with a Russian, married him and ended up making my home there for the next decade.

My husband, Costya Gagarin, and his mostly artistic and intellectual friends were rebellious children of the long years of stagnation under Leonid Brezhnev. None was a dissident as such, but in minor ways each kicked against the communist system. They listened to Western radio stations, went to church because the official ideology was atheist and dodged the draft, with increasing desperation and inventiveness after Brezhnev invaded Afghanistan in 1979.

Some slit their wrists or feigned mental illness to avoid going to that war. Costya, a carpenter who grew up in a village near Leningrad, had another trick. He knew that call-up papers went out every spring and autumn and that his local recruiting colonel didn't work too hard. So every time conscription season came round, Costya went logging in Siberia, to return only when he knew the man had filled his quota.

*… every time conscription season came round, Costya went logging in Siberia …*

Costya then apologized for being late and promised to be on time for the next draft, which satisfied the paper-pushing Colonel Rakitin, because the young man never actually refused to serve the Motherland. Later, the colonel died and the Army forgot Costya.

But the KGB nearly wiped the smile off his face in 1987 when he said he was marrying me. East–West love was still not accepted. The Army, at the prompting of the KGB, went to recruit Costya for Afghanistan. It was only the intervention of British diplomats, preparing a visit to Moscow by Margaret Thatcher, which saved us from becoming a human rights case.

Ironically, I am the one of our circle who ended up in Afghanistan. 'You did my "international duty" for me,' Costya says, using the euphemism by which the Soviet authorities described the sojourn of poor Russian boys in a proud Moslem land that was determined to eject them.

So, I share common memories with Russian men in their forties, from General Alexander Lebed to the sad wrecks who sit in wheelchairs begging in the tunnels of the Moscow Metro. It is hard to explain to non-veterans, but life will never again be so intense for us as it was in Afghanistan, a place where we experienced unimaginable horror, but also beauty and love.

WESTERNERS HAD SAT DOWN to Christmas dinner on 25 December 1979, when Soviet tanks rolled over the border into Afghanistan to start what was to be a decade of war. Retired KGB officers have told me that their then leader, Yuri Andropov, was against the adventure, but that he was overruled in the Politburo by Brezhnev. The troops went in on Christmas Day in the hope that the West would not immediately react.

Their reasoning was sound enough. Reuters World Desk in London, for example, was running on a holiday roster. There was a duty editor – we had a quartet of them working in rotation whom we called 'Four Horsemen of the Apocalypse' – plus a handful of sub-editors and the trainee. That was me. We had a busy day.

The invaders assassinated Afghan President Hafizullah Amin and replaced him with their puppet, Babrak Karmal, justifying the invasion by arguing that political instability threatened to spill over and undermine the Central Asian republics on the Soviet side of the border. To some extent, that was a legitimate concern. The fundamentalist Taliban rulers of Afghanistan would, years later, seem a risk to the security of newly independent former Soviet republics, such as Tajikistan and Uzbekistan. But if the Russians had studied the experience of the nineteenth-century British Empire in Afghanistan they must have seen that, by invading a nation of warrior tribes, they had stirred a hornets' nest. A British army had been massacred on a retreat from Kabul.

The fractious Afghans soon united to face an infidel Soviet foe. Pakistan and the United States gave support. The rugged mountains were an ideal base for guerrilla war. Moscow replaced Karmal with another puppet, Najibullah, but it made no difference. The Afghans hated the alien presence, except perhaps some women who benefited from educational and work opportunities that Islam would have denied them.

Brezhnev hung on at the top of the Kremlin – he had been there since he deposed Khrushchev in 1964 – until he died in

1982 and Andropov succeeded him. But he was by then himself too old and sick to introduce reform and was dead in 15 months.

CHANGE CAME WITH GORBACHEV. He found the courage to admit the error of the Afghan war, cut Soviet losses and beat a humbling retreat. Most Russians welcomed this, but communist hardliners were unhappy. Dissatisfaction over the public humiliation would be a factor in the August 1991 abortive coup against Gorbachev, after which – although he survived for a few months – he was too badly weakened to hold the Soviet Union together. Boris Yeltsin dismantled it.

The Kremlin had kept Russians in the dark about how they were losing the Afghan war, although people drew their own conclusions as the bodies came home in sealed zinc coffins. In my husband's village of Kirovsk alone, six victims of the war lie in the cemetery beside recruiting colonel Rakitin. Foreign correspondents were kept out of Afghanistan and the only ones who got in did so with the Mujahadeen guerrillas.

But in April 1988, when it was clear that the occupation was coming to an end, the Soviet Army gave journalists access to bases in Kabul. Costya and I had been married for only a year. He was very much against me going to the war zone that he had so studiously avoided himself. 'It's not a job for a woman,' he said.

I quickly squashed that first flicker of Russian sexism in our marriage and told him, 'A Reuters correspondent goes where he or she is sent and the spouse had better not argue.' To his credit, he accepted that and took on what I now know is the harder role – that of being the one who stays behind and worries.

I WAS NOT THE ONLY WESTERN WOMAN on that trip to Kabul. There I met Sîan Thomas, a flamboyant character from Wales who was working on contract for Yorkshire Television. She had flame-red hair that fell to her waist and dressed in Soviet helicopter-pilot overalls. I was a dull mouse beside her, but even I must have seemed outrageously exotic to the Afghans.

We had no problem as women, however, in that strict Moslem society. The Afghans had one rule for their own females and another for us, creatures from another planet. Indeed they could not have been more gallant. I remember an official shinning up a mulberry tree to pick me a basket of mulberries. And on another occasion, when I naively wandered alone into a slum and suddenly found myself surrounded by dozens of ragged children – a more frightening experience than you might imagine – a delightful English-speaking doctor rescued me.

I learnt that, if I did not want to be lynched, it was better to speak English than Russian in the bazaar. In fact, knowing how much they were detested, Russian civilians rarely ventured from their safe suburb of Mikroravon. I was told that two army wives, bored with their isolation, had disguised themselves in yashmaks to go to market. They were shrouded from head to foot, but their European height and white hands gave them away. A mob was so enraged by this act of disrespect, it tore them limb from limb.

> I learnt that, if I did not want to be lynched, it was better to speak English than Russian in the bazaar.

The defeated Soviet military did not try to restrict journalists' movements but, given the tension in Kabul and my inexperience of Moslem society, I was glad enough most of the time to keep tight hold of my minders. Army press officers took us on trips to barracks, where we did our best to interview inarticulate spotty conscripts. I still have a poster that one of them, called Fedya, gave me, showing the three acceptable hair cuts in the Soviet Army: short, shorter and very short.

It brought tears to my eyes to see the empty beds of those who had been killed. According to official figures, the Soviet Union lost 13 000 men in the war – compared with America's 45 000 in Vietnam. Most of the conscripts came from poor homes in the Russian provinces, not privileged apartments in Moscow or Leningrad.

That is not to forget the atrocious suffering on the other side. Afghanistan, with a population of 17 million, lost one million, with thousands maimed by mines. A lingering memory is of a newly dug Moslem cemetery on a hillside. There were no gravestones, just black flags fluttering in the wind.

I JOINED PHASE ONE of the Soviet withdrawal in May 1988, when a convoy of tanks left Jalalabad in the south. Then bases further north were gradually dismantled until General Boris

Gromov, head of all Soviet forces in the country, shepherded the last troops over the Amu Darya river into Uzbekistan in February 1989.

Soviet officials in Kabul told journalists they could ride in the tank convoy from Jalalabad, provided they understood that their safety could not be guaranteed. Although the Russians were leaving, the Mujahadeen had not forgiven them and were refusing to guarantee them safe passage through the Black Mountains, which they controlled.

At Kabul airport, I got a God-given chance to duck respectably out of going on this frightening trip. The officer in charge took a look at the journalists waiting to board the transport to Jalalabad and declared that he was not taking the four women. Apart from me, there were women correspondents from Germany, Sweden and Spain. I marched up to him and shouted, 'If women can give birth, they can handle war.'

**'If women can give birth, they can handle war.'**

'Get on the plane, then,' he said.

I soon wondered what on earth I had done. We took off on the last flight into Jalalabad before the Soviet defences around the airport there were dismantled. The plane let out flares to draw off the Afghans' heat-seeking US Stinger missiles – a decisive weapon in the war – as I found myself sitting next to Marco Politi of the Italian newspaper *Il Messaggero*. He took my hand in a comradely way. 'I'm afraid it's a bit sweaty,' I said. He admitted he was a coward too.

WHEN WE LANDED AT JALALABAD, the night air was rich with tropical scents. At that moment, with my feet on the ground again, I was as sure as I have ever been before or since that there is a God. We were taken to a hotel for a news conference and the Mujahadeen shelled us in a desultory way, just to say they were there. For the night, Marco and I split up. I shared my room with a Finn and a Swede, who decided to fortify themselves for the tank ride ahead with whisky. They admitted next morning it had been a mistake.

I lay in my narrow bed, listening to the croaking of frogs. Shortly before dawn the muezzin called the faithful to prayer, when I got up and went to the rusty shower. I remember looking at my legs in a strangely detached way and wondering if, in a few hours' time, I would still have them.

Fear is always worse by night than in the daytime. It was good to find Marco again at breakfast. We ate flat bread and hard-boiled eggs, then went to the parade ground of the Soviet Army base to hear a speech from the commanding officer and watch the tanks line up to depart. Since I came back to Moscow, I have made friends with various Afghan war veterans, including a man called Oleg, whose badly burnt face looks like melted candle wax. He lives on a paltry invalid benefit, but writes poetry rather than complain. Unfortunately, I have no Russian comrades from Jalalabad, only Marco. This was because we were put on an armoured personnel carrier with a pro-Soviet Afghan rather than a Russian crew and the language barrier prevented us from conversing during the trip.

We were given the choice of sitting inside the APC or on top of it. We were told that inside, we would have no chance if we ran over a mine, but on top we could be vulnerable to snipers. It was as hot as an oven inside and we chose to sit on top. I wore white and put flowers in my army hat in the hope that the Mujahadeen would see I was an English lady.

We set off and the journey was not nearly so terrible as I had imagined. True, I got hit in the mouth with a lump of dried camel dung when locals lined the road to throw bouquets. I was lucky a stone or even a grenade had not been in the flowers, because this was an orchestrated farewell ceremony that resentful residents of Jalalabad were made to join.

BUT THE REST OF THE JOURNEY, through stunning mountain scenery, was the trip of a lifetime. Having watched military parades on Red Square and been choked by tank fumes, I had been afraid we would be inhaling the exhaust of the vehicle in front of us the whole way. Instead the tanks, APCs and lorries quickly spaced themselves out and we breathed fresh air.

With the Mujahadeen possibly lurking behind every rock, we could not afford to stop until we reached Kabul, a day's drive up the road. The guerrillas did shoot at us, but as soon as the puffs of smoke from their guns got too close, swarms of wasp-like Soviet helicopter gunships clattered up into the air to protect us.

The movement of the APC was so gentle – 'like a gondola', Marco said – that we relaxed enough to sleep part of the way.

The hell came when a desperate desire to use a lavatory wiped out all my previous thoughts of mortality. The men did not have a problem, because they could just urinate off the side of the moving tanks, but I was stuck. That, I discovered later, was the real reason why the commander had not wanted women on the trip. At last we halted when a tank ahead broke down. We were sitting ducks, but with no thought for that I jumped down and went joyfully behind a boulder. Soon the convoy set off again. We did not have much further to go. Shortly before Kabul and out of danger, we joined all the dusty soldiers who leapt fully clothed into a river.

At Kabul, the journalists left the convoy, which would continue trundling up the road for four more days until it reached the Soviet border. Marco returned to Moscow, leaving me a pressed flower and a note that said: 'Since it is a rare privilege to share fear, do not forget your friend from Italy.' I never have.

Later I flew to see the tanks finally cross the Soviet border at Termez. One soldier tossed me a bouquet. I caught it. The soldiers roared their appreciation. I was the girl with the flowers, symbol of their return to life.

> Shortly before Kabul and out of danger, we joined all the dusty soldiers who leapt fully clothed into a river.

# THE FALL OF THE BERLIN WALL

TOM HENEGHAN

FRONTLINES 39

## THE FALL OF THE BERLIN WALL | TOM HENEGHAN

# In the end, it needed just a few

months for communist East Germany to fall apart. Over the summer of 1989, East Germans used holidays in Hungary and Czechoslovakia to flee in their thousands through a collapsing Iron Curtain to the West. Democracy activists defied the state in peaceful protest across the country and by early November, they were so confident that they publicly lampooned their leaders. I was the chief correspondent for Germany, based in Bonn. Sensing that anything could happen now, I headed for Berlin to lead the Reuters reporting team.

**Bemused East German border guards look
on as crowds demolish the Berlin Wall**
09 November 1989

© Reuters. Photo by David Brauchli

GÜNTER SCHABOWSKI LOOKED FLUSTERED as he shuffled his papers. He'd just mentioned to a news conference, almost as an afterthought, that East Germans could travel freely to the West. Reporters wanted more facts. When would this new law come into effect? Would it apply to West Berlin? Shrugging, the East German communist official scanned the Central Committee resolution he had just read out. He hadn't even looked at it before making the announcement, but now he needed an answer. When another reporter asked when the guidelines would apply, he responded hesitantly, 'As far as I know, right away. Immediately.' And how could they leave? Schabowski briefly wondered to himself if the Soviet Union had agreed to all this – but the new East German communist party leader, Egon Krenz, had handed him the text with the words, 'Announce this, it will be a bombshell.' So he read on, 'Permanent emigration can take place at all East German border crossings into West Germany and West Berlin.'

It was 9 November 1989, shortly before 7 pm, and this East German Politburo member had effectively announced the end of the Cold War by mistake. The Central Committee had planned to put an embargo on the hastily drafted text, but none was indicated on the piece of paper that Schabowski had been given. Baffled journalists just had to write what they had heard.

**... this East German Politburo member had effectively announced the end of the Cold War by mistake.**

**'East Germany has decided to let its citizens emigrate directly over the border to West Germany, communist party media chief Günter Schabowski said on Thursday,' the urgent Reuters despatch read. 'The new ruling comes into effect immediately, he told a news conference.'**

THE COUNTRY HAD BEEN SHAKEN by protests for months, tens of thousands of East Germans were fleeing through Hungary and Czechoslovakia, and the hard-line communist leadership was disintegrating, but was the Berlin Wall really open? Were all the hurdles to travel simply abolished? Had the Cold War actually ended – not with a bang but a whimper? There were about a dozen staffers in the Reuters bureau that day,

all with years of experience, and none of us could really be sure.

What an end it was! Within hours of the clumsy announcement, hundreds of thousands of East Germans massed at crossing points along the Berlin Wall and the East–West border, demanding the right to travel. The numbers overwhelmed the border guards, who tried to get them to go home. Even the Stasi security police, who had kept an arm-lock on the frontiers, couldn't hold them in. Encouraged by Soviet leader Mikhail Gorbachev's *perestroika* reforms, East German protesters had marched for democracy, free speech and free travel and had come eyeball-to-eyeball with their communist masters – and the communists blinked. They didn't start shooting. The Party was afraid of the people. By 4 November, hundreds of thousands demonstrated in East Berlin to laugh at an emperor who had no clothes. Just one more push and the last taboo would fall. The mishandled travel law provided it. In but a few hours, the East–West divide would be dumped on the garbage heap of history.

Some East Berliners turned up at the Bornholmer Strasse crossing soon after the live East German television broadcast of Schabowski's news conference ended, but most were at first as confused as we were. Many went to their local police headquarters to start the slow process of getting exit visas, but the officers had no instructions. By jumping the gun and declaring free travel immediately, Schabowski had sidestepped the lumbering bureaucracy that was supposed to control any exodus.

Even so, Doug Hamilton, the first Reuters correspondent to visit Checkpoint Charlie, found the famous crossing point all but deserted up to an hour after the announcement. 'There must be some mistake,' one border guard said when shown the official ADN news agency report on the new law. 'It's not good,' a quick-witted colleague blurted out. 'We'll lose our jobs.'

FOR MOST EAST GERMANS, the full effect of Schabowski's slip only came at 8 pm, when West Germany's ARD television began its evening news report with the blunt headline: 'East Germany opens its borders'. After that, people rushed to the nearest crossing. Pubs and restaurants emptied as customers paid up and hurried West. Parents woke their children and threw coats over their pyjamas to bring them out to be part of history. As the crowds swelled at the eight exits through the Wall, confused border guards vainly tried to get them to go home. The people responded, 'Open the gates! Open the gates!'

The Bornholmer Strasse guards tried to ease pressure by letting some of the loudest protesters through at around 9 pm. Instead of letting off steam, that only spurred the crowd. With no clear orders on what to do, passport officer Harald Jäger called his Stasi superiors at 10.30 pm and barked down the line, 'We can't hold out any more ... I'm shutting down the controls and letting the people out.'

The crowds burst through the Wall like champagne spraying out of a bottle. Once in the West, strangers hugged like long-lost friends. Easterners raced to visit Western relatives. There were whoops of joy as the smoke-belching Trabi cars inched through the crowds, but also bitter tears as Germans recalled the years of separation and the brutal shooting of those who tried to escape. East and West Berliners scrambled on the Wall at the Brandenburg Gate – for which, before, they too could have been shot – and started hammering away at it for souvenirs. There was only one word for all this and almost everybody seemed to shout it: '*Wahnsinn!*' 'Madness!'

WRITING THE MAIN NEWS STORY in the East Berlin office that night, I felt the weight of history falling away by the hour. The claustrophobia of a communist dictatorship was dissolving and decades of injustice were coming to an end. The most potent symbol of the Cold War division was nothing more now than a traffic bottleneck. For someone like myself, who had observed communist countries for almost 20 years and moved in and out of them freely, while the people I reported on could not, the Wall's fall prompted a mixture of joy and something, I suppose, like indignation.

The gravity of the hour echoed in the wrap-up that I filed late that evening.

**'Embattled East Germany threw open its prison-like western borders to its frustrated people on Thursday ... a stunning concession in a country that tried to pen in its citizens with the Berlin Wall, barbed wire, attack dogs and automatic firing devices trained at fleeing refugees.'**

I recalled that more than 225 000 East Germans had given up on their communist homeland and left for West Germany already that year. West German estimates put the total of those wanting to leave at between 1.2 and 1.4 million of the country's 16 million people.

Once the initial news was out, Reuters correspondents headed away from the office to begin reporting scenes of joy and celebration at every border crossing they visited. It was happy news and we got swept up in the party. Martin Nesirky, our East Berlin correspondent, used his special border pass to slip over to the Western side of Checkpoint Charlie just before the floodgates opened. The first East German across, a young man named Jens Richter, stumbled in a daze and was almost run over at the nearest intersection. 'I never thought I would ever touch West German soil,' he said. West Berlin buses quickly stopped charging fares because so many East Berliners, with no West German pfennigs, were getting on asking to go to Kurfürstendamm, the glittering main thoroughfare of the West. Shaky telephone lines overloaded as East Berliners stormed phone booths to call home and tell their surprised families, 'Hey, guess where I am!' Over in the East, where public telephones were few and far between, Martin's wife Loraine ran back and forth between Bornholmer Strasse and their apartment to call me with the latest news.

After midnight, when all the crossing points were open, the rush of freedom was intoxicating. 'The Wall is gone!' they were chanting now. Even stodgy East German television and radio caught the fever, broadcasting live from the scene with unscripted interviews with ordinary people. Their reporters loosened up so quickly that only the occasional Eastern phrase or telltale nasal accent from Saxony gave viewers a hint this was not a West German station. The communist party was finished – the reunification party beginning. The mood changed again as I crafted the next Reuters wrap: 'Berlin erupted in an East–West festival on Friday ...'

Later in the night, the flow reversed and exhausted East Berliners tramped back through the Wall to go home. One man

> ... East Berliners stormed phone booths to call home and tell their surprised families, 'Hey, guess where I am!'

explained that he was on the early shift at his factory. 'Going to West Berlin was as good as going to Australia for me. It was just as far away. Now I've been there and back while my children were home in bed. I can't believe it.' A young couple said they had to be home to see the children off to school. East German radio and television seized on the fact so many were coming back voluntarily, saying that showed they supported the state, but that wasn't what people were saying. They had called their rulers' bluff and won. They had visited the West now. Many were stunned to see just how affluent it was. They might not all want to live there, but they were sure that they wanted its freedom and prosperity.

As the night gave way to a chill dawn, I sensed that, if the Berlin Wall could fall so easily, the unimaginable could happen. The end of Communism and the reunification of Germany – maybe even the dissolution of NATO and the Warsaw Pact – all seemed possible now. Less likely, but not ruled out, was a crackdown: but it was only much later when secret files were opened and memoirs written that we learned how some in the KGB did apparently urge Gorbachev to order a military response.

He decided against it after an assurance that things were under control from West German Chancellor Helmut Kohl – who would soon canvass Moscow to support reunification and then achieve that. Even so, the East German military put a crack rifle division and a paratroop regiment on combat alert and, two days after the Wall opened, hard-line Defence Minister Heinz Kessler was still considering using troops, but he had to concede it was too late for that now.

*... two days after the Wall opened, hardline Defence Minister Heinz Kessler was still considering using troops.*

THREE DAYS AFTER the Wall opened East German soldiers demolished sections of the double wall at Potsdamer Platz, in the heart of pre-war Berlin, and the mayors from East and West met in the middle of the old no man's land. Waiting on the Eastern side for the ceremony, a pensioner told me that the last time he had been there was to demonstrate during the 1953 uprising that was crushed by Soviet tanks.

'Last Sunday, I would not have dared come this near to the Wall for fear of being arrested,' added a younger man who had his small daughter on his shoulders. When the little girl got impatient and cried to go home, her father apologized, 'She's too young to understand what all this really means.'

The pensioner smiled weakly at the two of them and then turned away. 'Maybe it's just as well she doesn't,' he muttered.

# MANDELA IS FREE

JONATHAN SHARP

FRONTLINES 40

## MANDELA IS FREE | JONATHAN SHARP

# The white South African police officer,

sitting in a shabby bar, said he felt low. The previous evening, he told me,
he'd wandered through a park hoping that a black would mug him. Then he could
draw his pistol and kill him, claiming self-defence. Nobody did try to mug him –
and that was why he was depressed. I had just begun three years for Reuters in
South Africa that would be climaxed by the story of the release of Nelson Mandela
in 1990. I'd reported from China in the Cultural Revolution and covered the
Lebanon civil war, but apartheid sent a chill up my spine. The policeman that
evening didn't sound like a troubled soul making a drunken confession. It was just
a matter-of-fact grumble about a wasted evening.

**Nelson Mandela walks to freedom after
27 years in prison**
11 February 1989

© Reuters. Photo by Ulli Michel

I SOON DISCOVERED THAT THAT POLICEMAN was by no means alone among South African whites in his attitude to the black majority. I learned to dread conversations when someone began with a disclaimer about being a racist. A white South African friend said that a teacher at his school used to tell his pupils, 'I am not a racist. I just can't stand blacks.'

Then, as I contemplated writing a story on race, I saw an Indian clerk in a shop spray a can of air freshener at a departing black messenger and heard the venomous hiss of 'chocolate soldier'. Suddenly my story was more complicated than I had supposed. The image of a land where the white bad guys were always utterly beastly to the downtrodden black good guys had truth in it, but it was hopelessly simplistic. In a country where racism was not only recognized, but institutionalized, there were enmities of undreamed complexity.

*… I saw an Indian clerk in a shop spray a can of air freshener at a departing black messenger …*

Some of the most brutal violence of the 1980s was not between whites and blacks, but among the black people of deceptively peaceful-looking rolling countryside around Natal province's Pietermaritzburg. We used to call it a turf battle between supporters of right- and left-leaning political groups, but there was also a strong tinge of tribal rivalry. As for the five million whites, they were a far from uniform collection. There were English speakers and Dutch-descended Afrikaners, hard-line rightists who esteemed Adolf Hitler and a liberal crust who agonized over injustice and even risked their lives in the struggle to dismantle the system. Then there were communities of Indians and mixed-race coloureds, each meticulously labelled in the apartheid rulebook.

Nor was it true that the distribution of South Africa's wealth was along apartheid lines. To be sure, you had only to compare living standards in the plush northern Johannesburg suburbs with those in the adjacent black township of Alexandra to see stark injustice, but not all blacks were poor, nor all whites rich. Soweto, the township outside Johannesburg that is synonymous with the anti-apartheid struggle, boasted a BMW dealership.

In 1988 Anton Lubowski, a leftist white lawyer, told me that the white-led government had a key trump card to play in its campaign to end South Africa's pariah status with a wider world – the release of Nelson Mandela. 'And they will play it soon,' he said. Lubowski, who would soon suffer the fate of other left-wing activists and die by an assassin's bullet, had no inside knowledge of government plans. But he was convinced, as were many people of varied persuasion, that the release of the world's most famous political prisoner was inevitable, the only question being the timing.

MANDELA – IN JAIL SO LONG that few could even remember what he looked like – had already been moved from Robben Island to Pollsmoor prison at Cape Town. Speculation about his release, which would routinely rise to fever pitch among the foreign and local media on the faintest whisper of a rumour, intensified in 1988 when he fell ill and was rushed to hospital. So convinced were some that South Africa's biggest story for a generation was set to break that TV crews and journalists like me spent a nervous two weeks outside the Cape Town hospital to see if an elderly black man, said to be slightly stooped, would walk out the door. One of us feigned illness to try to get in to the heavily guarded wing where we thought he was, but the ruse failed.

The government gave no hint of its plans. Its relations with the foreign media, at best brittle, had not been eased by a bizarre episode when some of us were invited to a government reception. Incongruously, it was held in Pretoria's main prison. This was also the only jail where death sentences were executed, by hanging. Inmates served us wine and canapés and we asked them what they had been convicted of. 'Robbery. Would you care for some more white wine?'

*Inmates served us wine and canapés and we asked them what they had been convicted of.*

Suspecting it all to be a joke in poor taste, I asked an official why the prison had been selected for the get-together. He replied, without a trace of irony, 'We heard they do good catering here.' He was stunned and vexed when several stories, including that on Reuters, portrayed it as perhaps the oddest social event anyone had ever experienced.

In 1989, P. W. Botha, the head of state who was nicknamed the 'Crocodile', had a stroke and was bundled from office by colleagues, to be replaced by F. W. de Klerk, a mild-mannered lawyer who seemed an unlikely figure to transform South Africa. 'Nothing in his past seemed to hint at a spirit of reform,' Mandela would say in his autobiography, *The Long Walk to Freedom*, and an aide called Stoffel van der Merwe told foreign correspondents over lunch not to expect drastic change soon. Was Mandela's release on the agenda? No comment.

But events were moving faster than 'Waffle Stoffel', as we called him, let on. Mandela had already been in secret talks with white leaders, among them the supposedly implacable Botha, and on 10 October 1989 it was announced that Walter Sisulu and seven former Robben Island colleagues were to be freed. De Klerk also moved unexpectedly soon to ease the policy of apartheid. Black and white could now bathe from the same beaches.

Reform was in the wind and we at Reuters needed to be ahead, and dreaded being behind, on the sensation of Mandela being set free – but how would we find out from authorities who were so unforthcoming?

WE GOT SOME HELP FROM AN UNLIKELY SOURCE, a very senior and rather mysterious policeman who was introduced to me in a Pretoria street by a South African journalist friend. At first we knew him only as Vic. I've never found out why, but he did indeed prove not only informative but friendly. I take no credit for having cultivated him as a source. He just decided to help us where and when he could. He said the timing of the Mandela release was known only to a few insiders, but the prospect was that it would happen around the end of January or early February in 1990 – vague enough but priceless information at the time.

Still, despite this help from a source who, with memories of Watergate, we predictably called 'Deep Throat', we had an uneasy Christmas. The government gave jangled nerves a reprieve by saying that nothing would be done over either Christmas or New Year, but that did not halt a stomach-churning flow of rumour. There were hoaxes too. The police played one of the cleverest and cruellest of those. They invited correspondents, including Reuters Brendan Boyle, for a canoeing trip in a remote region along the Orange River –

then casually turned on a radio that broadcast what sounded like a news report that Mandela was free and Britain's Margaret Thatcher had flown out to see him. 'I thought my career was over,' said Boyle. It was a fake. The police, anyhow, found it funny.

With Boyle safely back on base in Cape Town and the Reuters team of writers and photographers in place, the moment arrived.

On Saturday 10 February, I was watching the police spray mace at some demonstrators, who were protesting against an unauthorized tour by English cricketers, when Bill Maclean, on duty in the Johannesburg office, called to say that de Klerk had scheduled a news conference for later that afternoon. It could only concern one thing. I managed to find Vic and he divulged that, yes, the release would probably be the next day. So it was. After roughly 10 000 days in prison and at the age of 71, Mandela walked through the gates with his fist held high, his wife Winnie at his side.

'When a television crew thrust a long dark and furry object at me,' he would recall, 'I recoiled slightly, wondering if it were some newfangled weapon, developed while I was in prison. Winnie informed me it was a microphone.'

A WEEK LATER, I stood outside a tiny shabby so-called 'matchbox' house in Soweto. It was his old home, to which he had returned after a wild round of speeches, rallies and news conferences. Much of the media feeding-frenzy had subsided and on that Sunday there were just me and a crew from a French television station, waiting to see if he had anything left to say. Eventually, courtly and cordial as ever, he came out to shake hands and tell us he simply wanted 'to spend Sunday at home'.

... he came out to shake hands and tell us he simply wanted 'to spend Sunday at home'.

But he knew that his destiny was never to sit out a quiet old age. His freedom and the end of the ban on his African National Congress were only steps on a long trek for South Africa, as it struggled to avoid a race war and in its transition from white rule to democracy. The argument that white South Africa had always made in justifying a reluctance to free Mandela was that there could be no guarantee that it would not unleash violence on a scale unheard of even in the darkest days of apartheid. If the worst fears proved unfounded, peace and harmony were elusive. A legacy of apartheid lingered. The squalor and degradation of the black townships remained. For Mandela himself, the marriage with Winnie, that somehow survived 27 years of his incarceration, ended in divorce.

But in 1994, when the first all-race elections were held, black and white stood together in patient lines at polling booths, with an equal voice on who should rule their nation. Back on a reporting visit for a month in that year, I heard everywhere the buzz phrase of the 'New South Africa'. Everyone at least tried to be politically correct. White housewives kept their black maids, but spoke of 'my domestic helper'. Police spokesmen, who once barely gave me the time of day, greeted me as a lost brother, going to some length to supply information that I used not to waste my breath asking for. Unbelievably, the minister in charge of the armed forces was black, and a communist.

I'll bet that the murderous policeman in the shabby bar, even if his gut views about his fellow South Africans are unchanged, will now have curbed his instinct to roam the park in the hope that he can shoot someone.

Everyone at least tried to be politically correct.

# ELEGY FOR YUGOSLAVIA

HUGH PAIN

## ELEGY FOR YUGOSLAVIA | HUGH PAIN

# In early 1992, the siege of Sarajevo

was just beginning and the Europe editor, Tony Winning, had a problem. The Bosnian war was clearly going to be nasty, brutish and probably not short, and it was no place to send inexperienced correspondents who hadn't reported warfare before, nor anybody who did not want to go. 'At the moment I've only got two volunteers and that's not enough to staff it,' said Winning. Well, I had covered several wars including the one in Croatia, and being a sub-editor on the desk in London had its limitations. 'Make that three,' I said.

**Displaced Bosnian Moslems in a makeshift
camp after fighting in central Bosnia**
Spring 1993

© Reuters. Photo by Corinne Dufka

I HAD DRIVEN OUTSIDE THE CITY in the office car to pick up petrol. A full tank now and some jerry cans on the back seat, so the car was a mobile bomb. It had been quiet when I left Sarajevo, but buildings beside the road were burning now and the firing was uncomfortably close.

An armoured car of the United Nations peace force in Bosnia used to stand sentinel along the airport road, under cover of a chicane of cargo containers, blocking your way until a flash of the pale blue UN press pass persuaded it to trundle aside. It had been there as I had driven out, but now it was gone – the soldiers had decided that nobody would be fool enough to travel through the middle of the battle.

I stopped in the shelter of the containers to consider the options. None beckoned. I could stay there or turn back to the sandbagged UN-controlled airport, which meant reversing the car in the open, or else I could blind on into town across an exposed fly-over and along a thoroughfare that, with good reason, was known as Snipers' Alley.

To this day, whenever I think of Snipers' Alley, there is always in my mind's eye the body of a young woman, hands still clutching her shopping bags, hair whitened by the morning frost, and the long trail of her blood across the road.

A gun shooting in your direction sounds sharper than one pointing away. A crack rather than a bang. So, even without seeing the bullets landing, I knew that a machine-gun that had opened up close by was telling me something, if only to go away. Wild animals in the face of death, beyond all saving, seem to achieve a kind of calm. Well, it wasn't like that. In sheer gut-wrenching panic, with no protection at all in what the military calls a soft-skinned vehicle – like its occupant – and knowing that the unseen gun could rake my little car whenever it chose, I slammed into gear and careered on into the town.

*... even without seeing the bullets landing, I knew that a machine-gun that had opened up close by was telling me something ...*

Why did they let me survive? Perhaps a target so defenceless was not worth hitting. More likely, it was because I had nothing to do with that day's quarrel – another tiny incident in the struggle between Croat and Moslem and Serb that flared for three-and-a-half years in Bosnia in the 1990s, as it has at intervals over the centuries and inevitably will again.

THERE USED TO BE SOMETHING immensely appealing about Yugoslavia – before it broke up, that is, and when Josip Broz Tito was alive, firmly in charge and keeping his distance from Moscow.

When Eastern Europe was virtually blotted from the Western map, its people never seen and its leaders all grey men in awful suits, the Yugoslavs enjoyed a freedom to travel and were allowed, as we found on holiday on the Dalmatian coast, to run their own businesses. The country was tatty around the edges, certainly, but the food was cheap and there was not that dreariness that socialism had come to represent. You found candour, fuelled by slivovitz, that seemed to reflect a way of life worth having. There were only two rules: no opposition politics and no talk about ethnic divisions. Well – going without politics must sometimes seem a kind of freedom, and who wants to talk about nationalities anyway?

As we found out, they all did.

We in the West were so naïve – so ignorant of the fractures just below the surface of central Europe. Like Czechoslovakia, Yugoslavia had always been there. It just was. All borders seem inviolable, until they are violated. How few of us understood that for all those years they had dreamed of throwing off the yoke of unity and of going their own ways. Conversely, I wonder how many of them would have gone ahead and done that if they had known how high the cost would be.

By the time I was assigned to Yugoslavia, Tito was long dead and the cracks had opened wide. Tiny Slovenia went first, after a brief and inglorious attempt to hold it in the federation by force. Then Croatia, the historic enemy of Serbia, refused to go on being ruled by a Serb-led regime in Belgrade – whereupon the 600 000 Serbs who lived in Croatia mobilized for battle.

They advanced within 12 miles of the capital, Zagreb, shelled Dubrovnik and destroyed the Baroque town of Vukovar, even though half its inhabitants were Serbs, replaying all the hatred of World War II, when Serb and Croat were on different sides, until the UN brokered a fragile peace.

SO TO BOSNIA. A virtually landlocked territory bigger than Switzerland, which its landscape often resembles, it was the furthest reach westward of the Ottoman Empire. Hence its Moslems – descendants of settlers or of those Slavs who had prudently converted to Islam. The Turks were succeeded by the Austro-Hungarian Empire, which brought with it a tide of Croats, while from the east the Serbs expanded into Bosnia to complete the job of making it a cockpit of three mutually distrustful peoples.

Even so, the war in Bosnia could have been avoided. The place had never been a state, so no one group could claim historic right to possession. A proposed federation, favoured by the Moslems and Croats, was a goal worth striving for, even if the Serbs opposed it. But then the European Union, fatally, told Bosnia that if it held a referendum that produced a majority for immediate independence, it would be recognized. So it did, and it did, and it was, and the Bosnian Serbs, outnumbered but not outgunned, took up arms rather than live under Moslem and Croat domination, as we always knew that they would.

*... the Bosnian Serbs, outnumbered but not outgunned, took up arms rather than live under Moslem and Croat domination ...*

Sarajevo is a long narrow city along the valley of the River Miljacka, where an easy-going cosmopolitan society was much given to sitting in the sunshine at outdoor cafés. It is also a city that, if an enemy holds the hills on either side of it, is spread below him only 500 yards away, perfectly indefensible.

A sniper has only to sight along one of the streets at right angles to the river and wait for something to move. A gunner need only work out the coordinates to drop a shell or a mortar bomb at will on a hospital or a power line or a queue of people waiting for bread. And for three-and-a-half years that is what they did.

It was not that the Serbs could not take Sarajevo. They did not want to. How much better to keep its 300 000 people penned inside, miserable and cold and afraid, and let the UN bring in just enough to eat to keep them alive, but undernourished – and then, now and again, harass the convoys or foray into a suburb to keep the pressure on. You have to remember that the Serb war leader, Radovan Karadzic, was a trained psychologist before the war, who had worked at the hospital that his troops were shelling.

War correspondents like to pretend that they've seen it all, but the agony of Sarajevo was weird – a medieval siege in the centre of Europe as the twentieth century neared its close; a war at once ideological, religious and tribal that was waged as the world watched in real time on television and to which it could find no prompt remedy.

The view in close-up was just what you saw on the television, only the suffering was more immediate. Every so often the Serbs would lob a few shells at the Holiday Inn, where the journalists stayed, to give us a sense of solidarity with the besieged people. But no one was deceived, because while they were cold and hungry and saw their children die for lack of simple medication, we always had our press passes and a shameful freedom to leave.

THE GREAT AND THE GOOD CAME and went too. Cyrus Vance and David Owen offered a peace plan, while the combatants wanted nothing but war. Lord Carrington, whose diplomacy had triumphed in Rhodesia, held a hurried briefing at the airport before departing, grey-faced, admitting that he could do no more. The UN deputy secretary-general, Sadako Ogata, tiny in helmet and flak jacket, and visibly terrified, discovered that guns are more powerful than a humanitarian ideal.

Daniel Moynihan, the chairman of the US Senate Foreign Relations Committee, ignored the snipers, and the advice of his own appalled aides, to stand on the spot where in 1914 the Archduke Franz Ferdinand of Austria had been assassinated – the act that triggered World War I and made the name of Sarajevo resonate in Europe's consciousness for most of the century, as it did again now.

Moynihan went to the Lion Cemetery above the town, and gazed silently at the rows of fresh graves overflowing down the hill and across a sports field beside the devastated Olympic Stadium. Having seen with fresh eyes what we were used to, he went home and at length, due no doubt in part to his influence, American firepower, for the third time in the twentieth century, imposed a kind of solution on a European war.

I was not there to see that resolution. In a snowy January, the third of the war, Reuters photographer Corinne Dufka and UPI (United Press International) correspondent Kevin Sullivan and I drove in an armoured Land Rover to a town called Gornji Vakuf, where the Moslem inhabitants were also besieged, this time by Croats. Don't ask. It's far too complicated.

Not a soul could be seen in the ruined streets, but hundreds of people huddled in cellars, waiting to emerge in the relative safety of the night.

I should have realized that the branch across the road was too neatly placed amid the rest of the rubble. That it had been put there deliberately. I slowed to walking pace and bumped over the log. There was a curious buzzing sound and I had just time to think that perhaps the car had a short circuit.

I DO NOT REMEMBER the sound of the anti-tank mine that we had run over. I only recall an almighty kick and a black cloud that blotted out everything. Like dying, presumably. Then the darkness cleared and we were still there, and the motor was running down, pumping out the lifeblood of its oil. Then silence.

Not for long. From the nearby hill the snipers started. It seemed unsporting but, after Sarajevo, it was what you'd expect. Kevin's legs were broken and Corinne had had her face gashed by her camera, which had been thrown up from her lap. I felt no more than shaken, with an odd fuzzy feeling in my feet, but I could walk. I dragged Kevin out of the wreckage to the cover of a wall, where he lay without enthusiasm beside another unexploded mine the size of a dinner plate. Then I went for Corinne, who was wandering dazed in the road, trying to staunch the bleeding with a scarf, but who, once behind the wall, promptly began taking pictures of the scene through force of professional habit.

I started off for the main road, ducking behind fences and buildings, hoping to flag down a UN patrol, but I'd not gone far when I met a posse of men with guns, the Moslem defenders of the town, stubble-cheeked and festooned with bandoliers like the bandits in a Western. They rose from out of the ground and rescued us. As, no doubt, they had placed the mines, it was the least they could do.

We were in a sector controlled by the British peacekeepers, so our hosts radioed to their local base and, after an hour, some of them bore us in their armoured cars away from this war that had abruptly ended for the three of us. The strange thing was that the doctors at the field hospital discovered that both my feet were shattered and I did not walk again for months.

BOSNIA LEFT SCARS, not only physical ones. Perhaps that was for the good, if it helped to cure an assumption – as arrogant as it was widespread – that Europe after the horrors of World War II was in some way inoculated and that concentration camps and mass killings could never happen there again. No one country has a monopoly of evil. Kosovo came next, or if you went to Moscow you'd watch television war footage that you thought must belong to the now familiar Balkans, until you realized that it came from yet another post-Cold War conflict, Chechnya.

The siege of Sarajevo left me with a kind of dazed astonishment – the same as our fathers must have felt in the far greater European conflicts of the century – that this could happen in an advanced society among educated and civilized men and women. People like us.

> I only recall an almighty kick and a black cloud that blotted out everything. Like dying, presumably.

## ANALYSIS OF A SPY

STEPHEN SOMERVILLE

FRONTLINES 42

**ANALYSIS OF A SPY** | STEPHEN SOMERVILLE

# 'So,' I said cautiously, 'you were a spy?'

I wondered how he would react, but he showed no emotion. He took time to consider his response. He looked around the restaurant and sipped his wine, reflectively. He was a courteous man, a journalist of the old school. It was 1994 and we were finishing a friendly lunch on the terrace of the Continental Hotel in the heart of Ho Chi Minh City, recalling bygone times. We'd last met nearly 30 years before, when it was wartime Saigon – I was Reuters bureau chief then and Pham Xuan An was the brightest, and best-informed, of the South Vietnamese press corps.

**Caical US special forces camp, Vietnam, taken by Stephen Somerville from a helicopter gunship**
November 1965

© Stephen Somerville

I WAS IN TOWN AGAIN now for the first time. I'd made a point of contacting An, because I was curious to know what he had really been doing during the war. The story was that he had been a communist spy or even a double agent, working for both the Viet Cong and the Americans.

He'd been a sophisticated and charming colleague, educated in France and the United States, who worked for Reuters and then moved on to an American news magazine. We used to meet on military operations, or wherever the news crowd hung out in those edgy Saigon days of the mid-1960s, as the war intensified and President Lyndon Baines Johnson threw in hundreds of thousands of American troops to fight what the US government saw as a communist attempt to overrun Asia. An was always worth talking to. His analysis of the internal power struggles in South Vietnam was particularly shrewd. He had a wealth of sources.

'So, you were really a spy?' My question hung in the air. It gave me time to look at him and think back. He had always been a cool character, unusual in the high-pressure news world, and he had not changed much over the years. More *gravitas*, a certain professorial distinction.

I waited and glanced around, seeing memories everywhere. The city was much as I remembered it. I knew there had been some years of austerity after the communist victory, but now it was a capitalist free-for-all again, building sites everywhere, black-market goods spilling across the pavements. The traffic at the crossroads outside the Continental was as chaotic as ever – a heaving mass of hooting buses, trucks, cars and '*pousse-pousse*' rickshaws. Motorcycles and scooters darted in and out, ridden at furious speed by young men in sunglasses, long-haired girls in flowing *ao dai* dresses hanging on behind. Only the US military dimension was missing.

The humid tropical heat was the same, of course, but not for us: the Continental terrace was now a chic conservatory, an Italian *trattoria* protected by plate glass and air-conditioning. In the old days, it had been an open grandstand, part of the dusty city street life, full of American construction workers, off-duty soldiers, child beggars, diplomats, journalists and, no doubt, a sprinkling of spies.

The real difference now, in 1994, was the absence of palpable tension. Saigon, during the war, was a city living on the edge. The mood was fatalistic. Business boomed by day; explosions and gunfire at night. The Viet Cong used to set off bombs at US military billets in the centre and lob mortars on the outskirts. The Americans replied with heavy artillery and air strikes by B-52 bombers on the surrounding countryside that shook Saigon like distant earthquakes. Obscure scores were settled in the streets with hand-grenades and rifles.

I JUMPED BACK TO THE PRESENT. As An was still silent, I repeated my question, 'All those years, with Reuters and then with the Americans, were you really a Viet Cong spy?'

He weighed the proposition and answered slowly, like an academic in a student tutorial.

'No, not a spy,' he said carefully. 'Not a spy. I prefer to say I was an analyst.'

We discussed the difference over coffee. Spies were operational, he explained, they were tactical agents. Analysts were strategic advisers. There was a moral difference, he said firmly. 'I never gave Reuters a wrong report. I never gave any information that did any harm. I never put you or any of my colleagues in danger. I provided analysis and interpretative reports for the other side, just as I did for the international press. I was a reporter, at two different levels.'

An explained that he operated like any other journalist – working his contacts, asking questions, trading information. He also provided assessments of US strategic thinking and estimates of morale and opinion in the United States and in South Vietnam, besides answering the 'What if?' questions that helped the communists to formulate policy. He knew everybody in Saigon, he said, including the CIA station chief.

But he denied strongly that he had ever been a double agent. He said he worked for the Viet Cong and the North Vietnamese because he believed in their cause.

'Were you a communist?'

'No, I never joined the Party. I had no interest in the politics. I was a patriot. I believed that the Americans, and the French before them, had no historic right to run our country. I would do the same again.'

Despite his cooperation, the communist authorities evidently

'Not a spy. I prefer to say I was an analyst.'

had their doubts about his loyalty. When they won the war in 1975, An and other agents were imprisoned in camps where they were ideologically re-indoctrinated. 'They thought I was too Westernized.' He smiled at the idea.

But it was easy to imagine why the hardened jungle-fighters might have been suspicious of the elegant Mr An, with his perfect French and English, his old-world manners and cosmopolitan culture. He survived the camps and was then rehabilitated and honoured for his undercover work. Now he lives quietly as a pensioner, evidently content with his role in the history of his country. General Pham Xuan An, retired.

Any regrets? Yes, he regretted that his communist partners did not always take his advice. After the spectacular surprise of the Viet Cong Tet Offensive in 1968, which penetrated the centre of Saigon, An said that he – 'and others like me' – urged an immediate all-out onslaught, to maximize the impact on American public opinion, but North Vietnamese commanders withdrew to rebuild their forces after they suffered heavy losses in US and South Vietnamese counter-attacks.

'I am convinced that the war could have been ended within a year, if only they had been able to press home their advantage at that time,' An said. The conflict dragged on for another seven years. There were other times too, he believed, when the fighting could have been ended if there had been better mutual understanding of each side's real interests and objectives – more attention paid to the work of the 'analysts'.

We reminisced some more, finished our coffee and parted on friendly terms. I certainly understood An's own objectives better, but I felt uneasy. I respected his motivation and admired his courage, but I was uncomfortable about the method. Journalism as a cover for espionage is common enough, but always to be deplored for the damage it does to our craft. I was not convinced by his moral distinction between tactics and strategy, either. I was worried about the means, if not the end.

So – spy or analyst? Traitor or patriot? A Graham Greene hero – the 'Quiet Vietnamese'? Whatever his eventual epitaph, Pham Xuan An was a very special war correspondent.

## THE VIEW FROM HANOI

*Pham Xuan An, known to us as Hai Trung, had studied journalism at an American university and worked for the Time-Life group for many years. He was a confidant of Tran Van Don and Tran Kim Tuyen, who worked hand in glove with the CIA. He was also close friends with American, British, French and Japanese journalists based in Saigon. He accompanied them into battle on American helicopters and then spread all sorts of stories on Radio Catinat, in other words the rumour mill which stretched the length of the bars and cafés of Saigon's main boulevard. At the same time, he despatched numerous valuable documents and photographs to Cu Chi for transmission to Hanoi. This intelligence network consisted of only two people, Pham Xuan An and a woman who acted as a courier. Amazingly, both of them were able to carry out this task for 20 years without once being exposed, and they were both honoured as heroes in 1976.*

Extract from Bui Tin (1995) *Following Ho Chi Minh – Memoirs of a North Vietnamese Colonel*. London: Hurst & Company.

# THE FRIGHT FACTOR

DAVID ROGERS

FRONTLINES 43

## THE FRIGHT FACTOR | DAVID ROGERS

# As a new millennium began,

the end of the Cold War and the collapse of Soviet Communism seemed to have changed the news agenda almost beyond recognition. The 'fright factor' for millions of people had gone elsewhere, out of big power politics. One legacy that had been handed on, however, by a century that now belonged to history, was the conflict in the Middle East. I was the chief news editor of Reuters when the year 2000 arrived, and, as I contemplated how the world looked then, my mind returned inevitably to the biggest story that I'd reported in my 33 years with the agency – the moment back in 1981 when I watched as the bullets of militant Islam tore through the fastidiously tailored powder-blue tunic of Anwar Sadat of Egypt.

**Islamic fundamentalist soldiers assassinate
Anwar Sadat, President of Egypt**
06 October 1981

© Hulton Getty

FOR A FEW SECONDS, I REMEMBER, many of us in the crowd thought that it was all part of the extravaganza of Egypt's annual 6 October Army Day parade. Perhaps a mock exercise was going on. We had seen the exotic camel corps. The latest medium-range missile had trundled by. So what now?

An air force aerobatics team was plastering smoke trail patterns across the sky above us when the soldier-assassins jumped from an army truck and ran towards the dais where Sadat sat. They lifted their rifles above the parapet, pumping round after round into his torso. Too vain or too brave, he wore no bullet-proof vest.

Twenty-five yards to Sadat's left and halfway up a grandstand, I was swept to the ground as people dived for cover. I groped for my binoculars and got a shaky close-up of the presidential box. It was a tangle of blood-smeared bodies. The gunfire petered out. Down on the parade ground, a presidential guard had trapped one gunman on the ground and began spearing him with his ceremonial lance.

Looking back now, it somehow seems that it was tragically fitting that Anwar Sadat should die such a very public death with the press so close at hand.

> ... it somehow seems that it was tragically fitting that Anwar Sadat should die such a very public death with the press so close at hand.

No Arab leader courted publicity so persistently, so openly. At a time when many of the region's rulers shied away from all but the most stage-managed contact with the Western media, Sadat turned to network cameras and newspaper interviews to help him gain support from the impoverished Egyptian fellahin, to woo American support, and money, and, fatefully for him, to make peace with Israel.

The Cairo foreign press corps, which in 1981 was one of the biggest in any capital, had seen a great deal of Anwar Sadat. However numbing his Fidel Castro-length speeches, however self-serving and egotistical his news conference responses, Sadat was accessible, unpredictable and he made news. We had witnessed the killing of someone who we knew well by an exploding force of Islamic militancy that we little understood.

As Sadat was taken to hospital in a helicopter – he probably breathed his last *en route* – correspondents and ambassadors picked themselves up and began calmly, if urgently, swapping accounts. It's almost ghoulish how, in such circumstances, journalists and diplomats so soon resume their normal activity of gathering and assessing information.

Was Sadat, who that summer had been the target of student as well as Islamic demonstrators, now the victim of an army coup? The behaviour of the generals and their edgy soldiery around us suggested otherwise. Most looked bewildered. One soldier strode over, gestured excitedly at my binoculars – did he fear they were a weapon? – and grabbed them from around my neck.

Months later, the assassins went on trial at a military base. Facing execution, they shouted mockingly from the wired-off dock and declared that they had been obeying God's will. Cries of '*Allahu Akbar*', 'God is Great', punctuated the proceedings. Among the young thrustful accused, restlessly pacing their courtroom cage, stood a still, seemingly blind old mullah in religious robes. Like many of the clerics who preach a fundamentalist Islam, from Palestine to Afghanistan, he carried an aura of calm conviction – and of inevitability.

NEARLY 20 YEARS LATER, as chief news editor, I mulled the challenges that faced our correspondents as we entered a new millennium. Islamic militancy, with its hidden resources and defiant appeal to frustrated Moslem masses, remained a powder-keg of a story. Almost everything else had changed.

As the clock ticked down towards midnight on the last day of 1999, the concerns in our bureaus around the globe were with technology and potential catastrophe – whether or not the 'millennium bug' would confuse the world's computers to bring down airplanes and space satellites, throw the exchanges into disarray, melt down nuclear power stations and unravel the internet. Reuters had spent a huge sum on back-up communications and it had put in place sophisticated contingency plans.

Then, one bureau after another began to report in. Communications and public utilities were 'A-OK'. The millennium disaster scenario faded fast. In an emptying newsroom there was a sense of anti-climax, little New Year revelry, but considerable reflection.

I know that when the late Sidney Weiland – a Moscow veteran and Cold War specialist – conceived the idea of this book, it seemed to us all that the story of the collapse of Soviet Communism was the big theme; a change so momentous that it would set the agenda and loom over the beginning of the new century.

But events had moved so fast – even China's communists were embracing the free market – that it now looked as if even the repercussions had begun to be absorbed. The direst predictions of how imploding East Bloc states might unleash a mass migration to the West, on a scale not seen since the Germanic tribes broke in on a collapsing Roman Empire, were already looking very exaggerated.

The Middle East smouldered on, and the Kashmir dispute, too, went unresolved, but forgotten was the ideological rivalry that, for decades, had permeated in some form or another almost every news event, be it war, politics, technology, even sport. The backdrop to international news of the second half of the twentieth century had disappeared. No more simplistic good against bad guy. In the fragmented era now that the Cold War was over, it was all so much more complicated.

The most interesting 'global giants' now were perhaps the multinational corporations, some of them as ambitious as the ponderous superpowers in their prime and far more innovative. For many people, if they had the leisure to think about anything beyond the next meal, the most worrying threats came not from politicians in Washington or Moscow, but from terrorism, drugs cartels, global warming, genetically modified crop experiments or AIDS. If scientists in the last century had managed to clone Dolly the Sheep, what would they achieve in the next?

Even the wars were more complicated. It really was easier to explain Korea or Vietnam to a world audience than ethnic and religious strife in Chechnya, Sri Lanka or the Balkans.

The last conflict that I helped to cover was the 1991 Gulf War, which could be billed, if crudely, as Saddam Hussein of Iraq versus Virtually the Rest of the World.

In the media war, round one went easily to Reuters. Our correspondent in Kuwait, Hamza Hendawi, gave us a beat of 42 minutes on the Iraqi invasion across the desert. It was a whopping old-fashioned scoop and Reuters took out advertisements in the newspapers to proclaim the success.

Then, new technology changed the whole game. An era of instant satellite communications – ushered in most spectacularly by the live coverage by Cable News Network (CNN) of the night-time bombing of Baghdad – put a huge, and some would argue excessive, premium on speed. Speed. Don't-worry-about-the-detail-too-much speed. For a while, the reporter with the best satellite telephone was beating the reporter with the best story.

THE OLD NEWS AGENCY ADAGE – first secure your communications – had never been so valid, nor so costly. At the start of the Gulf War, satellite phones were weighty, the size of a large suitcase, and were accompanied by a transmitter dish as big as a dustbin lid. They took hours to set up. But month by month the sat phones got more cute and portable, so that by the time General 'Storming' Norman Schwartzkopf sent in his armoured divisions to evict the Iraqis from Kuwait, dozens of journalists had them. Those who had not, begged to borrow from colleagues. The charges per minute remained dazzling – Reuters took a big hit when a correspondent had his phone confiscated by a Scottish regiment and then had to pay the bill for all the calls from the sands of Saudi Arabia home to Glasgow!

Sat phones went beyond enhancing operational efficiency in the field. They helped liberate foreign correspondents from censorship.

That day in Cairo when Anwar Sadat was gunned down, my big fear was that I wouldn't be able to file my story; that the Egyptian authorities would react like other governments had done in similar circumstances and cut communications with the outside world. They did not, but elsewhere in the Middle East, including Israel, censorship could have been expected.

My other fear was that I would get caught in the snarl of Cairo's traffic and take hours to reach the bureau. Actually, it was light on that day, the city strangely subdued, and I drove, or, in truth, raced to the office remarkably quickly.

Neither of those fears would have weighed on my mind if I had had a satellite telephone in my pocket. Standing metres

> Sat phones went beyond enhancing operational efficiency in the field. They helped liberate foreign correspondents from censorship.

away from where Sadat was assassinated, I would have delivered a faster account. It might well have been more vivid, more impressionistic. Perhaps it might have included less background and analysis, with no office files or consultation with colleagues to help me, but weigh up the pluses and minuses of new technology's impact on news coverage and, thankfully, it's a huge plus.

On my first foreign posting after I joined Reuters in 1967, in West Africa, I had to file by cable and literally pay for every single laboriously counted word. Delivery took several hours. In the new millennium the correspondent transmits the story by telephone and the internet, fast and cheap, whether from home or up the Amazon.

The themes that run through many of the accounts in this book – the struggle to file copy and the ingenuity that it often required, the battles with censors, the sense of being remote – are unlikely to feature so prominently when the reporters of the twenty-first century recall their experiences.

# AFTERWORD

IT IS A PRIVILEGE of journalism that reporters in the course of their work may witness history in the making. News agency journalists are no exception, and the accounts in this book exemplify the resourcefulness, determination and, sometimes, bravery of Reuters reporters past and present, as they recorded and interpreted world events. These 'snapshots of history' tell the untold story behind the headlines. They are the next best thing to being there yourself – on the battlefield, aboard a presidential aircraft, at an execution, or on a film set in Hollywood. As personal stories, they offer a new take on familiar events. But they also give an insight into how journalists operate, into the challenges and rewards they enjoy, into the risks and dangers they can sometimes face. At another level, then, this book is a tribute to all Reuters staff who have been killed or wounded in the pursuit of truth.

For journalism can be dangerous to the practitioner, lethal even. In the year 2000 alone, Reuters journalists were caught up in eighteen violent incidents across the globe. In last year's most serious incident, veteran Reuters war correspondent Kurt Schork was shot dead on a jungle road in Sierra Leone, victim of a rebel ambush which also killed Miguel Gil Moreno, an Associated Press cameraman. Kurt was the eighteenth Reuters journalist to be killed on assignment since 1937. Overall, more than 750 journalists around the world have died in the course of their work in the past fifteen years. Already this year, several Reuters staff have been shot at, beaten or wounded by shrapnel covering the Israeli-Palestinian conflict on the West Bank, currently one of the most dangerous areas for journalists.

The Middle East conflict is one legacy of the last Millennium stretching into the new. The new millennium also inherited the uncertainties and complexities that filled the vacuum left by Soviet communism's demise. The post-Cold War order has fragmented the world, blurred boundaries, changed the nature of conflict itself. As big power politics waned, ethnic conflict, breakaway states, religious fundamentalism were given the space to take their place. As a result journalists probably face more, not less risk when working in many areas of the globe.

The lightning speed of technological change presents an entirely different sort of challenge for working journalists. The latest satellite 'phones' are smaller and lighter than ever before and can send text and images almost instantly, from almost anywhere, however remote or inaccessible. Journalists can now 'file' their reports, pictures and video footage directly from wherever the news is happening – liberated not just from their reliance on fixed communications back at the office, but also, oftentimes, from government censorship and propaganda. News releases and key background information are available online, at the touch of a key, ready for instant use. But then, so are propaganda and disinformation – and distinguishing between what's bona fide and what's not is often much more difficult and challenging than it may seem.

In this challenging environment, our talented journalists embrace the Reuters principles of accuracy, speed and freedom from bias – traditional values that underpin our reputation for integrity and objectivity, and which apply across the board, to all we do, whether writing about a civil war or a corporate takeover battle, taking photos of a riot, or capturing on video the victims of a drought. Our reputation as one of the world's trustworthy sources of information means the Reuters brand is recognized and valued everywhere truth itself is valued. In a world of furious change, this reputation at least has remained a constant, as the chapters in this book will illustrate.

GEERT LINNEBANK, EDITOR-IN-CHIEF, REUTERS

AUTHORS' BIOGRAPHIES

## DOON CAMPBELL

*D-Day: A beach in Normandy*

Doon Campbell was born in Scotland in 1920 and began his career in journalism at the age of 18 with the *Linlithgowshire Gazette*. He joined Reuters in 1943. As a war correspondent, he was mentioned in dispatches and awarded the American Glider Wings and Combat Star after taking part in the Rhine crossing in 1945. World leaders he interviewed included Mahatma Gandhi and Mao Tse Tung. In 1952 he became deputy chief news editor of Reuters and, in 1958, news manager. In 1963 he was made editor and deputy general manager. He was appointed an Officer of the Order of the British Empire (OBE) in 1984 for services to journalism. His autobiography, *Magic Mistress*, was published by the Tagman Press in 1999.

## RONALD BEDFORD

*Death before noon*

Ronald Bedford was born in England in 1921 and entered journalism in 1938 as a junior reporter on the *Wakefield Express*, before moving to the *Daily Mirror* in Manchester in 1943. He joined Reuters in 1945 and was chief UK reporter, before returning two years later to the *Mirror*, where he remained until he retired in 1986. He specialized in science and medicine, and in 1962 became science editor of both the the *Daily Mirror* and *Sunday Mirror*. He was particularly interested in space flight, but also reported the development of human organ transplants and the field of 'test-tube baby' technology. In 1982 he was appointed an Officer of the Order of the British Empire (OBE).

## DEREK JAMESON

*Who, what, when, where and why?*

Derek Jameson, born illegitimately in 1929, grew up in poverty in London's East End. He spent 16 years at Reuters and was a senior executive on his departure to learn the skills of newspaper production. Over the years he worked in every editorial department and went on to become managing editor of the the *Daily Mirror* and editor of the *Daily Express*, *Daily Star* and *News of the World*. In 1984 he changed course completely and turned his talents to radio and television. He now lives in semi-retirement on the Sussex coast with his third wife, Ellen. He is pictured above in the Reuters newsroom in 1946.

## DON DALLAS

*A tyrant and his birthday balloon*

Don Dallas was born in England in 1915 and joined Reuters as a sub-editor in 1939. He served in Civil Defence Casualty and Rescue during World War II, before returning to Reuters to be posted to Moscow in 1947. Later assignments included six years' editing a service for North America of news from Russia, Eastern Europe and China, and a spell as editor of the Reuters African Report. He was seconded to UNESCO to help establish news agencies in Libya and Malaysia, and he taught journalism in Africa before retiring in 1980. His book *Dateline Moscow* was published by Heinemann in 1952. He was made an Officer of the Order of the British Empire (OBE) for services to journalism in Malaysia.

## PETER JACKSON

*Ascent of Everest*

Peter Jackson (pictured in the Himalayas) was born in London in 1926. After serving in the Royal Navy, he graduated in history from Cambridge University and joined Reuters as a trainee in 1950. He flew as a reporter on a pioneering RAF flight over the North Pole in 1951 and covered the Iranian oil crisis, before being assigned to Pakistan in 1952. Collaboration on the Everest story led to his marriage to Adrienne Farrell and their life-long work together as foreign correspondents and wildlife conservationists. Top stories they reported included scoops on Himalayan expeditions, including the American success in 1963. After leaving Reuters, he became chairman of a panel of eminent international specialists on wild cats.

## ADRIENNE FARRELL

*Ascent of Everest*

Adrienne Farrell was born in England in 1920 and graduated in French from Hull University College before working during World War II in the naval section at Bletchley Park, where the German Enigma code was broken. She joined Reuters in 1945 and served as a foreign correspondent in Geneva, Rome and New Delhi. She married fellow correspondent Peter Jackson in 1954. She shares her husband's enthusiasm for wildlife and, after retirement from Reuters, edited yearbooks for the World Wildlife Fund, as well as collaborating with Peter in producing books on tigers, other wild cats and elephants. She is pictured above with her husband, Peter Jackson.

**SIDNEY WEILAND**

*Russian secrets and spies*

Sidney Weiland started working as a journalist for provincial newspapers in 1945, aged 17. He joined Reuters in 1949, covered various events in Eastern Europe and was appointed as a correspondent in Moscow in 1953. He did two tours in Moscow, interspersed with assignments in Yugoslavia, India, Washington and New York, and spent eight years in Vienna as Eastern Europe correspondent. He was Reuters diplomatic editor from 1980 to 1986. After retirement, owing to ill health, he established East European media training courses for the Reuters Foundation and later taught diplomatic journalism at City University, London. Sidney Weiland died in 1999.

**JOHN EARLE**

*B and K*

John Earle was born in 1921. In World War II, he was commissioned in the Rifle Brigade and served in the Western Desert before joining the Special Operations Executive and parachuting to join the partisans in Serbia in 1944, in an operation designed to sabotage the Danube. After graduating from university, he trained as a journalist with Reuters in London and Bonn, and the agency made use of his Yugoslav experience by posting him as Belgrade correspondent from 1953 until 1957. Later Reuters assignments were as chief diplomatic correspondent in London until 1962 and chief correspondent in Rome (1962–7). He then worked for *The Times*, until he retired to live in Trieste in 1986.

**ALECO JOANNIDES**

*Paratroops and necrophilia*

Aleco Joannides was born in Greece in 1922 and joined Reuters in Athens in 1951. Covering the Anglo-French Suez invasion of Egypt was among his earliest assignments with the agency, in a career lasting 36 years. He later became chief correspondent or manager in Cairo, Algiers, Lisbon and Rio de Janeiro. As Middle East manager from 1975 to 1978, he had the uncomfortable task of moving regional headquarters from Beirut to Bahrain as Lebanon flared in civil war. In the eight years until he retired in 1987, he was media services manager for Europe, based in London.

**RONALD FARQUHAR**

*Revolt in Hungary*

Ronald Farquhar, a Glasgow Scot, joined Reuters in London in 1952, after five years with Scottish and English provincial newspapers. As well as covering the 1956 Hungarian uprising and its aftermath, he reported from every other communist country in Europe during a career of 32 years with Reuters that included assignments as correspondent in Prague, Beijing, Belgrade, Warsaw and Geneva. He was chief correspondent for Eastern Europe, based in Vienna, in the early 1980s. He also worked in Frankfurt, Bonn and Berlin and helped to report the Winter Olympics of 1964 at Innsbruck and 1984 in Sarajevo.

**DAVID CHIPP**

*The day I stepped on Mao's toes*

David Allan Chipp was born on 6 June 1927. He was educated at Geelong Grammar School in Australia, then saw service in Germany during the closing weeks of World War II, before graduating in history from King's College, Cambridge. He joined the Reuters sports desk as a graduate trainee in 1950 and changed to general news in 1952, serving as a correspondent in Pakistan, Burma and Indo-China. He was the first resident correspondent in Beijing from 1956 to 1958 and was manager and chief correspondent, Asia, until 1968, when he was appointed editor of Reuters. He joined the Press Association in 1969 as editor-in-chief.

**JOHN HEFFERNAN**

*Globetrotting with the President*

John 'Pat' Heffernan was born in England in 1910 and became a journalist, aged 19, as an editorial assistant with Central News Ltd in London, later becoming a desk editor with the British domestic Press Association news agency. He served as a major in the Army in World War II before joining Reuters to become, in 1952, the chief correspondent at the United Nations in New York. He was chief correspondent and later chief representative in Washington from 1957 until 1976. He was made a Commander of the Order of the British Empire (CBE) for services to Anglo-American relations. The above picture shows John (left) with President Lyndon Johnson.

**BASIL CHAPMAN**

*'They shoot like pigs'*

Basil Chapman was born in England in 1918 to a lifelong career in journalism, apart from six years' World War II Army service, which provided his first experience in 1940 of France. After the war he returned to a weekly newspaper, then moved to the *Continental Daily Mail* in Paris, where he rose to be deputy night editor before joining Reuters. After working in France for Reuters, he returned to London on a new world desk, set up to edit the global news file, as one of a quartet of world service editors or the 'Four Horsemen of the Apocalypse', as journalists were quick to call them. He returned to France when he retired, to live with his wife Hildegard in the châteaux region of the Loire valley.

**PETER B. JOHNSON**

*Private Presley*

Peter Johnson was born in England and served in the Royal Navy from 1943 to 1946, meeting his wife Elfi, a refugee from East Prussia, on a posting in Hamburg in that year. He worked for seven years in British provincial newspapers, before joining Reuters as a sub-editor in 1954. He opened the first Reuters bureau in East Berlin, before becoming bureau chief in Moscow and later Bonn. He was Berlin correspondent for the BBC (1965–71) and then, until he retired in 1985, a London-based BBC commentator. He has written two volumes of memoirs based on his diaries: *Reuter Reporter in Divided Germany 1955–58* and *Reuter Reporter and the Communists 1958–59* (Tagman Press, 2000).

**SANDY GALL**

*At gunpoint in Africa*

Sandy Gall was born in 1927 in Malaya, where his father was a rubber planter. Educated at Glenalmond and Aberdeen University, he joined Reuters in 1953 and worked in Berlin before reporting in Africa. He joined Independent Television News in 1963 and was a foreign correspondent, covering Vietnam, the Middle East, Afghanistan and the Gulf War, and a newscaster for *News at Ten* from 1970 to 1990. He was awarded the Lawrence of Arabia Memorial Medal by the Prince of Wales in 1987 and made a Commander of the Order of the British Empire (CBE) in 1988. He and his wife Eleanor, who have four children, live in Kent. His latest book, *The Bushmen of Southern Africa: Slaughter of the Innocent*, is published by Chatto & Windus.

**ROBERT ELPHICK**

*Oranges in Gorky Street*

Robert Elphick spent most of his life in journalism before becoming a spokesman for the European Commission in Brussels and London. He was Reuters correspondent in Moscow 1958–62, then was personal assistant to the general manager in 1962, followed by an assignment to Algiers (1963–4). He then joined the BBC, serving in Vienna as Central Europe correspondent (1967–70), spending much of the time in Prague. He moved to Bonn as BBC Television's first Europe correspondent in 1972 and had other lengthy assignments in India, Vietnam, Amman and Beirut. He joined the EC in 1977.

**ADAM KELLETT-LONG**

*'Die Grenze ist geschlossen'*

Adam Kellett-Long was born in Cape Town in 1935 and joined Reuters in 1958 as a graduate trainee from Oxford University. He was a correspondent in East Berlin (1960–2) before being assigned to Beijing for two years then, in 1965–7, to Johannesburg as chief correspondent in Southern Africa, where stories that he reported included the assassination of Prime Minister Hendrik Verwoerd and Rhodesia's Unilateral Declaration of Independence. As chief representative, West Germany, from 1970 to 1972, he oversaw the establishment of the agency's German-language service. He resigned in 1989 to work for the Red Cross in London and Geneva, before retiring on health grounds in 1993.

**ANNETTE VON BROECKER**

*Swans, spies and a greenhorn with red gloves*

Annette von Broecker was born in 1940 in Berlin. She joined Reuters there as an editorial assistant in October 1959 and during 35 years with the agency she had assignments in Germany, Czechoslovakia, Austria, Italy, Yugoslavia and Iran. Stories that she reported, besides the Powers–Abel spy swap, included the 1972 Munich Olympics and the overthrow of West German Chancellor Willy Brandt, as well as the abduction and murder of Italian Prime Minister Aldo Moro and Iran's Islamic revolution. She also covered the deaths and elections of two popes in 1978 and travelled in Africa with Pope John Paul II. She was Reuters editor for Germany from 1983 until she retired in 1994. She now lives in Berlin.

**GERRY RATZIN**

*The Hammarskjoeld mystery*

Gerry Ratzin joined Reuters from university as a trainee in 1957. After spells on the sports and general desks, he was assigned to Moscow, then spent two years from 1960 to 1962 in the Congo and West Africa. He was a correspondent at the United Nations in New York for six years, before becoming chief representative in India from 1970 to 1975. He then served as personnel manager in Europe, before being appointed in 1985 as European manager of Reuters pictures service, based in Brussels. From 1987 until he retired in 1994, he was human resources manager in France. He lives with his wife Betty in London.

**FREDERICK FORSYTH**

*The American bomber*

Frederick Forsyth was born in England in 1938 and attended the University of Granada in Spain. He served in the Royal Air Force and then became a journalist on the *Eastern Daily Press* in 1958. He was a Reuters correspondent in Europe from 1961 until 1965, then worked for the BBC, before publishing his first book, *The Biafra Story*, in 1969, a non-fiction account of the Biafran War. The first of his admired best-selling novels, *The Day of the Jackal*, appeared in 1971 and, like *The Odessa File* (1972) and *The Dogs of War* (1974), drew on his experiences as a foreign correspondent. His later novels include *The Devil's Alternative* (1979), *The Fourth Protocol* (1987), *The Negotiator* (1989), *The Fist of God* (1994) and *Icon* (1996).

**ANTHONY GREY**

*Ming Ming, me and Cat-Strangler Chi*

Anthony Grey became a journalist on the *Eastern Daily Press*, from where he joined Reuters in London in 1964. He served as a Reuters correspondent in East Berlin and Prague, before being assigned in 1967 to Beijing, where he was to spend more than two years in solitary confinement as a prisoner of the Red Guards. His first book, *Hostage in Peking*, was an account of that experience during the Cultural Revolution. He drew on his experiences as a journalist in Asia to write a series of internationally acclaimed best-selling novels: *Saigon*, *Peking* and *Tokyo Bay*. He is now a publisher, having founded the Tagman Press, as well as an author. He is pictured above with Mr Chi.

**JOHN CHADWICK**

*Back to Balfour*

John Chadwick (left) was born in 1929 and, after graduating in English from Manchester University, worked for the *Bury Times* and *Bolton Evening News* before joining Reuters. An early story was the ill-fated romance between Princess Margaret and Group Captain Peter Townsend. In seven years in the Middle East, he led the Cairo and Tel Aviv bureaux, and other foreign assignments included the United Nations, Bonn, Stockholm, Copenhagen, Geneva, Rome, Karachi and Istanbul. Since Reuters, he has written reviews for *Jazz Journal* and articles on travel, jazz, film and literature for the *London Magazine*, the *Guardian*, the *Australian* and the *Washington Post*, besides playing jazz piano.

**BRUCE RUSSELL**

*Dateline Hollywood*

Bruce Russell began in journalism in his native Australia on the *Melbourne Herald*, run by Sir Keith Murdoch (the father of the tycoon Rupert), before hitchhiking from Alaska to Brazil. His book, *Carnival Bound*, about his adventures was published by Macmillan in 1954 and dedicated to his mother 'who, ever since I was able to work, has never quite known where I was'. He then joined Reuters to report coups and wars in South East Asia and the Congo before being appointed correspondent in Los Angeles for ten years. He was bureau chief in Washington for 13 years before he retired in 1992. He and his wife now divide their time between Paris, the Pyrenees, Washington and Los Angeles.

**CHRISTOPHER ROPER**

*The death of Che Guevara*

Christopher Roper joined Reuters in 1964, aged 24, after graduating from Cambridge University, and arrived in Lima, via Buenos Aires, in September 1966, staying until the end of 1968. After a brief interlude in the City, where he was publisher (1970–82) of newsletters providing weekly political and economic reports on South and Central America, he fell in love with computers. In 1984 he founded Logotron, a leading supplier of computer software to schools; and another company, Landmark Information Group, to provide map-based environmental information to engineers, in 1994. He sees a common thread, in his otherwise disparate careers, in packaging and distributing information.

**RONALD CLARKE**

*The war America lost*

Ronald Clarke arrived on Fleet Street as an editorial office-boy and learned the beginnings of his trade, in between making several thousand cups of tea for sub-editors. He joined Reuters from the *Daily Telegraph* in 1960 and, after working as a desk editor, was posted to Vietnam as chief correspondent in 1968. This was followed by a spell in Beirut, covering Middle East clashes, before he became news editor in Washington in 1971, when he covered the Watergate scandal. Ending three years as editor for North America, based in New York, in 1978, he posted himself to Los Angeles and became a reporter again covering everything from Hollywood to earthquakes.

**JOHN SUCHET**

*Get it right!*

John Suchet began his career in journalism as a graduate trainee at Reuters, before leaving in 1971 for BBC Television News. In 1972 he joined ITN as a sub-editor and from 1976 to 1986 he was an ITN reporter and correspondent, covering major events across the world, including the Iranian revolution, the Soviet invasion of Afghanistan, Rhodesia, the Reagan presidency, and the Philippines revolution, when Cory Aquino ousted Ferdinand Marcos. He also reported from every country in Europe. For his coverage of the Philippines revolution, he was named TV Journalist of the Year in 1986. He is now one of ITN's best-known newscasters and in 1996 was named TV Newscaster of the Year.

**PATRICK MASSEY**

*Mideast: David and Goliath*

Patrick Massey joined Reuters in 1965, after a 12-year stint at the Associated Press of America. There he had acquired a taste for the life of the foreign correspondent, following assignments in Europe, Cyprus and most notably in the Congo. After 1967, he reported war in Jordan, Cyprus, Vietnam, the Indian sub-continent and Lebanon, as well as the troubles in Northern Ireland. He also covered a British political and diplomatic beat, and stories as diverse as plane crashes, train wrecks and the weddings of Princess Anne and Paul McCartney. In 1977 he returned to Israel as a bureau chief, followed by similar assignments in Cairo and Tokyo. He is pictured (centre) alongside a captured Syrian tank, during the Six Day War.

**PETER MOSLEY**

*Just what did he say on the moon?*

Peter Mosley was born in London in 1936 and started work as tea-boy at UPI, before he joined Reuters in 1957. As a senior Reuters correspondent and editor, he covered stories that included the assassination of President Kennedy, the Apollo Moon landing programme and the Soweto riots, which eventually led to the collapse of apartheid in South Africa. He was also science editor and later features editor. Since 1992, he has worked as a freelance journalist, author and training consultant, and has directed residential training programmes for the Reuters Foundation, running workshops in Africa and Eastern Europe as well as Britain He is a lecturer at Boston University's London school. Pictured is his NASA pass.

**RICK NORSWORTHY**

*Thrilla in Manila*

Rick Norsworthy was born in 1932 in Savannah, Georgia, where he began his career as a copy boy on the *Morning News*, before becoming a journalist at the International News Service in New York. When the 'I' in INS became the 'I' in UPI, he worked on several newspapers on the East Coast of America, before joining Reuters on the North American desk. He was soon a chief sub-editor in the London bureau and then news editor. During his stay in London, he also spent two years in Northern Ireland, before becoming editor, Asian services, based in Singapore in the final year of the Indo-China war, when he reported from Cambodia and Laos. He now teaches journalism.

**PAUL TAYLOR**

*'America cannot do anything'*

Paul Taylor was born in 1954 and joined Reuters in 1977 after graduating from Oxford. His first foreign assignment was to be a trainee in Paris where he interviewed Ayatollah Ruhollah Khomeini just before his return to Iran to assume supreme power there. He was later based in Iran before other postings to Germany, Belgium and Israel where, as chief correspondent, he reported the Palestinian uprising of the late 1980s. He was chief correspondent in Paris from 1991 until his appointment in 1997 as Reuters diplomatic editor.

**PETER GREGSON**

*The Iron Lady*

Peter Gregson was born in 1945 and joined Reuters as a graduate trainee from Leeds University in 1966. During 30 years as a correspondent, he was posted to Singapore, Hong Kong, China – memorably covering President Nixon's visit to Peking in February 1972 – and South Africa, where in 1995 he interviewed President Nelson Mandela. He also reported from New York, Washington – covering both the State Department and the White House – and Zimbabwe. He was Reuters UK chief political correspondent from 1987 to 1990, travelling extensively with Prime Minister Margaret Thatcher (pictured), and subsequently head of the London bureau responsible for general news coverage of Britain and Ireland.

**BERND DEBUSMANN**

*The censor used a silencer*

Bernd Debusmann began his career in his native Germany, where he joined Reuters in 1964. He has had assignments as correspondent or bureau chief in Vienna, Belgrade, Addis Ababa, Beirut (1975–80), Nairobi, Mexico City, Prague, Miami and Washington, as, for the better part of two decades, he reported on war and conflict in the Middle East, Africa and Latin America. He is now Reuters news editor for the Americas, based in Washington, where he lives with his wife, Mexican journalist Concepcion Badillo, and their son. Reuters twice nominated him for a Pulitzer Prize, for his role in the team that reported the Tehran embassy hostage drama and for his file on the Gulf War from Baghdad.

**NICHOLAS MOORE**

*Mr Shake Your Money*

Nicholas Moore was born in 1941 and spent his childhood in Africa. He joined Reuters as a trainee from Cambridge University in 1964 and reported from Pakistan, East Africa – where he covered the 1971 coup in which Idi Amin took power in Uganda – and the Lebanon, before becoming oil correspondent in 1980. He led a Reuters reporting team that in 1982 won the Prix Bernard J. Cabanes for covering the OPEC cartel. During the 1980s, based in Cairo, he was a roving correspondent in the Middle East with Saudi Arabia included in his brief, before he returned to oil at the end of the decade. He retired as training editor in 2000. He is pictured here with Saudi oil minister Hisham Nazer.

**CLARE McDERMOTT**

*Politics – the name of the game*

Clare McDermott was born in Edmonton, Canada, in 1928 and began his career in journalism in 1949 as a night-shift apprentice on the *Ottawa Journal*, after graduating from Carleton University. He joined Reuters in 1954 on holiday relief, during a hitchhiking tour of Europe, and served in London and Paris before being assigned to Beijing in 1960. He also reported from Vietnam, before becoming editor in Asia in 1969. He was sports editor from 1973 until 1980, when he became editor, general news. He taught journalism after he retired from Reuters in 1990. He is pictured reporting on the Tehran Asia Games of 1974.

**BERNARD MELUNSKY**

*How a Buddhist lama opened my eyes*

Bernard Melunsky worked as a correspondent in Germany in the early 1970s and in Asia from 1976 to 1983, where his assignments included those of chief representative in Thailand and chief correspondent for South Asia. Returning to London, he served for several years as features editor and was then a chief sub-editor on the World Desk until he retired in 1995.

**BRIAN WILLIAMS**

*'Mrs Gandhi is no more with us'*

Brian Williams is an Australian who joined Reuters in 1969 from the *Melbourne Age*. After working in New York, he spent three years covering the Vietnam and Cambodian wars, and later opened a new bureau in Sydney. He was based in Islamabad to report the Afghan war against the Soviet Union. He was chief correspondent for South Asia in New Delhi (1983–7) and then became media news editor for the Americas, before working in Asia as chief correspondent for Japan and North Korea, when he reported the Kobe earthquake. He became chief correspondent for Britain and Ireland in 1999, and has covered five Summer and Winter Olympic Games since 1972 in Munich.

## ALLAN BARKER

*Fear at the wheel*

Allan Barker, an Australian, was a Reuters correspondent and editor for more than three decades. In the early 1960s, when based in New York, he covered some of boxing's legendary fights, including the Clay–Liston encounter in 1964. He later held senior posts in Washington, London and East Asia before, as business news editor, he was asked in 1980 to set up new editing desks in London and later in New York that specialized in reporting economic and corporate news to the media. Now 67, he is retired and lives in Arundel, West Sussex.

## VERGIL BERGER

*Red Guards to Tiananmen*

Vergil Berger joined Reuters in 1958, after graduating from Cambridge University, and was a correspondent in Germany and Africa before moving to Beijing in 1964 for three years, when he reported on the Cultural Revolution. He led editorial teams in Switzerland and Germany, before he became chief representative for Japan, Korea and Taiwan (1977–81). Later, he was the Hong Kong-based managing editor for Asia and Australasia, with responsibility for China. He returned there in 1987 as chief representative, remaining until he left Reuters in 1992. Since then he has written and broadcast about China and Japan, and taught journalism and languages at Asian universities.

## HELEN WOMACK

*Moscow's Afghan Vietnam*

Helen Womack was born in Wakefield, West Yorkshire, and studied at the universities of Birmingham and Cardiff, before she joined Reuters in 1979. During nine years with the news agency, she worked in London, Vienna, Stockholm, Moscow and Kabul. From 1990 until 2000, she was a correspondent for the *Independent* in Moscow and is now a freelance writer. She is the author of *Undercover Lives: Soviet Spies in the Cities of the World* (Weidenfeld & Nicolson, 1998). She is married to Costya Gagarin. Helen is pictured (left) on an Afghan tank.

## TOM HENEGHAN

*The fall of the Berlin Wall*

Born in 1951 in New York, Tom Heneghan studied languages and international relations in New York, Boston and Göttingen, before joining Reuters as a trainee in 1977. He has been a correspondent in London, Vienna and Geneva, and a chief correspondent in Islamabad and Bangkok, as well as deputy news editor, Asia. As chief correspondent in Germany (1989–97) he covered its reunification and told the story of the first decade of reunited Germany in his book, *Unchained Eagle: Germany after the Wall* (Pearson Education, 2000). He is now chief correspondent, money, politics and general news, in Paris. He is married to French journalist Elisabeth Auvillain and they have three sons.

## JONATHAN SHARP

*Mandela is free*

Jonathan Sharp joined Reuters after graduating in Chinese studies from Leeds University in 1967. He has spent much of his career in the Far East, including two years based in Beijing during the Cultural Revolution, and he was also in Beirut during the first year of the Lebanon civil war. In Tehran in 1981, he covered the release of the US hostages who were held in the American embassy there for 444 days. He served extensively in Reuters North America, before a three-year spell in South Africa, climaxed by the release of Nelson Mandela in 1990. He now makes his home in Hong Kong, where he freelances, writing about aviation in Asia.

## HUGH PAIN

*Elegy for Yugoslavia*

Hugh Pain joined Reuters in 1977. After several Reuters assignments in Europe, he became chief correspondent, New Delhi. He later worked as a chief sub-editor in London and completed several new assignments in Central and Eastern Europe, including stints in the war zones of the former Yugoslavia. Since then, he has been back to Sarajevo, but not, so far, to Gornji Vakuf, where he was injured by a landmine during the Bosnian conflict. Hugh is pictured alongside his wrecked Land Rover immediately after the explosion.

**STEPHEN SOMERVILLE**

*Analysis of a spy*

Stephen Somerville joined Reuters as a trainee from Cambridge University in 1960. After a year in Geneva, he was assigned to Africa to cover the attempted secession of Katanga from the Congo. He reported the Vietnam War as bureau chief (1965–6) and then, as news editor for France, organized cover of the 1968 Paris uprising and the challenge by students and workers to President de Gaulle. As chief correspondent in Beirut, he covered the Middle East War of 1973 and Lebanon's descent into civil war. He was later a senior manager in France, the UK and Asia, and then director of corporate affairs and director of the Reuters Foundation, the news group's educational and humanitarian arm. He retired in August 2000.

**DAVID ROGERS**

*The fright factor*

David Rogers, who was born in England in 1941, worked as a journalist in Britain, the United States and Jamaica, before joining Reuters in 1967. He reported the final turbulent phase of China's Cultural Revolution in the mid-1970s and was chief correspondent in South Africa during the anti-apartheid protests there. He had several assignments in the Middle East, besides his posting to Cairo, when he witnessed the 1981 assassination of Anwar Sadat. He reported the 1973 Middle East War from the Arab side and the 1982 invasion of Lebanon from the Israeli side, and was Middle East editor, based in Cyprus, for the Gulf conflict of 1990 to 1991. He retired in 2000 as chief news editor of Reuters.